B. P. Pratten

Modern Scottish pulpit

First Series

B. P. Pratten

Modern Scottish pulpit
First Series

ISBN/EAN: 9783337237967

Printed in Europe, USA, Canada, Australia, Japan

Cover: Foto ©Andreas Hilbeck / pixelio.de

More available books at **www.hansebooks.com**

Modern Scottish Pulpit.

SERMONS

BY

MINISTERS OF VARIOUS DENOMINATIONS.

FIRST SERIES.

NEW YORK:

ROBERT CARTER & BROTHERS, 530 BROADWAY.

1880.

CONTENTS.

GREEN PASTURES: A COMMUNION SERMON.

BY THE

REV. SIR H. WELLWOOD MONCREIFF, BART., D.D.

" He maketh me to lie down in green pastures."—Psalm xxiii. 2.

No thought is more suggestive of animal refreshment and comfort than green pastures provided for a flock of sheep. The
remembrance of rich and healthy verdure, in the time of its
brightest greenness, is always full of pleasant ideas. Few impressions, derived from early childhood, are more agreeable than
those caused by association with the softness and beauty of a
natural carpet in the open air. We are disposed to feel, that, if
even man shows this delight in the green clothing of the earth,
much more must sheep luxuriate in it, finding in it both their
resting-place and their best nourishment. . . Therefore, as believers
in the Gospel, we are ready to accept of green pastures as the
best outward representation of the precious provision made by
our Shepherd-King for our spiritual resting, and our spiritual
refreshment. Looking at the words of my text in this point of
view, I propose to direct your attention

(I.) To Man's Want of Green Pastures.

(II.) To the Discovery of Green Pastures.

(III.) To the Experience of Green Pastures.

(IV.) To the Expectation of Green Pastures in Richer
and More Abundant Measure.

I. Let us attend to *Man's want of Green Pastures.*

In this bustling world it is difficult to enjoy a pleasant repose.
Even those to whom a full cup of earthly good has been vouchsafed are, to a great extent, prevented from partaking of it in
peace and tranquility. The hard-working servant of the community, whether it be by hands or by brain that he chiefly per-

forms his part, is apt not only to feel a strong necessity for rest,
but to pant and sigh for a more retired and soothing kind of rest
than his position often permits him to attain. The flock of a
faithful shepherd may be sufficiently fed for the preservation of
their lives, and even for the chief purposes of their existence,
through supplies of food furnished to them within the confine-
ment of a fold in some crowded locality. They may all have
opportunity for resting their wearied limbs upon some barren
rock or upon some dry and unfruitful plain. The hardness
of the surface may be alleviated by artificial means, and all care
may be taken to secure their substantial comfort. But something, in such circumstances, would still be felt wanting. The
green verdure of a fresh and rich pasturage, in a fertile valley,
is longed for as a precious boon,—needful for the full accomplishment of their purpose of rest—precious from its satisfying and
exhilarating tendency. " O for some quiet resting-place," is frequently the utterance which, if it do not escape from the lips,
corresponds, at least, to the heartfelt desire, of many a labourer
in many a sphere. " O for some rich refreshment, far away
from the pressure of the busy throng with which I have to do !
O for green pastures !" is the aspiration of not a few sons and
daughters of Adam, who, crowded together, are compelled to do
their work, and receive their nourishment, in the dry localities of
busy money-making and hard worldliness. " O for the softness
and beauty of a holiday life, enjoyed for a season with a chosen
number of loving friends !"

There is a kind of dryness in the soil of earthly life, there is
a kind of hardness in the track of earthly ways, the evil of which
the greater part of men do not perceive, and which no retirement
from the world will cure. " Oh !" says the genuine Christian to
himself, " the soils on which I naturally tread are all dry and
parched—the walks that naturally lie before me are all hard and
stony ; because the burden of guilt presses heavily upon them,
and because I find in them no foundation for peace with God, and
no vigorous strength wherewith to serve Him. But Jesus has
given me peace through His precious blood, and Jesus pours down
His Spirit's influence for the refreshment of those that seek Him.
O, how shall I enjoy more abundantly the presence of Jesus with
my soul ? How shall I feed more pleasantly and quietly on the
Bread of Life ? O for quiet spiritual resting-places ! O for a
rich exercise of faith ! O for freedom from the dust of secular
concerns ! O for green pastures !"

II. Let us attend to *the Discovery of Green Pastures.*

We can easily conceive of a poor, wandering, lost sheep, stumbling in darkness; and, when light shines forth on the scene around, perceiving no place of comfort, and no promising path. We may picture to ourselves its disconsolate wanderings to and fro, even while no enemy appears, and its despairing cry when the wolf is seen approaching. Let us suppose also that, in the very crisis of the animal's fate, a strong step and a vigorous arm are interposed between the ravager and his victim. Let us look upon the shepherd, suddenly appearing in dark and wonderful conflict with the beast of prey. Let us see him shed his blood. Let us see him give his life to save that lost and foolish sheep, and let us observe the means of safety thus secured. Let us imagine the shepherd, recovered from fearful wounds and risen from the grasp of death, coming forth to guide the wanderer to the true fold. Let us fancy his hand pointed to a green spot far off, and the trembling animal beginning to discern something of the brightness of that spot, through the mists which are gathered on the immediate scene in which it moves. Then cheerfulness would revive in its heart. Then the instinct of hope would cause it to follow joyfully the footsteps of its deliverer.

We are warranted by Scripture in applying this analogy to the case of a once lost, but now recovered sinner.

The blindness of all men by nature is great and deplorable. We wander far from God, without knowing what we are doing. The child perseveres in its wayward courses; the young man or young woman pursues with eagerness the paths of earthly gaiety; the prosperous man of business becomes more and more intent, every day, upon his schemes of aggrandisement; the ambitious leader of a party sees nowhere to halt in his exciting career. These are all taken up with their several objects. They often think themselves wise in their generation. They often obtain the approbation of admiring circles gathered round them. But often they are all blind to the true character of the roads which they are rapidly traversing. Often they are blind to the danger of the dark mountains which they are approaching, and to the spiritual barrenness of the soil in which they are sowing their seed. But suddenly some one among them is awakened to the terrible certainties of his lost and wandering state. Conviction of his guilt, and experience of his corruption, have opened his eyes to discern a fearful abyss before his feet. He knows not which way to turn. The guilt of his sin stares him in the face.

The wrath of God breaks forth into view, as a stern reality. The devil's power over him becomes manifest. The gates of hell are visible to his conscience, standing open for his reception. Trembling on a desolate spot, far from the fold of God, he beholds the approach and hears the sound of a roaring lion, or a howling wolf, close at hand. But what steps are these that come between him ͮ and the enemy? Here is a countenance of love, and an arm of strength. Here are garments stained with blood. Here is the Good Shepherd giving His life for the sheep. Here is one who has vanquished the destroyer and driven him away. Here is the seed of the woman bruising or crushing the serpent's head. Here is one lifted up on the Cross—the Son of God suffering in the flesh—that, believing on His name, I may have pardon and peace through His blood. Here is Jesus, the resurrection and the life. Here is Jesus, the Shepherd-King, restoring my soul, standing by me in the darkest waters, with His rod and staff, to bring me to His Father's everlasting refreshment on the other side of Jordan. Here is a beloved One who will make me to lie down in green pastures. My guilt is all blotted out through His great sacrifice; and the mighty working of His Spirit, having regenerated my soul, is now preparing me for the full enjoyment of Himself and of His Father in Him, through the action of a faith that ͮ worketh by love. Thus have men and women, otherwise worn out and depressed by the ills that flesh is heir to, and by indescribable sorrows, found delightful consolation for their desolate and bereaved hearts. Thus also have even the lambs of the flocks been enabled in early days to lie down in pastures, the greenness of which on earth has been speedily exchanged for the everlasting freshness of a heavenly resting-place.

III. Let us attend to *the Experience of Green Pastures.*

It is one thing to enter into the beauty of a description; it is another thing to have personal experience of what is described. It is one thing to behold the picture of a rich and fertile pasture-land; it is another thing to be in actual contact with richness and fertility in the locality of our dwelling-place. It is one thing to see green pastures afar off, or even to descry them nigh at hand within fences that exclude intruders; it is another thing to feed upon them and lie down in them. It is one thing even to find an entrance to them for the first time, and to obtain a bare taste of their excellency; it is another thing to understand and appreciate them by a good experience of their preciousness. I may hear the

Good Shepherd's voice calling to me while I wander on the mountains of vanity. I may listen to His call. He may lead me over difficulties to His bright pasture-land. The sight of it may delight my soul. I may set myself without delay to feed upon it. I may eagerly repose my wearied spirit upon its soft embrace. I may thus be ready to exclaim, with adoring gratitude, "He maketh me to lie down in green pastures."

But this exclamation, upon my part, will fall far short of the full meaning which the words of it bear in the lips of one who has long been personally conversant with the refreshment of those pastures. For such an one can talk of a prolonged enjoyment, for many days or years, of the Shepherd's care and provision. In speaking of what the Shepherd does, such an one declares the benefit constantly derived from the Shepherd's habitual course. / The sheep have been accustomed to know their Shepherd's voice, to follow His steps, and to rest and feed according to His guidance. They delight in the persuasion of a happy lot belonging to them, in which the experience of the past keeps them satisfied as to the present and the future. "I know in whom I have believed," says one of them, "and I am persuaded that He will keep that which I have committed to Him against that day." "I know my Shepherd," says the established believer; "I feel that I am safe under His teaching, that He gives me habitual peace, and that He sustains me by habitual grace. My provision is good and sure. For He maketh me to lie down in green pastures."

The Psalmist refers, not to one pasture only, but to pastures. The field of enjoyment to which Jesus introduces the once wandering soul is extensive. The provision of the field is various. When brought to be at peace with God, through the blood of the Cross, the soul is set in a large place. The power, the wisdom, and the goodness of the Almighty have prepared innumerable sources of pleasure for His intelligent creatures. The treasures furnished by divine loving-kindness are inexhaustible. But guilt and corruption shut out the sons and daughters of man from the true benefit of creation, and its teeming wonders. I cannot safely be at peace in my prosecution of useful or pleasant inquiries into nature's operations; I cannot, with solid satisfaction, stir up my mind to the consideration of divine attributes, or human character, while I know that condemnation awaits me as a sinner, and I know not how or where to find a refuge. I am therefore in straits of soul, even while the sources of a heaven-born joy are spread bountifully around me. But when my eyes have been

opened to discern the way of peace with God through faith in a
crucified Saviour; when I have discovered the Eternal One in my
own nature, beckoning to me, and calling me as my tender-hearted
and loving Shepherd; when His voice has raised me from the
death of trespasses and sins; when I have seen Him giving His
life for the sheep; and when I have been freely invited to trust
entirely in the shedding of His precious blood for the pardon of
my sin, and in His life-giving Spirit for the sanctification of my
soul,—now I feel that I have been born again into a new land of
liberty and consolation. Now I see all the precious things of
God's workmanship, all set before me for my sanctified use and
enjoyment. Now, with an enlarged heart, I see how I can run in
the way of the Divine commandments. And the more that I continue to follow the footsteps of my Lord, in the employment of
earthly opportunities, or in the improvement of spiritual blessings, the greater reason do I find for saying, at every stage of my
progress, "He maketh me to lie down in green pastures."

The chief of those pastures to a fervent believer, will always
be found in the rich soil of the Divine Word. The language of
patriarchs and prophets, compared with that of evangelists and
apostles, never ceases to furnish an increasing source of rest,
consolation, and spiritual growth for the sheep of Christ's fold.
They take an unspeakable delight in studying the ways of God's
redeeming love. They rejoice to meditate on the glory of Jesus.
They see Him, the Lamb of God, in the excellency of unspotted
holiness and purity. They see Him in the astonishing light of
His own self-sacrificing devotion. They see Him, the Great
Antitype, in whom all the Scripture is fulfilled. They see all the
strength and all the beauty of Divine promises gathering round
the person of their glorious Shepherd. Their souls are ravished
in the contemplation. Their hearts are mightily moved within
them, while they taste of His fellowship. They rest upon Him.
Their souls live by His strengthening power. They are refreshed
and invigorated, daily and hourly, by the views of Him to which
faith leads them. They feel that their life is hid with Him in
God. They count all things but loss for the excellency of the
knowledge of Him. Their hearts are set upon Him. He fills
them with joy and peace. Each of them is well prepared to say,
as the result of a constant experience, "He maketh me to lie down
in green pastures."

IV. Let us attend to *the Expectation of Green Pastures in greater and more abundant measure.*

Experience of past love is the strongest foundation for the anticipation of future love. Experience of exquisite delight and substantial kindness gives a certainty to the hope of increasing joy, and more abundant favour from the same hand. The fact that the habit of my neighbour or my relative, in his dealings with me, is to impart enjoyment, tends to assure me that he may be relied upon for continued and enlarged efforts towards my happiness. He that maketh me to lie down in green pastures is the very one from whose power I may hereafter expect a provision of green pastures in larger varieties and in greater richness. "He that spared not His own Son, but delivered Him up for us all, how shall He not, with Him, also freely give us all things? He that gave Himself a sacrifice for sin, how shall He not, with exuberant loving-kindness, extend to us every demonstration of His liberal and tender beneficence? That Good Shepherd, who has given His life for the sheep, how shall He fail to make His goodness abound toward them, with mighty overflowing, in the pastures which He provides for their enjoyment?

Have you tasted and seen, my brethren, that the Lord your God is yours? Have you known and felt that Christ, your Saviour, is precious? Have you found a sweet resting-place, amid earthly trials, for your wearied and famished souls? Looking to the Lamb that was slain, have you welcomed and embraced a peace of God that passeth all understanding? Burdened with guilt, and overcome by corruption, have you been enabled to delight yourself with the blotting out of sin and the possession of Heavenly strength, through faith in the precious blood of Jesus? Has there thus been opened up for you a bright oasis in a wilderness of sin and death—a blessed spot of verdant ground, inviting you to a sure and safe repose—a place of refuge, in which you cannot be injured or destroyed, because it is a rock of strength, and in which you can be more than satisfied, because it is fertile in all that can minister to your comfort and joy. Weary and heavy laden in your souls, have you thus attained to rest? Hungering and thirsting, have you thus fed upon unspotted righteousness, and been sustained by the springs of spritual life? Have you learned, in the school of Jesus, through deep acquaintance with His Word, to cherish a hidden joy, which no man can take from you, even though the hardest earthly trials seem to have hemmed

you in, and threaten to overwhelm you ? Has the thought of
Christ and His cross bestowed upon you a wondrous elevation of
spirit, the high pleasure of which is never approached by the men
of the world, even when their corn and wine do most abound ?
Have you thus lain down in the green pastures of the Gospel ?
Have you thus put yourselves with joyful confidence into the
hands of Jesus, your Good Shepherd, and experienced abundantly
the tenderness and fulness of His unremitting care for all your
need ? Do you thus know, as matter of habitual thankfulness,
that *He* maketh you to lie down in the green pastures ?

O, then, you have a bright expectation that your spiritual provision will not only abide for your repose and sustenance, but
will minister to you fresh satisfaction every day.   The exercises
of prayer and meditation on the Divine Word produce, by the
Holy Spirit's effectual work, a growing enjoyment.   Rich fruit
springs up out of these exercises.   The operation of faith
strengthens faith, so that believers abound in hope.   You have
much to try you.   You have a large share of the ills that flesh is
heir to.   Peculiarities in outward position and inward temperament bring many perplexing clouds to hide the face of God from
your souls.   But you have felt and tasted the green pastures.
Your hearts have been lifted up through the peace-speaking
blood of Jesus.   The Spirit of Jesus has taken of the things of
Jesus and shown them to your souls.   Your persuasion has become stronger, that He who has begun a good work in you will
perform it unto the end.   Therefore you feed by faith upon Jesus,
the Bread of Life, and you discover more of His strength and
excellency, the more that you seek Him as your refuge in trouble,
and your support in weakness.   You have received great things
from Him, and you expect greater things.   There may be much
before you, on the path of your natural life, which has a disheart-
ening appearance.   But Jesus is all the more full of light, the
greater the darkness through which He shines upon you.   Your
refreshment and nourishment in Him do not depend upon the
sufficiency of external means.   His pastures are all His own—
the pastures of one who bestows life in the midst of death, and
who, having given His life for His sheep, will help them more
and more abundantly, the more that they need His help,   He
leads them to a rich variety of green pastures.   That rich variety
will be enlarged, the more frequently that their faith makes trial
of His faithfulness and love : according to their faith it shall be
done unto them.   If you trust in Jesus, you may expect to find

His pastures brighter and more sustaining, on each occasion of your secret converse with Him before the throne of grace, on each occasion of your searching into the declarations of His Word, and on each occasion of your active service to Him among His people, or in the world. The more that you look upon Jesus, the more shall you see of His bounty and glory ; the more simply that you trust in His words of promise, the better experience shall you have of His fellowship. Thus, the spiritual feeding of believers in the green pastures brings them continually onward, to an improved spiritual growth, and introduces them continually to extended views of the provision made by their Shepherd for their peace and consolation. They thus come into a habit of strong expectation. They expect richer greenness and wider fields of pasture. And they are not disappointed. For faith, in proportion to its exercise, leads the soul, on an ever-rising path, towards the fulness of spiritual joy. Are you strong in the Lord, my friend, and in the power of His might ? O, then, you are looking for a greater strength through the increasing exercise of your faith. Do you feel yourselves weak in faith, while you cling, even in darkness, to the strong hand of your glorious Shepherd ? Then you expect that He will not only take you off the hard and barren ground, to which your own waywardness and the allurements of the world have brought you, but that He will give to you a richer taste of His exquisitely soft and soul-sustaining pastures than you ever had before.

And if such expectations spring from the exercise of faith in any circumstances, much more do they arise in the mind when Jesus specially invites His people to a feast of good things. Many of you, my brethren, have sat in former days at the table of your Lord. I trust that many of you have tasted of His rich loving-kindness, in the breaking of bread and the pouring out of wine. I trust that you have partaken spiritually of His refreshment and His nourishment, while you were eating and drinking in remembrance of His death. But if He have thus made you lie down in His green pastures, while He came near to your souls with peculiar tenderness and power through the medium of His special ordinance, He has surely taught you to expect a more abundant fulness of enjoyment when He repeats His invitation. Now, surely, you may look out intently for a brighter greenness in His pasture than you ever saw before. This day, assuredly, you have ground for expecting that you shall taste, more largely than you ever did before, of His delightful provision for your wants.

Some of you may intend, on the present occasion, to feed upon your spiritual provision in a manner unknown to you at any previous period. You may not have sat at the Lord's table in time past. You may now have formed the resolution, for the first time, of showing forth the death of Jesus in the feast of the Supper. Led by the Spirit of God to feel your need of Jesus, the love of Jesus may now, for the first time, constrain you to honour Him by a public profession of your attachment to His name. Or perhaps you feel and know, that, though outwardly engaged in this celebration before, your hearts were not truly in it. Perhaps you have recently awakened from delusive dreams; perhaps now, for the first time, you have come towards the table with a true sense of your own sinfulness, and with a true knowledge of the excellency that is in Jesus. Then you are indeed welcome to this feast! But if you have thus been enlightened to know your Lord, you have been taught by him to expect great things, while, by faith, you seek to feed upon Him in His own appointed way. You have learned, through converting grace, that He maketh you to lie down in the green pastures; and now it is your hopeful and fervent desire to experience the richness of those pastures in an extraordinary manner. Now you seek, along with your brethren, to delight yourselves by a special participation in the provision made for your souls. May the Holy Spirit bless your endeavours, and satisfy your believing desires.

But if, even on earth, we are called to expect green pastures in richer and more abundant measure, how great ought to be our expectation of heavenly rest and heavenly nourishment beyond the grave! If Jesus make us to lie down in green pastures amid the adverse elements of a corrupt world, and in opposition to the impulses of corrupt nature, what must be the richness of those fields for our enjoyment which He is preparing for His chosen ones around His Father's house on high? Let us eat and drink in strong faith here, that, throughout our earthly pilgrimage, we may lie down with sweet satisfaction in the green pastures. But let us have the eye of faith habitually fixed on the purer and greener pastures of the Heavenly Canaan. Let us be always full of expectation as to the joy which we shall share, when brought in safety to the complete possession of the inheritance which is incorruptible and undefiled, and that fadeth not away.

The peculiar excellency belonging to the pastures of Christ's inheritance, while it is laid hold of in faith during the continuance of our trials upon earth, is their tendency to become all the greener, and all the more nourishing, in very proportion, not only to the weariness which they are designed to remedy, but even to the afflictions and harassments, the pressure of which nothing else can overcome.   Those afflictions and harassments are signs, to our natural minds, of the desolation and woe which follow in the train of sin, and which will reach a fearful consummation in eternity. But to the spiritual mind—the mind visited from on high by the light of God's reconciled countenance in the face of Jesus Christ— they appear as the means whereby our gracious Father is preparing us for a higher appreciation of what He has in store for us beyond the grave.   He is reminding us thereby, that, through suffering, Jesus won for us our salvation from the devil; and that now, through suffering, Jesus is bringing us into conformity to His own likeness, and thus fitting us the better for the fulness of His own enjoyments.

TRUE HAPPINESS: A LECTURE.

BY THE REV.

ROBERT JAMIESON, D.D.

ST. PAUL'S CHURCH, GLASGOW.

" A good name is better than precious ointment, and the day of death than the day of one's birth. It is better to go to the house of mourning than to the house of feasting ; for that is the end of all men, and the living will lay it to his heart. Sorrow is better than laughter ; for by the sadness of the countenance the heart is made better. The heart of the wise is in the house of mourning ; but the heart of fools is in the house of mirth."—Eccl. vii. 1-4.

THE design of the early part of this book is to take a just and dispassionate estimate of all the objects on which mankind are most commonly prone to found their happiness. After a very full and extensive survey of the whole field of human labours and enjoyments ; after having subjected to a searching scrutiny the pleasures of sense, as well as those of taste and imagination, and last of all, money itself,—to which, in the eyes of most men, the greatest importance and value are attached,—Solomon arrived at the conclusion, that, whether as regards the nature of those things themselves, or the concurrent testimony of all experience, they are incapable of affording to a being, constituted as man is, full, solid, or lasting satisfaction. The happiness after which all so eagerly pant, and which yet so few succeed in drawing from the sources at which they repair to seek for it, must consist of something not external, something not subject to the accidents of time or chance, something which is intrinsically suited to the constitution, character, and capacities of the human mind. And now, therefore, at this part of his treatise, the inspired writer proceeds to recommend several means for fortifying the mind against the seductive influence of those things by which men are so apt to be captivated and ensnared, and to shew the way in which good may be got out of the evils which so largely abound in the world. Many of the observations that he has made will appear strange and paradoxical to the unthinking, who form the largest and most numerous portion of mankind. But a little calm and patient reflection will satisfy every intelligent mind that the course, recommended by Solomon, has not only a direct tendency to promote the good that is sought, but, as all observation and experience attest, does actually, in the ordinary course of things, secure it. He begins with the influence of a good reputation : " A good name is better than precious ointment." A good name is used here synony-mously with a good character ; this is a possession whose value, both as a source of happiness to the individual himself, and a means of usefulness in the world, it is impossible to overestimate. To acquire a great name—whether as the owner of a princely fortune, or the achiever of high deeds of gallantry and prowess— whether as having advanced the interests of learning and science, or as the defender of the honour and liberties of one's country— to acquire a great name, in any department of human exertion, and to have national centenaries observed in one's honour, is the lot and privilege only of a few. But it is within the reach of all to attain a good name—a name for piety and virtue : and wherever it is well known and established, it secures to its possessor, in the con-scious enjoyment of the respect and esteem of the world, a source of happiness, which no wealth, however ample, no fame however brilliant, no rank however high, can ever confer. The man to whom that good name belongs may be a man of small or limited means ; he may move in a humble and obscure condition ; or he may have few or none of the vaunted accomplishments of the world to recommend him. Yet, if he is a man of genuine piety and high-toned virtue ; if he is known to be a person whose integrity and uprightness have always preserved him, and who, in some trying vicissitudes of life, has shewn a sincere and inflexible regard to the law of God and the interests of truth and righteousness :—such a man has not only a wellspring of peace and joy in his own breast ; but, in the eyes of the world, will secure to himself a measure of respect and honour which no earthly dignity, and no worldly possession, can ever give. In this view, the value and ad-vantages of a good name are great, and are here shewn by a com-parison which the countrymen of Solomon could fully appreciate : it is said to be "better than precious ointment." That is, rich oils and sweet odours, in the use of which people in the warm countries of the East take so great delight, are not half so grate-ful, or so valuable, as a good reputation. In a hot and sultry climate, the languishing natives find strong or sweet-scented per-fumes a great refreshment. A person who comes into a room

redolent with Sabæan odours, is sure to attract notice and collect
around him delighted groups of the company; or perhaps the
precious ointment may be of that strong aromatic odour, which,
on the very entrance of the individual who carries it about or
upon him, will diffuse its powerful fragrance all around the
place where they are met. In this respect, "a good name is
better than precious ointment." For, bad as the world is, a
good name diffuses everywhere an attractive influence. In
this changing and uncertain scene, where vicissitude and trial
are the common lot of humanity, the very best of men, as well
as persons of an opposite description, must experience reverses.
But, let a man be known as acting on the high and unvarying
principles of piety to God ,and fidelity to duty, and the conscious
possession of a good name will prove to him an inward source
of comfort and support, which, next to the favour of God and the
approval of conscience, gives, of all things, the most grateful,
refreshing, and delightful pleasure, to a well-constituted mind.

Moreover, a good name is better than precious ointment, inasmuch as it diffuses itself far and wide, and confers upon its
possessor an extensive means of usefulness. Who needs to be
told, that the good name which Joseph had earned, by the exhibition of the purest and rarest virtue, was a great means, under
God, of his being invested so rapidly with irresponsible power,
and of the king of Egypt placing unbounded confidence in the
wisdom of his plans, and the benevolence of his administration?
Who needs to be told that the good name for piety and unpre-
tending valour which the son of Jesse had early established, led,
in the course of Providence, to his securing the devoted affections
of a youthful band, by whom he was successively raised to the
thrones of Judah and of Israel? What reader of the New
Testament needs to be told that the good name, possessed by
the Roman centurion in Capernaum, as a sincere and disinter-
ested worshipper of God, was the true reason why the elders of
that city, sinking all their prejudices as Jews, went in a body
to Jesus, and implored his sympathy and aid for recovery of
the dying servant of the devout soldier? And,—to adduce only
one other Scripture example,—who needs to be told that the
good name for judicious and active charity, which Dorcas had
gained in Joppa by her labours of love, was the occasion of the
deep and unfeigned regret which her sudden removal had produced? The same value is attached to a good name, and similar
advantages accrue to its owner still.

Who, that reflects but a few moments, can find any difficulty in drawing abundant illustrations from the records of modern or contemporary history, to confirm the truth of the statement before us, that "a good name is better that precious ointment?" Have we not had many, many instances, in the church as well as the world, among the laity as well as the clergy, in private as well as public life, of individuals who, having been known and distinguished for their piety and genuine worth, found it verified in their own experience that "a good name is better than precious ointment?" The tradesman who, in the limited circle of his acquaintances and associates in business, is known for his amiable disposition, and by his habits of strict, unbending uprightness, and integrity in speech and conduct, has gained the character of an honest man; the private individual, who, with time and ample means at command, is ever ready to devote them to the cause of benevolence and charity; the magistrate who is zealous in employing the official influence he possesses in promoting the interests of truth and righteousness amongst the people over whom he presides; the minister, who is the honoured and successful instrument of enlightening the minds of men in the mysteries of divine truth, in cheering the hearts of multitudes who are weary and heavy laden, and in diffusing the odour of sanctity in many a family, where he is known and valued as a preacher of the glorious gospel; the christian lady, who visits in the huts and hovels of the poor, and who, by her active beneficence, clothes the naked, or feeds the hungry, and by her pious conversation, comforts the mourner, or animates the sick and the dying:—that friend in the social circle; that magistrate in the city where he resides; that minister in the hearts and homes of his people; that lady in the huts and hovels of the poor,—all know, feel, and exemplify, in their own experience, the truth of the declaration, that "a good name is better than precious ointment." They know, and feel, and exemplify it in the respect and esteem that is cherished for them while living, in the deep and unfeigned sorrow that was expressed for their loss when they die, and in the extent to which their children, long after their decease, feel how valuable is the inheritance of a good man's name. Let it be our care and ambition, in dependence on Divine grace, to aim at the establishment of a good name for Christian wisdom and virtue among the wise and good; and it will impart a far higher enjoyment to the mind, it will open a far larger opportunity of usefulness it will reach farther and last longer than the influence of either worldly rank or worldly wealth. And when we are gone, it will be a never-failing source of pleasing and grateful recollection to our families, that, though they may not boast of a long and illustrious line of ancestry, they have the inheritance of a good man's children—they are the children of parents who have passed into the skies.

"Better," says Solomon, "is the day of death than the day of one's birth." Of course, it is with reference to a good name that this statement is made, and it is only in connection with such a name that the statement can be considered as holding true at all. For, every dictate of reason as well as every doctrine of revelation tells us, that, if there is a world beyond the present, it will be well there only with the righteous; and that, as death is the medium through which we are ushered into that other state of being, it can be viewed with feelings of welcome only when there is the good hope of its being the precursor of a happy change.

It is, however, somewhat paradoxical,—nay, not a little at variance with the prevailing and ordinary sentiments of mankind,—to assert that the day of death is better than the day of one's birth. Is it not reckoned a subject of joy and congratulation among families, when a child is born into the world; and are we not in the habit of observing, or at least remembering, the day of our birth, as an event worthy to be held in happy and grateful memorial? True. And, seeing that life is an inestimable blessing, a gift of our bountiful Creator, who has sweetened and enhanced its value by the addition of other nameless and numberless blessings, it would betray but a small sense of obligation, if we could ever think of our birth without feelings of gratitude and joy. Looking, however, at the beginning and end of the present life in a religious point of view, and especially through the glass of the Gospel, it is a great and glorious truth, that, to every man who, through faith in Christ, has got a good name, the day of his death is better than the day of his birth. The day of our birth introduces us into a world of sin and sorrow, of trial and suffering, of pain and uncertainty—a world where change reigns over every person, every object, and every scene—where we are in a state of constant, often painful discipline; and objects the most valued, friends the most dear, ties the most close and sacred, are liable at any time to be severed, and pierce our hearts through with many sorrows; whereas, in that higher state into which the good man is ushered at death, the course of things is altogether different. There, there is no sin, no suffering, no sorrow, no separation of friends, no law but

the light and easy law of love, no change but into higher and
fuller degrees of enjoyment, no object for the heart to rest upon,
but what yields pure and everlasting satisfaction. It is, in fact,
a state in which the grosser elements of the body become refined
and etherealized, where the intellectual and moral faculties of the
soul are expanded into their full maturity. It was this view that
led Paul to say that " he longed to depart." It was the sentiment
of a man raised to a Pisgah height, from which he took a survey
both of the present and the future world ; it was the power of
faith and of Divine grace which had given him so complete a
triumph over the fear of death, that he could even long for it,—
long for that death, which, through itself an evil,—the extinction
of natural life and the punishment of sin,—is welcome to the
believer on account of that with which it is connected, being the
gate of heaven, the pathway of glory, the commencement of our
nobler existence, the expansion of our highest powers,—above all,
our admission into the Saviour's presence, and all the indescribable joys of immortality. It was the same view that led the
primitive Christians to think the day of death better than the day
of their earthly birth. That event, which neither the reflections
of reason nor the aids of philosophy could enable the heathen
around them to view without horror, was contemplated by the
early followers of Jesus, not only with submission, but with joy.
Looking upon that event as introducing the soul into the immediate enjoyment of heaven, and as only lulling the body into a
state of temporary repose, from which it would be eventually
awakened to join its sainted partner in the realms of bliss, they
mingled their natural lamentations at leaving the world, with joy
that they were about to enter upon a scene where all the
powers of their nature would be expanded to their full maturity
and be exercised in perfect blessedness ; and accordingly, they
were accustomed, in the fashion of the primitive age, to speak
of death as a birth, and of their believing relatives, when they
died, as then for the first time being born. Let us, like the
apostles and the Christians of the primitive age, be leading the
life that now is by faith in Christ ; and, in anticipation as well
as in reality, the day of our death will be better than the day
of our birth.

In the next verse, we have another paradox of Solomon's, in
the statement, " It is better to go to the house of mourning than
to the house of feasting." It is perfectly lawful for us, as Christians, to go to both. Neither our religious profession nor our
B

religious principles lay us under any restraint; and He to whose
life and conduct we are taught to look, as our great Exemplar,
participated in the festivities at the wedding occasion in Cana, as
well as joined in sympathetic sorrow with the mourning circle at
Bethany. It is natural for us, however, to prefer going to the
house of feasting. Possessed of a sentient and susceptible nature,
whose lively feelings give pleasure when they are called into
exercise, it is natural for us to like being present at a scene which
is dedicated to hilarity and joy. And, moreover, we may receive
good there; we may find opportunities of promoting the glory of
God and doing much good to others there, as well as in places
of a different description. But, while it is quite possible that we
may be benefitted when in the company of the wise and good,
enjoying "the feast of reason and the flow of soul,"—and there
are many such occasions which will bear reflection,—it is far more
probable that those who sit at the festive board are light and
frivolous, bent on mirth, anxious to "drive dull care away," and
too prone to indulge the bodily appetite. And, most assuredly, a
frequent repetition of such scenes,—a daily, continuous round of
festivity, when a large portion of the day is spent in preparing for,
and the entire evening devoted to, mirth and festive amusement
—is a course of living, the very reverse of favourable to reflection. And hence, in the gay world, there is and can be no
religion. Time as well as inclination for serious thought is lost;
and a state of mind is superinduced, which finds the retirement
of solitude irksome and painful, and the excitements of society
necessary to its enjoyment of life. Compared with such evil
habits, "it is better to go to the house of mourning than to the
house of feasting;" for there, one is naturally led to reflection,—
drawn, in accordance with the spirit of the place, into serious
thought; and we have an opportunity of learning, in the society of
the mourning relatives, that useful and solemn lesson which is
fitted to make us wiser and better. And what is that important
lesson which we are taught in the house of mourning? "That is
the end of all men." It is the end of man here; a final period to
his present existence, a termination of his sensual pleasures, a
stoppage of his worldly labours and schemes, a separation from
the society of his friends, a removal from "the earthly house of
this tabernacle," of which he may have been for years the tenant,
never to have a renewal of the lease, or to inhabit it again. It
is the end of all men. As it was the end of all the generations
that are past, so it will be the end of the present and future genera-

tions also. All have sinned, and death passes upon all men. It is
the end, too, to which we ourselves, as individuals, in our turn must
come, and there is no escape from this inevitable doom. That is
the great lesson to be learned in the house of mourning—a lesson,
however, not so much of knowledge as of admonition: "The
living will lay it to his heart." It were well if they would. And
assuredly, if any outward circumstances can make an impression on the heart, it is the removal of relatives and friends—
the removal of those who once took as lively and active a share
in the business and enjoyments of life as ourselves, but who
are now insensible to all that formerly awakened their interest,
or roused their energies, and cut off entirely from the world
of living men. But, alas! the living often fail to lay it to
heart. How often, when visited by domestic bereavements,—
deprived of the child of our hopes, or the partner of our affections,—have we been led to think about our latter end; but
time passed away, and our minds, with wondrous elasticity,
adapted themselves to the altered condition of things, and we
have found ourselves engrossed with the world and its concerns,
as much as if there would never be an end of our connection with
it! Nay, living in the midst of a vast population, we are almost
daily—at least, weekly—called to go to the house of mourning, to
accompany the remains of some acquaintance or fellow-citizen to
the grave. And in the solemnities of the religious service—in the
pomp of the funeral cavalcade—in the procession of the mourners
who go about the streets—in the lowering of the coffin into its
narrow receptacle, and the hoarse, hollow sound of the clods that
shroud it for ever from view, we are taught the impressive lesson,
"That is the end of all men." But, ah! how seldom, how little
do the living witnesses of the scene "lay it to heart!" These are
lessons given us by the Great Teacher in His providence, enforc-
ing, by all the impressive solemnities of the house of mourning,
the lessons taught by the still, small, but Divine voice of His
Word; and it is our fault if we do not profit by them to anticipate this certain event in our future history, and be taught so to
number our days that we may apply our hearts unto wisdom.
Let us ever—while we go to the house of feasting, and relax in
the pleasures of society—let us frequently, in thought, go to the
house of mourning, and familiarize our minds with its lessons.

The same paradox, so far as it relates to the sentiment, is
repeated in the 3d and 4th verses: "Sorrow is better than
laughter; for by the sadness of the countenance the heart is

made better. The heart of the wise is in the house of mourning; but the heart of the fool is in the house of mirth." Sorrow is an abnormal state of mental distress occasioned by the loss of some valued object—the removal of some dear friend; or it is a melancholic depression of spirits,—the worst of all kinds of sorrow to bear. Now, sorrow is not said here to be either a good or a desirable condition in itself. And it is especially necessary to notice this, as the calumny has often been thrown out against religion, that this is the habitual cast of mind it produces; that it is the parent of gloom, the source of despondency; it exiles its friends from many enjoyments they might otherwise have had, and fills their minds with gloomy anxious thoughts about futurity. The spirit of the Gospel, when rightly understood and thoroughly imbibed, is the reverse of all these allegations; and although, in the life of our Lord and great Exemplar, there is no recorded instance even of a smile, yet not only is it the tendency of the Gospel to produce cheerfulness, but there are many express commands to seek it, as, "Rejoice evermore." And who has better cause for cheerfulness and joy than Christians, who know that, through their faith in the Saviour, they are in friendship with God; and that the whole range of worldly pleasure and enjoyment, within the limits which reason and conscience approve, is as open to them as to any class of people in the world? Sorrow, then, is not here commended as a good and desirable condition in itself, much less is it spoken of as an effect of the Gospel; but it is said that " sorrow is better than laughter;"—that laughter which bespeaks the vacant mind; and the sentiment that underlies these expressions is, that a staid, serious, reflecting state of mind, such as is generally a concomitant of sorrow, is far more likely to lead to self-knowledge, and good and happy results on the heart and life, than that habitual levity which runs in a perpetual course of pleasure, and which is a determined enemy to all reflection. In illustration of this, I may refer to a well-known anecdote in the life of a celebrated wit and comedian. A person, labouring under a sad depression of spirits, one day waited upon a physician, and introduced himself by saying, " I am sad, unhappy, and depressed; everything I have tried has failed to relieve my distress, and I have come to you in the hope that you may be able to relieve me." " Go," said the physician, " to Shuter, who will help you; his exquisite humour, which has so often entertained me, will now prove the most efficient medicine." " Alas!" replied the stranger, "I am that Shuter, who used to keep crowded houses in a roar of laughter, and after whom multitudes eagerly ran, for the amusement of their idle hours. But I am myself now the victim of uncontrollable melancholy, and I would give all I possess in the world to obtain one day of comfort."

So true is it that a wounded spirit is hard to bear, and that the gay scenes of the world cannot relieve it. Men, in such cases, say, " Go to the theatre and the ballroom;" but Solomon, the inspired preacher, says that sorrow is then better than laughter; for, by the sadness of the countenance, the heart is often made better. Sadness is often a means of leading to seriousness; and that affliction which impairs the health, diminishes the family circle, or overtakes the estate, may have a salutary influence upon the mind—make such impressions upon it as will give a new and a more spiritual direction to the whole current of the thoughts and the affections—make it more meek, subdued, and humble,—more loose to the world, more penitent for sin, more careful and assiduous in its attention to Christian duty. My friends, perhaps some of you, in the day of adversity, were led to consider; and that affliction which, on its first arrival, you deplored as a sad and calamitous event, proving the occasion of leading you to consider, stands ever afterwards associated in memory's page with the brightest spots in your personal history. And in that adoring retrospect which, in heaven, you will take of the way by which you have been brought to that glorious kingdom, you will tune your harps with a firmer hand and to livelier notes, when you remember it was by the sadness brought on your countenance that your heart was made better. Ponder, then, the spirit and purpose of the paradoxical but important statements made in this passage; and, while " the heart of fools is continually in the house of mirth," remember

" 'Tis greatly wise to talk with your past hours,
And ask them what report they bore to heaven "

TRUE
PRINCIPLES OF CHRISTIAN ECONOMY:
A SERMON.

BY THE

Rev. JAMES R. M^cGAVIN, D.D., Dundee.

TAY SQUARE U.P. CHURCH, DUNDEE.

" To what purpose is this waste ? "—Matt. xxvi. 8.

There is a wide and irreconcilable difference between common opinion, and the estimate which God, in His Gospel, forms of men and things. What the world despises, God esteems; what the world forgets and overlooks, God records and perpetuates. Thus, in the sacred narrative, deeds and persons are brought into prominence, and divinely applauded, when this is what we would least expect; and Scripture calls that noble, heroic, and blessed, which multitudes would pronounce mean or low-spirited, —just because the wisdom of this world is foolishness with God, and " He hath chosen the weak things of the world to confound the mighty, yea and things that are not, to bring to nought things that are, that no flesh should glory in His presence."

We have a marked example of this great truth in the uniform action of our blessed Saviour. His whole career lay far away from the walks of the world's admiration; and the individuals whom He admitted into His confidence, and the actions He approved, as well as the principles of morality and obedience which He taught, were a grand protest against the hollow selfishness and painted hypocrisy around Him. When He called children to His arms, while the world frowned and rebuked; when He commended the Canaanitish woman, the Samaritan, the Centurion, the poor widow casting her mite into the treasury; while He ignored the needless profusion of the rich, and scorned the false pretences of the Pharisee,—you mark the essential contradiction between the world's shams and the Saviour's sincerity, and the glory with which He adorns the modest but genuine principle, which lies concealed from the world's notice, because, like the largest and brightest gems, it is overlaid beneath the mass of the worthless materials around it.

In confirmation of these great truths, we are invited to witness a humble repast in a mean suburb of Jerusalem, along with the Son of God. Neither the place, company, nor circumstances seem to invite public notice; and yet Scripture testimony lingers over the scene, as pregnant with precious truth and eloquence to all ages.

An obscure female villager comes forth to pay a tribute of homage to our Lord, as rare as it was seemly and merited. The act might have been allowed to pass without notice; but the gift was very costly, and the expense immediately provokes worldly grudges and opposition. The Saviour Himself comes forth to the vindication and defence of this devout offering. While the selfish and sordid company assail the extravagance and condemn the waste, the Saviour repels the charge, and honours the munificence of His disciple; and we see here precisely the grand controversy which has been waged, ever since, between Christ and human selfishness, as to what is real extravagance and genuine economy, when the world cries out, "To what purpose is this waste?" and Christ affirms, "She hath wrought a good work upon me; she hath done what she could."

The subject this text summons us to consider is,—What is waste, and what is proper expenditure, or true economy? It is plain that Christ and the world are in direct antagonism on this subject; and it is a solemn duty which we owe to Christ and to ourselves, to determine on whose side we are prepared to take our place. This is all the more imperative, inasmuch as the discreditable and unkindly taunt of the text came, not from open and avowed enemies, but from the ranks of the twelve Apostles; for, while Judas is the speaker, it is added by one of the Evangelists, "And so said they all." In considering this theme, let us first correct and challenge the world's charge of waste; and, secondly, vindicate and explain true Christian expenditure.

I. *Let us here seek to challenge and correct the world's charge of waste brought against this and all similar acts of homage to Christ.*

Waste, properly defined, is a useless and prodigal expenditure,—the dissipation of resources and property by extravagance

and wanton misuse. This seems a singular charge to bring
against religious service. We would have been inclined to look
in other channels for the implication. Where shall we find this?
In wealth running to waste, in countless millions ruining property and families, blasting health and reputation, as it sweeps
successive generations into bankruptcy, dishonour, an untimely
grave, and an undone eternity. Where? Certainly that waste
is not seen in feeding the hungry, soothing the sick, comforting
the wretched, or saving the lost. No! Sin is the parent of
extravagance, the mother of waste, and it is never satisfied in
offering continual hecatombs of victims on its blood-stained
altars. But there are prudent and careful people, most likely,
to be found in the Church, who are shocked at all waste,
wherever they find it; and they are not slow to cry out against
the extravagance which they are continually detecting in the
Church of God. They never cease to wonder what all these
modern schemes of benevolence mean—where all the money
comes from,—how some of their neighbours have got so much
money to give away, and so little sense to keep it,—how the
world got on before Bible, and Tract, and Missionary Societies
existed; and what it is to come to, with its Ragged Schools,
and Evangelistic Services! Is the world the better of all these
schemes, and is there not a large measure of waste in them?

Now, we ought to feel thankful to any who can help us
to save our money; but, before this charge of waste is made,
we have a right to ask how much of this wasted money they
have advanced. It is an easy and common thing for persons
to take the charge of their neighbours' affairs, and to blame
them for mismanagement; but we challenge the right of this
censorship. The Master sits over against the treasury, and
every one is responsible only to Him for the use of His talents.
It is significant, that while this charge of waste is always made
against others, by those whose own property is not at stake,
they are generally the individuals who boast that no one will
blame *them* for waste. Whether this be to their credit or not,
depends on what idea we attach to waste. There are other sins
besides extravagant expenditure, for which God will punish;
and if we are free from the sin of being spendthrifts, are we
sure that we are equally free from the no less accursed sins
of avarice, dishonourable selfishness, undue hoarding, or keeping back from God that which He has given us to distribute?
But there are notions current in the world, on the subject of

giving to God, which are monstrous and absurd, a few of which only, for the present, we can notice and correct.

And, *first*, let us mark, in opposition to selfish policy, that as *hoarding* is not always *saving*, so neither is expenditure always waste. If we want to know the true law of life, we must learn it from the works of God, and His administration of providence. In all His dealings with His creatures, exuberant and overflowing bounty is everywhere apparent. "He openeth His hand, and satisfieth the desire of every living thing." His showers fall copiously everywhere, on mountain, waste, and fruitful field. His sunshine streams down from the heavens with no restraint or stint, to fill all surrounding space with His glory, while it brightens the earth with its beams,—fructifying the soil, flushing the fields with fairest flower and fragrant fruitfulness. Yet here, while there is constant expenditure of light and heat, there is no real waste; because all this vast outcome of goodness goes back, in richest recompense of blessing, to its Parent Benefactor, to fulfil its perennial circuit of usefulness. The same principle of generous expenditure forms the life and success of commerce. A man of mean and sordid habits toils away with antiquated and worn-out machinery, because he dreads the expense of refitting or repair, only to find that his inferior goods, produced at higher cost, have fallen out of demand in the market; while his more discerning neighbour economises cost of production, and improves the quality of material, every day. by using the latest and best machinery,—no doubt, at great expenditure, but this is more than repaid to him by increased production and larger profits.

Now, we say to the penurious and selfish worldling, Take a lesson from the trustful and calculating man of enterprise; for, be assured of it, the same principle prevails in our stewardship with God's bounty, as in the right management of the world's business. You blame the generous man, who bountifully gives of God's goodness to bless others, and you say he is wasting his means; but you forget that these gifts are never lost; they form the best investments in all his business; they bring down the blessing of God, "which maketh rich, and He addeth no sorrow with it;" they fall, like this woman's ointment on the Saviour's head, on the homes of sickness, sorrow, and sin, to relieve their misery and save their souls; and they come back to his own soul, in fragrant odours of prayer and thanksgiving, sweeter than all the spices of Araby, and more precious than Ophir's gold.

Again, does the selfish man congratulate himself, when he has refused some urgent opportunity of doing good, that, whatever conscience or the world may say of him, he has at least saved his money ? He is mistaken. There is no safe keeping of that which vexes and displeases God. It may seem to lie safely in the selfish man's coffers, but there is a canker or a curse in it. What, if it has created yonder bad debts, involving a loss of hundreds, more than he saved by his ungenerousness? What, if the money kept back from God's purpose should help to lead to ruinous speculations, or bad investments, or to bring down the thunder-crash of commercial ruin, which scatters far and wide, in a moment, the grasping accumulation of years ? Even if the avaricious man, who withholds from God more than is due, seems to accumulate his gains in peace, what is it but waste ? It lies useless to him ; the care of it eats his flesh, as it were fire ; as wealth increases, he can take less use of it, and is haunted with the dread of poverty. He gathers it for his own children, it may be, to rob him and break his heart by their dissipation and folly. No! there is no greater evil under the sun, and it is "common among men; a man to whom God hath given riches, wealth and honour, so that he wanteth nothing for his soul of all that he desireth; yet God giveth him not power to eat thereof, but a stranger eateth it: this is vanity and an evil disease." Really, there is no safe investment in this life except the bank of faith, of which God has the key; and we need to be reminded every day,—"There is that scattereth and yet increaseth ; and there is that withholdeth more than is meet, but it tendeth to poverty."

But there is another fallacy of the ungenerous and selfish, suggested by the text, viz., that everything is wasted that is given to Christ. It was but little personal kindness that was ever paid to Christ on earth, by any of His followers. He who gave to men all things richly to enjoy, and who came to give His life a sacrifice, got nothing back. Even these, His own followers, who had for years received the richest blessings at His hands, when was it that any one of them ever showed that Saviour a personal kindness ? And yet, now, when a loving and grateful female would soothe that fevered brow, and weary head, by the balm of generous affection, even this small kindness must be rebuked by His disciples—called waste —and claimed for others, rather than for that lone, loving Spirit, who had none to pity Him. Thus the Saviour's heart was broken by reproach on earth; and thus it is now, that men, who are fed by His bounty, and loaded with blessings from His hand, are not ashamed to refuse to give back to Him some small dole, to lighten the burden of human misery, or to save ruined souls. "O Conscience! thou art fled to brutish beasts, and men have lost their reason!"

But is it really so,—that money given to Christ is lost? Impossible! Many costly sacrifices have been offered on earth to the Saviour. I see Moses spurn riches, and royal honours, to endure affliction with the people of God. I find that Paul counted all things but loss, for the excellency of the knowledge of Christ Jesus. Were these lives wasted? No: their names are imperishable as the truth for which they died.

Finally, it is the fallacy of the selfish, that, while they will not make sacrifices for Christ, they think they have a right to prevent others; but this will not exempt us from doing our own duty.

II. *What the world calls waste, as done to Christ and His cause, the Saviour Himself commends, as duty, which secures our truest, interest, and honour.*

This act of Mary was a simple and sincere tribute of homage to her Saviour, prompted by a sense of grateful love, which could not be suppressed, for benefits which could never be compensated. If we are Christians at all, we owe everything to Him for salvation, which it cost Him His life to procure for us; and the least we can do is, to consecrate that life to Him who has redeemed it. The Saviour, in visible person, is no more on earth, and we cannot now show Him any mark of personal homage; not less true is it, that He is beyond the need of any gift or service of any of His creatures. Certainly, for the love He bears us, He expects and claims our hearts and the devotion of our lives. Not otherwise can we attest the reality of our redemption; and the welfare and happiness of our own souls are bound up in this love-labour. Christ has left His cause and people to represent Himself on earth; and everything that is dear to Him will be precious to us, precisely in proportion as His Spirit is in us. We cannot now, like Mary, anoint that blessed head, because it needs it not, having ceased from all its throbbings of anguish, and long passed the humiliation of burial; but can we not visit the fatherless and widows to bless them, comfort the broken-hearted, and rescue the perishing ? You may discern, in a soul saved through your instrumentality, the reflection of Christ's person. The work itself is so heavenly and Godlike, that it is worth more than all the wealth of the world to secure it ; nor can loftier renown, or richer blessedness, belong to man, than when Christ says, "Inasmuch as ye have done it unto the least of these my brethren, ye have done it unto me." If we ask why Mary brought this alabaster-box, the readiest answer is—because she had nothing else so precious. Hers was a love that must honour the presence of the Lord, and nothing was sufficiently costly to express her obligations to Him who had done everything for her soul. Every sacrifice was too little. This might have been her whole life's savings; and, in parting with it, she may have exposed herself to poverty for all her future career ; but, to express her love for the Redeemer, she poured out her heart along with it. It was the tribute of a soul that gave itself up along with its offering, which, more than all the perfume of the ointment, was precious to Christ, and caused Him to vindicate and applaud her, as He said, "Verily I say unto you, Wheresoever this Gospel shall be preached, in the whole world, there shall also this, that this woman hath done, be told for a memorial of her."

Now, how should you and I express our obligation to Christ as this woman did ? We owe Him as much, if He is indeed our Saviour ; and we cannot serve Him with love which costs us less, if we are partakers of her spirit. May we not make sacrifices to Him of our money, our time, our talents, our life ? Is there no sweet recompense in the approbation of Him who has done all for us ? Ah! not one effort of the loving is lost. All shall be recompensed at the resurrection of the just.

What was counted waste here is fragrant with the love of Christ, and turns into treasure which is stored up in heaven. The cup of cold water given shall not lose a disciple's reward. Be assured, therefore, that the real waste of life is in the world's service. Whether you serve that world by hoarding, or by spending on your own lusts and amusements, you will find that these things carry with them no satisfaction, bring back no fragrant memories, no blessed recompense. But you will find that they who serve sin with the most lavish expenditure, learn, when too late, that they have sacrificed their souls for that which cannot profit them. On the other hand, let it sink deeply into every heart, that what the worldly call "waste,"— the soul that counts all things loss for Christ,—the life that is

spent in lessening the miseries of mankind, and seeking to convert sinners,—the silent sufferer, whose existence has been meek
and happy endurance of evil for Christ's sake,—those who live—

"The world forgetting, by the world forgot : "

these, after all, are the ornament, defence, and glory of society,
the salt which preserves it from corruption, the true and imperishable riches, which invest time with its best wealth, and
accumulate glorious treasures for eternity. And when the world
and the works that are therein shall be burned up, what alone
shall survive the conflagration,—what but those deeds, formerly
despised, that were done from love to Christ ? And when all
those shall be swept away into everlasting destruction, who
know not God, and obey not the Gospel of our Lord Jesus,—
who are they that shall shine forth like the sun in the kingdom
of their Father, but those who have poured out their hearts,
like Mary, at Christ's feet, and emptied the treasures of their
life, like precious ointment, in His cause, till the earth has been
filled with the fragrance, and it floats upwards, to be treasured
as the sweetest incense of immortality ?

Thus have we shortly set before us, the world's false estimate of deeds done for Christ, and the Saviour's commendation
of those deeds as the truest riches. It is for each of us to ask
ourselves on which side we take our stand,—with those who
do nothing for Christ and His cause, or with those who are ready
to embalm His blessed cause with all that we hold dearest,
even to the consecration and sacrifice of life itself ? Let us
not forget, that, if we are prepared to be workers for Christ,
and desire to secure His commendation, we must bear much
obloquy and misrepresentation. Let us be faithful, and we
shall be fearless. It is a small matter for us to be judged of
any man's judgment. The grand secret of good-doing is, doing
work for Christ. Many such opportunities lie open to us in
walks of love and usefulness around us ; and if God is willing
to employ you or me in such glorious work, let us know that
no higher blessing can belong to us than to save souls from
death, and hide a multitude of sins ; for "they that be wise
shall shine as the brightness of the firmament ; and they that
turn many to righteousness as the stars for ever and ever."

FELLOWSHIP OF CHRIST'S SUFFERINGS:

A SERMON.

PATON J. GLOAG, D.D.,

GALASHIELS.

"That I may know Him, and the power of His resurrection, and the fellowship of His sufferings, being made conformable unto His death."—PHIL. iii. 10.

IN the verse from which these words are taken, St Paul expresses his earnest desire to "know Christ,"—that is, to know Him experimentally as his Saviour; and "the power of His resurrection,"—that is, not the power by which He was raised, but the almighty power which His resurrection exercises on believers; and "the fellowship of His sufferings, being made conformable unto His death."

By "the fellowship of His sufferings," we are not here to understand *a participation in the sufferings of Christ, inasmuch as He was the substitute of sinners.* It is true that believers have, in this manner, in a certain sense, fellowship with Christ in His sufferings. Not only do they share in the advantages derived from these sufferings, but the sufferings themselves are in an important sense theirs; they are sharers in them. Christ stood in our room and stead; what He suffered was the punishment of our sins—the penalty attached to our disobedience. "He bore our griefs, He carried our sorrows; He was wounded for our transgressions, He was bruised for our iniquities." And therefore His sufferings may be regarded, in a peculiar sense, as ours, so that we, as it were, suffered in Christ; we died with Him in His death; "Our old man," as St Paul expresses it, "was crucified with Him." And hence, all believers who have a saving interest in these sufferings may be said to know experimentally "the fellowship of His sufferings." But still I do not think that this is the meaning which the apostle intends to convey. It does not appear that he here alludes to the sufferings of Christ in their expiatory nature, but merely to sufferings in general. And although we may be said to have fellowship with Christ, even in His expiatory sufferings, yet this is not a very obvious sense of the expression, nor is it one which, I think, would recommend itself to the Philippians as the meaning of the apostle.

Nor, again, is there any necessity to understand the expression as *metaphorical*,—that we have fellowship with Christ in His sufferings by being spiritually made conformable unto His death. This is, indeed, the sense which most commentators attach to the words. They represent the apostle as meaning that, as Christ died, so are we to die to sin; that, as Christ was nailed to the cross, so are we to crucify our corrupt passions; that, as Christ suffered in the body, so are we to suffer in the spirit. And, indeed, an important truth is expressed by this meaning—a truth elsewhere adverted to by the apostle, as when he says, "I am crucified with Christ, nevertheless I live; yet not I, but Christ liveth in me; and the life which I now live in the flesh, I live by the faith of the Son of God, who loved me, and gave Himself for me." But, still, this is not the import of the text; it is not the truth conveyed by these words of St Paul. It is a real, and not a mere metaphorical fellowship to which he adverts, a true participation with Christ in His sufferings,—drinking the same bitter cup of which He drank,—treading the same path of sorrow which He trod. St Paul here expresses his desire to share with Christ in His sufferings, and, if need be, to be conformed to His death,—like his Master, to suffer the agonies of crucifixion, or at least to die a martyr's death.

Now this is a strange desire of the apostle,—fellowship in suffering: a choice which certainly few of us would make. We wish to have fellowship in joy—to be made partakers of others' happiness, not of others' miseries—to frequent the house of feasting in preference to the house of mourning. We seek how we can pass most comfortably through life, experiencing the fewest inconveniences. But the apostle desires fellowship, not in joy, but in sorrow; he seeks to drink, not the cup of pleasure, but the cup of woe. It would not have been surprising, had the apostle desired fellowship with Christ in His glory, to live under the sunshine of the Redeemer's love: or had he desired fellowship with Christ in His resurrection and victory over death, in His ascension and session at God's right hand. But the wish here expressed is fellowship with Christ in His suffering, in His bearing the cross, rather than in His wearing the crown; conformity to His death, rather than participation in the glories of His resurrection-life. And yet, we cannot suppose that the apostle desired suffering for its own sake, but rather for the sake of those inestimable benefits which fellowship in suffering would confer. He knew well that the order of God's kingdom was, first the cross, then the crown; first the battle, then the victory; first the toil and heat of the day, then the rest; first fellowship with Christ in suffering, and then fellowship with Christ in glory.

In discoursing on this subject, I shall, in the first place, inquire in what sufferings we can have fellowship with Christ; and, in the second place, consider the benefits arising from fellowship in suffering.

I. *In the first place, then, we have to inquire, in what sufferings we can have fellowship with Christ.*

It is not in this passage only that we are taught that believers have an actual fellowship with Christ in suffering. The same assertion is made in other portions of the Word of God. "As," says St Paul, "the sufferings of Christ abound in us, so our consolation also aboundeth by Christ." "If children, then heirs, heirs of God, and joint-heirs with Christ; if so be that we suffer with Him, that we may be also glorified together." And again, "If we suffer with Him, we shall also reign with Him." Now, as I have already said, it is not necessary to understand these and such like expressions figuratively,—to hold that they allude merely to a spiritual conformity to Christ's sufferings,—a crucifixion of the flesh, with its affections and lusts. It is an actual sharing in suffering, a real participation in the same sorrows which were experienced by Christ. Believers are conformed to Christ. They have to drink of the same cup of which He drank, and to be baptised with the same baptism with which He was baptised. They must experience similar feelings—similar sorrows as well as joys. He is the Church's great model, of which all believers are copies. Believers must walk in His footsteps; Gethsemane and Calvary are stages on the road to glory. "Our sufferings are but the lengthened shadow of the cross."

But, to be more definite: In what particular sufferings may we be said to have fellowship with Christ? And, *first*, let us answer this question negatively, and point out some sufferings in which we cannot properly be said to have an actual fellowship with Christ; and, then, *secondly*, let us mention those sufferings which are common both to Christ and His people—in which they have a similar experience.

1. *First*, negatively, believers cannot have an actual fellowship with Christ *in His atoning sufferings*. In our introductory remarks, I observed that believers may be said to have fellowship with Christ even in these sufferings; this, however, is not an actual fellowship, but, so to speak, one by substitution. The sufferings of Christ formed the atonement for our sins; by them the justice of God was satisfied, and His law vindicated; by them, merit was obtained to procure the pardon of the guilty. There is an entire singularity in these expiatory sufferings; they are unique among all the sufferings in this universe. Into their mysterious nature we cannot enter; to His atoning sufferings, no sufferings of ours can have any resemblance. We cannot be partakers in them. No man can make any atonement for his own sins: far less can he offer any sacrifice for the sins of others. There is no such thing as creature-merit—no such thing as one creature enduring the penalty of the law for another. Paul, indeed, in a remarkable passage, speaks of filling up, by his sufferings, "that which is behind of the afflictions of Christ in His flesh, for His body's sake, which is the Church;" but by this cannot possibly be meant the completion of Christ's sufferings, as if they were imperfect, and as if Paul and other saints had to supply what was defective; or as if, according to the doctrine of a corrupt church, these sufferings of Paul were works of super-erogation. It is merely meant that Paul endured His portion of suffering for Christ's sake, as a member of the mystical body, the Church. Christ's body, the Church, had its complement of suffering to endure; and Paul, as a member of that body, by his sufferings, filled up his part which was wanting,—in the way of completion, indeed, but most certainly not in the way of atonement.

Nor can we have any fellowship with Christ *in those sufferings of ours which arise from guilt*. As we cannot be partakers with Christ in His atoning sufferings, so neither can Christ be a partaker with us in those sufferings which arise from actual sin. Much of our misery arises from personal guilt. There are the

C

accusations of an accusing conscience, the sense of guilt lying heavily upon the soul, the feeling that such a wicked action is ours, that it is stereotyped against us in the records of eternity. There are the fears of coming wrath—the terror of the Almighty which drinketh up our spirits. There is the sense of the Divine displeasure—a feeling that we have offended the Author of our being. There is the loss of character—the blasting of one's own reputation. There are all the other pernicious effects which sin often entails on ourselves, as the loss of health, the displeasure of the good, the desertion of friends, the degradation into which vice sinks us. And there are also the evil effects which our sins bring upon others,—upon our families, upon the Church, upon society at large.

But it would be impious to suppose that Christ was, in any sense whatever, a partaker of these sufferings. "He was holy, harmless, undefiled, and separate from sinners." In whatever sense He bore our sins, in whatever manner they affected Him, we must not for a moment suppose that He ever felt any of those regrets which we feel on the commission of sin; He must have been infinitely removed from all sense of sin arising from its actual commission; no feeling of guilt ever distracted the tranquillity of His soul; no such bitter ingredient was ever mingled in His cup of sorrow. In such sufferings, He can have no fellowship, no communion with us. They are sufferings to which none of His can bear any resemblance.

There is yet another class of sufferings, under which many of our troubles are included, of which we do not read that Christ was ever an actual partaker: I allude to *bodily affliction.* Of the many sufferings which Christ endured, we are not informed that He suffered from disease; we are never told that He was sick or unwell. This, indeed, may be said to be mere negative testimony, which proves nothing; but still, I am inclined to think that, if Christ had suffered from disease, it would have been mentioned. He was liable to many sinless infirmities, such as weariness, hunger, thirst, want; but sickness does not seem to have been one of them. I do not at present inquire into the reason of this exemption, I merely mention it as a remarkable fact. But, although Christ did not suffer personally from bodily afflictions, yet there is an important sense in which He was a partaker of these sufferings. His deep sympathy for others, His sensitive tenderness of heart, His boundless compassion, caused Him to feel keenly the sufferings of others, to put Himself in their place, and to appropriate to Himself their sorrows. And hence the Evangelist interprets the saying of the prophet thus: " Himself took our infirmities and bore our sickness."

2. *Secondly*, and positively, believers are partakers with Christ in those sufferings which arise from persecution for righteousness' sake. It is evident that it is primarily to these sufferings that Paul alludes here and in other portions of his epistles. "That I may know the fellowship of His sufferings, being made conformable unto His death ;" thus he expresses his readiness to endure the same persecutions which Christ endured, and, like Him, to end his life on the cross. And again, in this same epistle, he says: " Unto you it is given, on the behalf of Christ, not only to believe, but also to suffer for His sake." And St Peter calls on his converts to " rejoice " in persecution, inasmuch as they " are partakers of Christ's sufferings." Now, such sufferings constituted a large portion of the outward bodily sufferings of Christ. His whole life was a life of persecution for righteousness' sake. No sooner was He born than Herod sought to slay Him. During His public ministry, His enemies continually assaulted Him, endeavouring to ensnare Him in His words, and more than once conspiring to put Him to death. And at last they apparently triumphed over Him; they mocked, reviled, and maltreated Him ; they scourged and crowned Him with thorns, and at length put Him to an ignominious death. And in this respect the Apostles were conformed to their Master. They gained the reward of those who were persecuted for righteousness' sake. The world crowned them with the martyr's crown. Paul had his wish largely gratified. He partook in full measure of the sufferings of Christ; he drank deeply of the Saviour's cup. "Even unto this present hour," he writes, " we both hunger, and thirst, and are naked, and are buffeted, and have no certain dwelling-place; being reviled, we bless; being persecuted, we suffer it; being defamed, we entreat; we are made as the filth of the world, and are the offscourings of all things unto this day." It is true, and we bless God for it, that we are not now liable to sufferings of precisely the same nature. The days of persecution are now happily passed away, never more, it is to be hoped, to return. The principle·of religious toleration is now recognised as an undisputed maxim. But still, I believe that if a man maintains a very high standard of religion; if he lives an exalted, godly life in Christ Jesus; if he condemns the world by the holiness of his conduct, he will meet with persecu-

tion in the way of petty annoyances, designed misconceptions, and coldness of affection. The world is still the same in its aversion to the children of God; believers must still be conformed to the sufferings of Christ.

Again, believers are partakers with Christ in those sufferings which arise from sympathy with the distressed. These also constituted a great part of the sufferings of Christ. He felt keenly for human woe; every distress which He witnessed impressed itself, like a photographic picture, upon His soul; every cry of anguish which He heard was re-echoed from the depths of His Spirit; and perhaps, apart from His last sufferings, there is no scene of His life so affecting, and none that was the cause of such anguish unto Him as when, with weeping eyes and a breaking heart, He pronounced the doom of Jerusalem; it was infinite compassion weeping over the lost. " We have not," says the apostle, " an High Priest, who cannot be touched with the feeling of our infirmities, but One who was in all points tempted like as we are, yet without sin."

Now, in this respect, all believers must be conformed to the Master. The same sympathising, loving spirit which animated the Son of God must animate them. If we do not put ourselves in the place of our fellow-sufferers, if we do not weep with those who weep, if we do not endeavour to lessen the miseries of men, if we do not feel for the misfortunes of our brethren, if compassion is not substituted for selfishness in our hearts,—in a word, if we have no fellowship with Christ in His sympathetic sufferings, we are not His disciples, we have not imbibed His Spirit.

Believers are partakers with Christ in those sufferings which arise from grief for sin. Much of the sorrow of Christ must have been occasioned by His unavoidable intercourse with the wicked. When infinite purity comes in contact with wickedness, feelings of sorrow and moral indignation must be the result. How distressing must it have been, then, to the pure mind of Jesus, to hear the impious words which were uttered, to see the wicked actions which men did, to think also on the end to which all this wickedness inevitably led—to see God dishonoured and man ruined. And so it is with all true believers. The very sight of wickedness must be the cause of sorrow to them. The state of the world around them,—the abounding of iniquity,—the open and outrageous transgression of many,—the vice, and degradation, and moral ruin of multitudes among them,—the

shame and dishonour which the wickedness of professing Christians often brings upon the Saviour's cause,— the wickedness
of the neighbourhood in which they dwell—the drunkenness,
the Sabbath profanation, the blasphemy which everywhere
abound; the miseries which wicked men bring upon themselves
and others, both in this world and in the next—must necessarily
be peculiarly afflictive to all true Christians. In all these sufferings, then, believers have fellowship with Christ.

Believers are partakers with Christ in all those sufferings
which arise from spiritual distress. We would not have supposed that Christ would ever have been exposed to such sufferings; on the contrary, we would have imagined that, as God's
well-beloved Son, He would have enjoyed an abiding sense of the
Divine love; that, however threatening the storms abroad, there
would be perpetual sunshine in His soul. But there are, in the
life of Christ, intimations given us, once and again, that He knew
what spiritual distress was; as in the agony of Gethsemane,
when He offered up strong crying and tears unto Him who was
able to save Him from death; and on the cross of Calvary, when
He complained of spiritual desertion. There is most certainly a
mystery hanging over these sufferings of our Lord, which we
cannot penetrate; this is one of those things which angels desire
to look into.

Similar sufferings are experienced by believers. They have
their seasons of spiritual distress, when the light of God's countenance is obscured. Their spiritual joys and hopes are often
withdrawn, and there is the absence of sensible tokens of God's
love. They sometimes feel as if God had deserted them, and had
for ever withdrawn from them His grace; and thus they are
constrained to cry out with the Psalmist, "Hath God forgotten
to be gracious? Hath He in anger shut up His tender mercies?"
Now, it must be to them a blessed consideration, that they have
a Saviour who can sympathise with them in these sorrows, that
they have fellowship with Christ in these sufferings.

II. *But let us consider, in the second place, the benefits arising
from fellowship in suffering.*

"It is better," says the wise man, "to go to the house of
mourning than to the house of feasting. Sorrow is better than
laughter: for, by the sadness of the countenance, the heart is
made better." Uninterrupted prosperity has a prejudicial influ-

ence over our spiritual nature. It is not good for a man to be always fortunate; success is more frequently a curse than a blessing. Prosperity enervates character, weakens our moral powers, and tempts us to indulge in sloth and carnal enjoyment. We are thus led to forget God; we do not feel the sensible tokens of His presence; we are not alive to our need of Him, and are thus led to self-dependence and arrogance of mind. The world also insinuates itself into our hearts; we seek our happiness in it, and make its riches or honours the chief objects of our pursuits. The school of prosperity is unfavourable to the cultivation of religious feelings; there is much to tempt and draw us aside from God. On the other hand, in the school of adversity, we may form those habits and imbibe those feelings which are conducive to our moral training; here we may learn those lessons which will be useful to us in a world of glory.

Suffering purifies the soul. Affliction is a furnace which purifies. The spirit, loaded with the dross of earth, is purified by trial: the dross is removed, and the grains of pure gold remain. The evils contracted by prosperity are removed by adversity. We are withdrawn from the world; we lose our taste for its pleasures, its riches, and its honours; we are made sensible of its vanity. Our passions are mortified; our pride is humbled under a sense of our own infirmities; our covetousness is overcome by experiencing the vanity of riches; our ambition is weakened by the disappointment of our hopes; our lukewarmness gives place to fervency on the threatened approach of death; and our hard hearts are softened by an actual experience of suffering. So also our graces are confirmed and strengthened; our faith in God and Christ, our sympathy with the distressed, our patience in suffering, our resignation to the Divine will, our hope of heaven, our dependence on God,—all these graces are exercised by suffering; and thus it is that suffering, in various ways, improves our moral character. "God," says the apostle, "chastens us for our profit, that we might be partakers of His holiness."

Suffering draws forth the better qualities of a man. There is something in trial which stirs a man's nature to its depths, weakens what is evil in him, and brings to light what is good. How often do we see men improved by trial! Many a man, for example,—perfectly listless and insipid in prosperity, without character, devoid of animation, entirely negative and unmeaning, useless and destitute of energy, a mere cipher, whose death would be unfelt save in his own family,—is rendered truly noble by adversity, exhibiting virtues which he was never before known to possess, performing Christian works for which he once appeared totally unfit. Even bad men do sometimes, by the noble manner in which they bear adversity, by their heroic demeanour under trial, by the fortitude with which they meet their doom, command our respect, and almost, in our view, atone for their crimes. In many such cases, doubtless, affliction has had a sanctifying efficacy. So also, good men are often vastly improved by affliction. Qualities, formerly latent in the soul, are called forth. Noble feelings,—such, especially, as all the gentle graces, and all the passive virtues,—which were never known to exist, spring, as it were, into being. The seeds of virtue germinate in the hot-bed of affliction, spring up and flourish, and bring forth fruit unto eternal life. It is thus that suffering often makes a man a nobler character, a more marked being—not a mere insignificant unit, but a true man; one who feels that he has a life to live, a destiny to work out, and a character to form. "It was good for me," says the Psalmist, "that I was afflicted, that I might learn Thy precepts."

Suffering enables us to comfort others. Affliction is the great school wherein we are trained to do good to our fellow-men; here we are taught the art of sympathy. We thus learn to feel for others, to sympathise with them, to relieve their necessities. We are not only thereby stirred up to acts of benevolence, but we are taught how best to perform them; not merely to relieve the distressed, but to sympathise with them in their distresses; to remember them that suffer adversity, as being ourselves also in the body, liable to the same calamities. There is a great difference in the manner in which distress is relieved. One person may give largely of his money to the poor, but never come personally into contact with them; such a person experiences little advantage from his charity. But another person mixes with them, visits them in their houses, enters into their feelings, sympathises with them in their troubles; and thus, while in a more effectual manner he relieves their wants, he has at the same time his own heart improved and made better. Prosperity may induce a man to be benevolent; but he cannot, without adversity, enter deeply into the feelings of the distressed. The grace of sympathy is best learned by personal suffering. And hence it is that, in trouble, we seek for comfort from those who have been similarly tried, and who thus can have fellowship with us in suffering. Men liable to the same infirmities—not angels, however perfect, but who never knew what trial is—are our comforters. "God," says the apostle, "comforteth us in all our tribulation, that we may be able to comfort them which are in any trouble, by the comfort wherewith we ourselves are comforted by God."

And lastly, suffering prepares for heaven. "Our light affliction," says the apostle, "which is but for a moment, worketh for us a far more exceeding and eternal weight of glory." We have already seen, in part, how it does so. It purifies the soul, improves our moral character, weakens our corruptions, strengthens our graces, draws forth our better qualities, and makes us sympathising, loving, and compassionate. Habits, also, which shall be useful to us in another world are formed by suffering, and could not be acquired by prosperity. In suffering, we are taught our continual dependence on God; then all the passive virtues are exercised, the gentler graces flourish, heaven and the things of heaven occupy our thoughts, faith exhibits to us the abodes of the faithful, and love to Him who died for us, and who sympathises with us in all our troubles, is strengthened and confirmed. The more the soul is purified by trial, the better is it prepared for the mansions of glory. The greater the trials, the sweeter the promises. The heavier the cross, the brighter the crown. The more plentiful the precious seed of sanctified affliction, the more abundant the harvest of joy. And as we are now partakers of the sufferings of Christ, we shall, in a future world, be partakers of His consolations; here, we are made conformable to His death,—hereafter, we shall be made conformable to His resurrection.

One caution, and with it I conclude. You must not imagine that suffering by itself produces all those benefits which are here mentioned; it does so only when accompanied by the operation of the Holy Ghost. The fire, which melts some metals, hardens others; some are improved by suffering, and others, by reason of their own perverseness, are made worse. It is only unto them who are duly exercised thereby, that affliction yieldeth the peaceable fruits of righteousness.

BLASPHEMY OF THE HOLY SPIRIT:

A SERMON.

BY THE

Rev. WILLIAM REID, D.D.,

LOTHIAN ROAD UNITED PRESBYTERIAN CHURCH, EDINBURGH.

"Wherefore I say unto you, All manner of sin and blasphemy shall be forgiven unto men : but the blasphemy against the Holy Ghost shall not be forgiven unto men. And whosoever speaketh a word against the Son of man, it shall be forgiven him ; but whosoever speaketh against the Holy Ghost, it shall not be forgiven him, neither in this world, neither in the world to come."—MATT. xii, 31, 32.

THE sin against the Holy Ghost has occasioned much perplexity. The learned have differed as to what it is, and the unlearned have feared lest they have committed it. The difficulty is so peculiar, and the distress occasioned by it is so great, that any attempt to solve the difficulty, and thereby remove the distress, is surely becoming.

Our Lord, you will observe, uttered the words before us on the occasion of delivering a man from a blind and dumb spirit. Many of those who witnessed this double miracle, saw in it a proof of His Messiahship, and gave expression to that conviction ; for we read, " All the people were amazed and said, Is not this the Son of David ? " That is—is not this the Messiah, the Christ ? But His inveterate enemies, the Pharisees, made the miracle the ground of the vilest slander, inasmuch as they charged Him with casting out devils by the power of Beelzebub. Now, if ever, it was necessary for Christ to speak, and to speak with no bated breath. Indeed, He might have done something more than speak. Had He struck these revilers dumb for their blasphemy, and blind with a more terrible blindness, He would only have visited their offence with the award which it merited. " But in wrath he remembered mercy." First of all, He defends

Himself from the wicked charge of being in league with the devil; and then, rising in all the majesty of insulted Divinity, He characterises their wickedness as blasphemy against the Son of man, and warns them that like treatment of the Holy Ghost, whose work was to succeed His own, would be unpardonable.

I purpose, then, pointing out wherein the sin against the Holy Ghost consists; and considering the question, Whether its commission be possible still?

I. *Observe, first of all, the sin spoken of in the text is described as blasphemy.*

It is common to speak of the *sin* against the Holy Ghost; but Jesus does not call it *sin* but *blasphemy.* Nor are they one and the same. All blasphemy against the Holy Ghost is doubtless sin; but all sin against the Holy Spirit is not blasphemy. We read of "grieving," "quenching," and "resisting" the Spirit. These are sins against the Holy Spirit, but they are not blasphemy. In one aspect, every sin that is committed is sin against the Holy Ghost; but we would not say that all sin is blasphemy against the Holy Ghost. Now, it is well to keep in view this distinction, as it greatly limits our field of observation—in fact, narrows it to a particular sin of a special kind, and thereby enables us to determine, with greater certainty, in what the sin really consists.

What, then, are we to understand by blasphemy against the Holy Ghost? To utter slanderous, abusive, defamatory, or malignant words, under the influence of vindictive feeling, against any one, is, according to Scripture, to blaspheme him. We, however, restrict the use of the word to God alone. When, then, abusive and defamatory words are uttered against God wilfully, knowingly, and malignantly, it is blasphemy.

Now, the charge which Christ makes against these Pharisees is, that they had blasphemed against Himself, and that, in the event of their resisting and misrepresenting the Holy Ghost in a like manner, they would commit a sin which is unpardonable. Observe: He cast out a devil, and He said He did it by the power of God. The Pharisees, on the other hand, asserted that He did it by Beelzebub, which, Mark informs us, was equivalent to charging Him with being in league with an unclean spirit— Beelzebub being so regarded; and this they said, rather than acknowledge His Divine commission, although they could neither deny nor explain away the miracle which He had performed.

Here, then, we have all the elements which go to establish the charge of blasphemy against these men, and the means of determining wherein the sin against the Holy Spirit still consists. Just as an abusive and malignant rejection of Christ, when He had afforded conclusive evidence of His Messiahship, was blasphemy against Himself; so now, an abusive and malignant rejection of the truth about Jesus is blasphemy against the Holy Ghost. It would surprise you, were I to enumerate the various sins which have been characterised as this blasphemy. Take the following as a sample:—sinning against light, denying the truth, denying the Divinity of Christ, resisting the Spirit, belying conscientious convictions, backsliding, apostacy, atheistical thoughts, doubts and unbelief, have all been adduced as instances of this sin. Doubtless, they are all sins which, if unrepented, may issue in the eternal ruin of the soul; but, notwithstanding, not one of them can be properly designated blasphemy. Why, then, specify various offences, as if they were this sin, when not one of them has the essential characteristics of blasphemy? Why thus needlessly increase the distress of anxious souls, when Christ but speaks of one, and that one so exceptional and peculiar that all may easily understand what it is? The fact is, it is not to be found in this sin or in that sin, but solely and alone in that which can properly be described as blasphemy, and that blasphemy against the Holy Ghost.

II. *The second thing to be observed is, that this blasphemy is described as a sin specially against the Holy Ghost.*

Now, why is it thus characterised, and not as a sin against the Father or the Son? We may rest assured that it is not because He is more sacred than the Father or the Son. The Scriptural doctrine of the Trinity is, that the Father, Son, and Holy Spirit are the same in substance, equal in power and glory. Nor is He called Holy because He is more holy than the Father or the Son, but because His great work is the production of holiness in the believing heart. The reason, then, why this sin is represented as specially against the Holy Ghost is, that in revilingly opposing the Gospel, the work of the Spirit is specially opposed. It is the Spirit who takes of the things of Christ and, through the Word, read or spoken, presents them to the mind. No minister or private Christian speaks the word which converts a soul, but under the immediate direction of the Holy Spirit. It is the Spirit who gives to the sinner that interest in divine things which secures attention to them when so presented. It is the Spirit, too, who gives the susceptibility which prepares for their due impression, and that love of the truth which inclines the soul to close with its overtures. Now, if all this be resisted, and, especially, if it be resisted with abusive language, it is easily seen how the sin thus committed is specially against the Holy Ghost, inasmuch as it is an impious defiance of His peculiar prerogative.

III. *The crowning fact connected with this sin is its unpardonableness.*

Once and again, Jesus declares that, for this sin, there is no forgiveness. The question then naturally presents itself,—When there is forgiveness for all sins besides, how is it that there is none for this? What sin could be more heinous than that which these Pharisees committed in alleging that Christ was in league with the devil? To treat the author of this most beneficent miracle as an impostor—to endeavour to disprove His claims as the Messiah, and thereby defeat His design to save the world —to confound a work of the God of Holiness with a work of a foul fiend—to call good evil, and evil good—to refuse to enter the kingdom of heaven, and to forbid those who would enter to go in—is a sin which mounts up in iniquity to the very heavens; and yet, even for this sin, there was forgiveness. Or, if there be a sin of greater heinousness, it surely must have been the murder of our Lord; and yet many of His murderers obtained mercy. In view of these facts, how is it that there is no forgiveness for the sin of which our text speaks? It cannot be because of any inadequacy in the merit of Christ's atonement. For " His blood cleanseth us from all sin." Nor can it be that the mercy of God cannot reach such a sin, for His mercy is infinite; and what limits can be set to infinitude? Nor can it be that the Spirit is unable to overcome the obduracy involved in such iniquity, for He is omnipotent. The truth is, that, properly speaking, there is no sin in itself unpardonable. To say that there is would be to contradict what Christ asserts in the 31st verse. The reason of the unpardonableness of this sin, then, is to be found, I apprehend, not in its turpitude, but in its nature, inasmuch as it discovers a state of heart resolutely opposed to the Spirit and to the truth. Dead in trespasses and sins, man does not spontaneously awake to spiritual life. The conviction of sin, faith in Christ, and repentance toward God, are all the works of the Spirit; hence, if the Word be neglected, and the Spirit scorned, it follows, as a necessary consequence, that pardon is impossible. Pardon depends on penitence—not that it is dispensed because of penitence, or on the ground of it; but because, in the very nature of the case, the absence of it precludes pardon. Even an earthly parent cannot forgive a child till it has exhibited a due sense of sorrow for its offence; and as sorrow for sin is unknown to those guilty of blasphemy against the Holy Spirit, their salvation is impossible. When, then, resistance is accompanied by blasphemous language, and this blasphemy is persisted in, up to a certain point, the grieved and insulted One ceases His gracious pleadings, and sets upon the soul the seal of final condemnation—a seal which no power in earth or heaven can possibly break. Where the line is which separates the sphere of mercy from the sphere of doom, no one can tell; but those who are persisting in a course of blasphemy, or abusive resistance to the Spirit and His work—either in attributing His work to evil influence, or denying its reality, or pouring contempt on His blessed name—may well fear.

IV. *The question here presents itself,—may this sin be still committed?*

I think it may. It is common with those who hold that these Pharisees had committed the unpardonable sin, and that its commission was limited to their time, to argue as if Jesus had performed this miracle by the power of the Holy Spirit, and that the sin consisted in ascribing the power by which it was performed to Satan. Jesus does indeed say—"If I cast out devils by the Spirit of God, then the kingdom of God is come nigh unto you." But observe; He does not say, "If I cast out devils by the Holy Spirit," but, "by the Spirit of God;" and if we turn to Luke's account of the miracle, we there find, instead of "Spirit of God," "finger of God,"—a figure significant of power. In performing miracles, He uniformly speaks as if the power by which He accomplished them was His own, or that of His Father. "The works which I do in my Father's name, they bear witness of me." "My Father worketh hitherto, and I work." It is no doubt true that we read of the power of working miracles as one of the gifts conferred by the Spirit, but it is to be observed that this was a power not conferred till the promised dispensation of the Spirit had come, and that then it was conferred on the apostles alone. Nowhere do we read

of its ever having been conferred on Christ. The fact is, in
virtue of His Divinity, He required no such endowment. He
even predicted that when the apostles should work miracles, it
would be in His name and by His power. Now, it is important
to keep this in view, in order to see that there is no ground for
the allegation that He wrought the miracle before us by the
Holy Spirit, and that therefore these Pharisees were guilty of
blaspheming Him. He wrought the miracle by His own power,
and hence we conclude that it was Christ, and not the Holy
Spirit whom they blasphemed.

Having cleared the ground of this objection, we are ready to
look at the evidence, which the passage affords, of the position
we hold. The simple fact that this incident is put on record at
all, and that not fewer than three of the evangelists quote our
Lord's words, is surely most significant. To suppose that He
denounced this sin in words so terrible—a sin, the bare possibility of committing which is fitted to awaken the most tor-
turing fears in sensitive souls—and that yet it could never be
repeated, is altogether at variance with what we know of the
mercy and tenderness of His character.

Observe, that our Lord specifies two sins—speaking against
the Son of man, and speaking against the Holy Ghost. Now, on
looking at the narrative, it appears that the sin, committed in
the present instance, was that of speaking against the Son of
man. He it was who wrought the miracle; and He wrought
it, as we have seen, by His own power; and He it was against
whom the malice of the Pharisees was aimed. Now, had they
been actually guilty of blasphemy against the Holy Ghost, Jesus
would doubtless have said so. Does He not, however, rather
intimate—by the antithesis which He presents between blasphemy against the Son of man and that against the Holy
Ghost, and by the pardonableness of the one and the unpardonableness of the other—that it was blasphemy against Himself
of which they had been guilty? Why speak of blasphemy
against the Son of man, if the sin which they had committed
was actually blasphemy against the Holy Ghost? And why
speak of the pardonableness of blasphemy against Himself, if
they had committed another sin which was unpardonable?
Would that not be to tantalise? But such a supposition is
utterly at variance with what we know of the tenderness of
the Saviour's character.

We regard Jesus as, in effect, saying—"Dreadful as it is to

speak disparagingly of the Son of man in this the day of His humiliation, when His true character is veiled, there is a day coming, when the evidence of My Divine commission will be complete, not only through the miraculous outpouring of the Spirit, but by the conversion of thousands to the Gospel; and, when that day comes, they who treat the work of the Spirit as they now treat me, shall, even in this life, pass from the sphere of mercy to that of inevitable doom."

One fact identifies this saying of Christ with the outpouring of the Spirit, beyond all dispute. If you turn to Luke xii. 10-12 you will read—"And whosoever shall speak a word against the Son of man, it shall be forgiven him: but unto Him that blasphemeth against the Holy Ghost, it shall not be forgiven. And when they bring you unto the synagogues, and unto magistrates, and powers, take ye no thought how or what thing ye shall answer, or what ye shall say: for the Holy Ghost shall teach you in the same hour what ye ought to say." These words seem to have been spoken on a different occasion from the present. From the first verse, we learn they were addressed to disciples; and from this fact we infer that the sin in question may be committed, not only by Christ's avowed enemies, but by those who confess His name. Observe then, that while, in the 10th verse, He repeats in substance the words of our text, in the 11th and 12th verses he predicts what actually took place immediately after the dispensation of the Spirit had begun on the day of Pentecost. For, when Peter and John were brought before the council, it is stated that, on Peter rising to speak, he was "filled with the Holy Ghost" (Acts iv. 1-8). And what was that but a literal fulfilment of what Christ predicted in immediate connection with the text as given by Luke? "For the Holy Ghost," he said, "shall teach you, in the same hour, what ye ought to say,"—conclusively showing that it was the dispensation of the Spirit which Christ had more particularly in view when he uttered the awful words of our text.

So far, then, from thinking, as some have done, that this sin consisted in ascribing the miracles of Christ to Satanic agency, and that it could only be committed during the period of Christ's earthly ministry, I rather conclude, on these grounds, that the Saviour specially pointed to that future which is our present, as the season of its commission.

V. Before concluding, it may be proper to ask if we can find, in our conduct or in that of others, the image of anything like this sin?

I think we can. From the treatment which these Pharisees gave to Christ, and from what Christ said respecting the sin in question, we have concluded that it consists in abusive and defamatory words, uttered wilfully and malignantly against Christ, when in the possession of adequate means for knowing the truth. Thus aided, we may have less difficulty in effecting its detection.

1st. There are the Jews. No people was ever so privileged, and no people ever so sinned. They were familiar with the types, sacrifices, and prophecies which pointed to Christ; and yet, when He came to His own, they received Him not. We can scarcely doubt that Jesus had in view the enmity which they were about to manifest to Himself and to His cause, when He uttered the words before us; and that, in His touching lamentation over Jerusalem, He regarded them as doomed for the commission of this sin: "O Jerusalem! Jerusalem! thou that killest the prophets, and stonest them which are sent unto thee, how often would I have gathered thy children together, even as a hen gathereth her chickens under her wings, and ye would not." One deed more—the darkest deed of all—and the cup of their iniquity was full. "His blood be upon us and on our children." Never was imprecation more terribly fulfilled. From that time till now, their hatred of Christianity has been proverbial. To spurn the very name of Jesus, and spit at the New Testament, is an every-day occurrence; indeed, to this day, they ascribe the miracles of Christ to the agency of the devil. Their fathers crucified Him as a blasphemer, and they still approve the deed. Though favoured with the Gospel from the very first,—for, when Christ charged His apostles to preach the Gospel to the whole world, he said "beginning at Jerusalem,"—though still possessed of the Old Testament Scriptures, which they prize with idolatrous fondness, and in which the character and work of Christ are set forth with almost New-Testament clearness, so that the Spirit of the Lord is but needed to transform their synagogues into Christian Churches; yet it is among them as an ever-resisted testimony for Christ. "For, even unto this day, when Moses is read, the veil is upon their heart." Now, we discover, in all this, the leading features of blasphemy against the Holy Ghost.

2nd. Another form in which the sin against the Holy Ghost now presents itself is that of scornfully resisting conscientious convictions. To know that the Gospel is true, and yet to reject it with scorn, and to persist in this course, is undoubtedly of the nature of the sin in question. There is a touching incident related in the life of the late Mr. Brownlow North. He had been frequently under the conviction of sin, and had even gone the length of attending the University, with a view to ordination in connection with the Church of England. Seasons of conviction were, however, succeeded by relapses into a state of spiritual indifference and worldly gaiety. At length, conviction came upon him in a manner not to be trifled with. I had better give the account of his final decision for Christ in his own words. " It pleased God," he says, " in the month of November, 1854, one night when I was sitting playing at cards, to make me concerned about my soul. The instrument used was a sensation of sudden illness, which led me to think that I was going to die. I said to my son, ' I am a dead man ; take me upstairs.' As soon as this was done, I threw myself down on the bed. My first thought then was, Now, what will my forty-four years of following the devices of my own heart profit ? In a few minutes I shall be in hell, and what good will all things do me, for which I have sold my soul ? At that moment, I felt constrained to pray ; but it was merely the prayer of the coward, a cry for mercy. I was not sorry for what I had done, but I was afraid of the punishment of my sin. And yet still there was something trying to prevent me from putting myself on my knees to call for mercy ; and that was the presence of the maidservant in the room, lighting my fire. · Though I did not believe at that time I had ten minutes to live, and knew that there was no possible hope for me but in the mercy of God, and that, if I did not seek that mercy, I could not expect to have it, yet such was the nature of my heart and of my spirit within me, that it was a balance with me, a thing to turn this way or that, I could not tell how, whether I should wait till that woman left the room, or whether I should fall on my knees and cry for mercy in her presence. By the grace of God, I did put myself on my knees before that girl, and I believe it was the turning-point with me. I believe that if I had at that time resisted the Holy Ghost—of course, I cannot say ; for who shall limit the Holy Ghost ?—but my belief is, that it would have been once too late. By God's grace, I was not prevented. I did pray ; and though I am not what I should be, yet I am this

D

day what I am, which at least is not what I was. I mention this because I believe that every man has in his life a turning-point. I believe that the sin against the Holy Ghost is, grieving the Spirit once too often."

I cannot, however, believe with him, that the sin of which he was in danger was that of blaspheming the Holy Ghost. No doubt, "the sin against the Holy Ghost is grieving the Spirit once too often." But it is grieving the Spirit once too often with malignant feeling and reviling words, and I am unable to gather from the life of this remarkable man that his persistent rejection of Christ was of this character. Doubtless, he was guilty of resisting the Holy Ghost, but not of blaspheming Him; and it is important to keep in view this distinction.

It is, I believe, no uncommon thing, in seasons of religious revival, to find those who have been deeply impressed, and who have almost been persuaded to become Christians, under the influence of the world or some cherished sin, not only to reject the truth, but to do so with oaths and cursing,—blaspheming the very name of Jesus and all things sacred. Nor is it uncommon for such to revile a work of grace in others. The conversion of a soul is a great work—a work of such excellence that it redounds especially to the glory of the Spirit. And this is a work frequently accomplished, not only in the case of well-trained, well-conducted, good-living, moral people, but, in numerous instances, in the case of those of openly irreligious life. Now, to revile such a work—to deny its reality—to ridicule the idea of the Holy Spirit having produced this wondrous change, or to ascribe it to hypocrisy, or to any evil influence whatever, bears a striking analogy to the sin under consideration.

3rd. Perhaps, however, it is in the annals of infidelity we must seek in our day for the grossest forms of this sin. Instances might be adduced, in which infidels, exasperated at their utter inability to disprove the evidences of Christianity, have given vent to the foulest blasphemy. Sitting in the chair of the scornful was not peculiar to the days of the Psalmist. By no feature is the aspect of our times more painfully characterised than by the bold and reckless hostility of ungodly men to Christ and the Christian cause. Boasting of their superiority to vulgar prejudice, and of their having based their belief solely on the discoveries of advanced science, they hold up to scorn the most sacred mysteries of our faith. Now, we can conceive of no sin coming nearer to that against which the Saviour warns us than sin like this.

> " Within this awful volume lies
> The mystery of mysteries ;
> But better had he ne'er been born,
> Who reads to doubt, or reads to scorn."

But, how different is all this from the spirit of those who dread the very possibility of their having committed this offence, —whose consciences are so sensitive that they would not cross a straw were it forbidden by God. Would such, I ask, willingly take rank with these atrocious transgressors? The very supposition shocks them. The truth is, not a few have conceived that they have been guilty of this sin who are utterly unable to tell what it is. If even learned men have found it encompassed with manifold difficulties, how can unlearned persons know that they have committed it? Ask any one who charges himself with this sin, what it really is; and you will find that those who think they have committed it have generally only some vague, undefined impression respecting it.

Those who dread they have committed this sin have chiefly to determine whether they have been indulging in malicious and abusive thoughts and words against the Holy Spirit and His work; and whether they have passed the fatal boundary-line which separates the sphere of mercy from the sphere of doom. To determine the former of these questions may be easy, but who shall determine the latter? For, while the nature of the sin itself may be easily determined, the fact of having committed it remains shrouded in mystery; and doubtless it is purposely so, to awaken fear and forbid the most distant approach to a region so awful. But this I may say—No one forsaken by the Spirit shall ever be possessed of a fear respecting it, such an one being incapable of that dread, owing to the very obduracy before which the Spirit retires; and hence, those who fear and tremble may confidently conclude, that, however long and however dark be the catalogue of their sins, this one is not of the number.

HEARERS OF THE GOOD TIDINGS ARE TO TELL THEM:

A SERMON.

BY THE

Rev. WILLIAM WILSON, D.D.,

SENIOR MINISTER OF FREE ST. PAUL'S CHURCH, DUNDEE.

"And go quickly, and tell His disciples that He is risen from the dead ; and, behold, He goeth before you into Galilee ; there shall ye see Him : lo, I have told you. And they departed quickly from the sepulchre, with fear and great joy, and did run to bring the disciples word."—MATT. xxviii. 7, 8.

"But go your way, tell His disciples and Peter that He goeth before you into Galilee : there shall ye see Him, as He said unto you. And they went out quickly, and fled from the sepulchre ; for they trembled and were amazed : neither said they any thing to any man ; for they were afraid."—MARK xvi. 7, 8.

THE good news of the resurrection, which had been announced by an angel to the women at the sepulchre, had a practical conclusion, as indeed, every gospel from heaven has, either expressed or implied. The glad tidings which had been preached to them were not designed to enkindle joy in their hearts alone. They were tidings of great joy which were unto all people—designed to be proclaimed from mouth to mouth, till the glad sound should reach the uttermost parts of the earth. The disciples of Jesus were not to constitute a new school, after the fashion of those of Greece or of Alexandria, with their outer and inner circles of truth, and hidden mysteries. They were messengers, missionaries, witnesses for Christ ; and what they had heard in the ear, they were to proclaim from the house-top. To them, there was no profane vulgar, who were to be driven back from the sacred temple. They were to be as a light set upon a candlestick, to give light to all. The knowledge which they received implied or expressed the obligation to impart it. They were to be dispensers of that grace of which they were made partakers, to reflect the light that was shining in their hearts, to be witnesses of the truth which they had been taught. This obligation had been laid upon them, from the first, by Jesus in the sermon on the mount; and, in the course of his ministry, it had been repeatedly pressed upon them. Whatever gift they might receive in the manifold grace of God, they were bound to impart to others, that their riches might become the riches of the world. For Christ was God's gift to the world, not to the Jews only, not to any particular nation, but to all men, Greeks, Barbarians, Scythians, bond and free; and whosoever received that unspeakable gift was under obligation to dispense its treasures, as he had opportunity, to all men. Always and everywhere, this is the Commission of the Church, and of every member of it. This is the charge given to all believers by him who came into the world to seek and to save the lost: "Go ye into all the world, and preach the Gospel to every creature;" preach it in the highways, and seek the lost in all places of their dispersion and seclusion; "and compel them to come in, that my house may be filled."

This wide field of operation, which embraces all the world, has, necessarily, various departments; and the Church which is evangelistic,—which is true to its high vocation, has various agencies at work in them. There are Foreign Missions, and missions to the dispersed of Israel, missions to our own countrymen dispersed over many lands, and missions to the neglected and ignorant within our own shores. It was thus from the beginning, from the day of Pentecost downwards. The proclamation of the glad tidings began at Jerusalem, where they had been announced to the disciples, and where there were so many who did not yet know them; but they were sounded abroad from that centre, over the three great Continents of the old world. The Home Mission enlarged itself into a Foreign Mission; and Paul, who was designated very specially as a Foreign Missionary,—one sent to the Gentiles, "to open their eyes, and to turn them from darkness to light, and from the power of Satan unto God,"—was also a colonial missionary, preaching Christ to the Jews in whatever town they had a synagogue.

But, besides all these departments of mission-work, there is another to which these women at the sepulchre were specially, and in the first instance designated. It is the innermost, but by no means the least important department of mission labour. The Church has a mission-field within herself, the cultivation of

which is essential to the existence and energy of all other missions. There must be light, and life, and strength in the Church
itself, if it is to become an evangelistic power in the world. The
root and source of that beneficence which it administers to the
world without, whether at home or abroad, is its own possession
of that grace which the Lord imparts. The Church must itself
receive and appreciate the glad tidings, ere it can be a faithful
and efficient instrument for sounding them abroad. The fountain must be fed by its secret springs, in order to send forth its
healing waters. In many respects, then, this innermost mission
which the Church has to carry on within itself is the most important of them all, because it is the originator and sustainer of
them all. This is a mission-field, which, though it lies so very
near us, is, I fear, very much neglected. Of one very important
department in this field, indeed, this cannot perhaps be truly said.
The ordinary ministry of the Gospel belongs very much to this
field of internal mission. That ministry, it is true, is not limited
to the Church. It has the high aim of turning sinners to God,—
of converting the ungodly. It reaches unbelievers, and, by the
grace of God, draws them to the living Saviour. But it is also a
mission to the Church itself, and is designed for the edifying of
the body of Christ. This is peculiarly and eminently the purpose of it, as is indicated in the declared design of Christ, in
conferring upon the Church pastors and teachers. It was " for
the perfecting of the saints, for the work of the ministry, for the
edifying of the body of Christ." But this work of ministry, or
service for edification, does not belong exclusively to pastors and
teachers. It belongs to every one who has received of the Lord,
to impart that which he has obtained. The Church is a body,
"fitly joined together, and it is compacted by that which every
joint supplieth." It exists under the conditions which belong
to bodily life, each member having its own function and office ;
and each, in the discharge of its own function, ministering
to the health of the whole body — giving that which it has
received, and performing that service for which it was designed.
It is an obligation resting on the members of the Church, that
they edify one another ; that they be not receivers only of that
which is ministered to them, but dispensers also of that which
they have received ; that they be not merely as those who sit
at table to be served, but that they gird themselves for service.
"For the body is not one member, but many. If the foot shall
say, Because I am not the hand, I am not of the body ; is it,

therefore, not of the body ? And if the ear shall say, Because I am not the eye, I am not of the body ; is it, therefore, not of the body ? If the whole body were an eye, where were the hearing ? If the whole were hearing, where were the smelling ? But now hath God set the members, every one of them in the body as it hath pleased Him. And if they were all one member, where were the body ? But now are they many members, yet but one body. And the eye cannot say to the hand, I have no need of thee ; nor again, the head to the feet, I have no need of you." That is to say, each member of this complex body has its own office and function, and, in performing the part assigned to it, ministers to the whole body. The ear hears for all the body, and the eye sees for it all, and the hand works for it all. They are not separate and independent, but are compacted together, and form one living organisation ; and the healthful existence of the whole depends upon the performance of its functions by each member. Each has its own work to do, according as God hath dealt to every man the measure of faith. Hence the repeated injunctions, running through all the epistles, "Exhort one another daily." "Edify one another." "Be not slothful" in your work, but "fervent in spirit, serving the Lord." The gift which the Lord bestows on any one member of the Church is given for the edifying of the body, and not of that one member only. That which belongs to one is the property of the whole body. This is the great mission belonging to every member of the Church. Even as regards temporal things, the Apostolic Church at Jerusalem had all things in common, and no man called his possessions his own. But this is always an obligation in regard to spiritual gifts, that we make our brethren partakers of them.

This was the mission to which these women at the sepulchre were designated. "Go quickly, and tell His disciples that He is risen from the dead." This was the gift which had been conferred upon them, even the information which filled them with great joy, that Christ was risen. It was not a joy which they were to hide in their hearts, but which they were commissioned to communicate. The other disciples were, as yet, ignorant,—as, indeed all the world was,—of this wondrous fact, which was so fitted to inspire gladness,—the fundamental fact in the Gospel, apart from which our faith is vain. They were instructed to go quickly and tell it. But they were not sent abroad to tell it to all the world, not even to proclaim it in the streets of Jerusalem. This was not their function. They were not designated as preachers of the Gospel, in the ordinary sense of that term. Their ministry was not public and official. It belonged to the innermost department of mission-work, by which the disciples were to edify one another. And, within this department, you will observe that women were preachers to the apostles themselves, and brought to them the fulness of the Gospel message. They were hastened on in their sacred embassage. There must be no tarrying in a work of such magnitude. The disciples must not be left to mourn in ignorance, while these women, in the light of their knowledge, had such great joy. That light must also be made to shine in the hearts of their brethren. It is true, indeed, that the angel might himself have been a minister of that joy which he urgently pressed the women to impart. He could have reached the disciples with this Gospel sooner than these women. But then, this is not God's method of edifying the Church. His beneficence is of a higher and wiser order than could be manifested by the employment of such an agency. The employment of created agency at all, indeed, is a proof of His beneficence. There was no apparent need, for example, that this Gospel should have been announced by an angel. The Lord Himself might have appeared to these women, and announced His own resurrection. But doubtless, in the first instance, it was given to the angels to preach this Gospel because it was such an honour put upon them to do it, and such a deep joy. The shepherds of Bethlehem, not many years earlier, had heard the choir of the heavenly host chaunting the gladdest song which created lips could utter. "Glory to God in the highest, on earth peace, goodwill to men." And now, when the great mystery of godliness had been unfolded to them, and as they looked into the unfathomable depths of Divine love, this glory and joy were again given to them, to be the first preachers of the resurrection,—of the conquest of death and hell by the Prince of peace.

But this blessed ministry was not to be exclusively theirs. It belonged appropriately to those whose nature Jesus had assumed. They also must be partakers of this honour and gladness. What a blessed thing it was for these women to have this ministry conferred upon them! How swiftly they would run to bring the apostles word! What a kindness it was to them to send them on such an errand,—that they should have to tell the disciples these glad tidings of great joy! Would it not have been to denude their calling of its highest privilege,

to be excluded from such a ministry as this? Could a greater
kindness have been shown them than to make them the bearers
of such a message, to put them in the position of flinging the
full burden of their gladness upon the hopeless and the darkened
souls of their friends?

What tenderness also, and what wealth of love, were manifested in the manner in which the angel gave them their charge.
It was much to say to them, "Go, tell the disciples;" but it was
more, when it was added, as Mark informs us, "Tell them, and
Peter." This reference to Peter personally must have opened
up their hearts to the full apprehension of the purpose of this
ministry of theirs. "Go, tell the disciples." It is great, and
seasonable news you have to communicate. Impart your joy
to them, but especially to Peter, who needs it most of all. Alas,
what a burden of sorrow must have been resting on his soul!
Oh, what a parting that was, between him and his Master, whom
he believed to be now lying in the silent grave! He had been
so forward, and full of zeal; he had been, among the disciples,
the most prompt and prominent in speech and action, and at
last had become so boastful and confident; and yet, the last
words his Master had heard him utter had been oaths and
curses, and a fierce denial of all knowledge of Him. It was
thus that the Master and the disciple had parted; and now, so
suddenly had death come between them, that there seemed to be
no possible means of reparation. Oh, what a burden of sorrow
there must have been pressing upon his heart: Peter, above all
men, needed to be comforted by this new Gospel; and therefore the angel said, "Tell Peter." It must have given a fresh
impulse to the speed of these women, to have a word to say to
him which would cleanse his foul bosom of that perilous stuff
which weighs upon the heart. This was a sort of ministry
which blessed those who exercised it, as much as those who
received it. And for this reason, doubtless, they were employed
in it. It was to them a fresh proof of the unwearied beneficence
of the Lord, who had risen as He said.

Nor let us think that these things belong to the past only
—that the joy and the profitableness of this ministry are beyond
our reach. "These things were written for our instruction,
upon whom the ends of the world have come." This mission,
in all its essential features, is part of our function. It is true
that we may not have to deliver to our brethren, as wholly a
new thing, a message so pregnant with health and salvation

as that which the angels communicated to the women at the sepulchre. We must be satisfied to minister, according to that which is bestowed upon us. But surely, there never comes a time when there is no need of such a ministry as this,—never a time in which some weak, struggling soul does not need the strength which a seasonable word can give,—in which a spirit, darkened by sorrow, does not need comfort,—in which some of us may not be as feet to the lame, and as eyes to the blind,—when the Word in which we have been taught to hope may not lift up the heart of the desponding. Only let us be willing to impart that which we have, to be bearers of one another's burdens, and helpers of one another's joys, and so fulfil the law of Christ. There are none who stand so high as to be beyond the need of our help. There are none sunk so low as to render our help unavailing. It is not good for us to be alone. It is best of all to be both the subjects and the dispensers of such a gracious ministry. This is what God designs in organising a Church,—in not leaving us as individuals to fight the good fight of faith, but in compacting us into a body in which each member may minister to the health and strength of all the rest.

Yea, it is good to remember that "those members of the body which seem to be more feeble, are necessary." These women at the sepulchre were well exercised in this truth. Had they not been ministers to the need of the Lord Himself? Had they not followed Him from Galilee in this work of ministry? And now they were taught that their service was still needed, if not directly by the Lord, yet by Him indirectly, in the persons of His disciples. They who seemed to be so feeble were necessary; and necessary, not in the lowest kind of service, but in the very highest,—such service as the angels from heaven delighted to render. They were sent with the glad tidings, not to some poor outcasts, but to the apostles, and chosen friends of the Lord, to carry comfort and joy to Peter, and to the rest who so sorely needed it. Even so, the feeblest members of the Church still may minister to the strongest, and the most ignorant to the most learned, and the poorest to those who are the most wealthy, and they who are taught, to their teachers. It belongs to the very constitution of the mystical body of Christ, that each member has something which another lacks; and each joint must supply its own strength for the compacting of the body. The most godly and well-instructed minister of the Church may receive edification, strength and comfort, and increase of faith and love from the feeblest of its members. It is a fact, pregnant with instruction, that these women were charged with this Gospel message to the apostles,—that the greatest truth the world has ever heard was committed to such ministers as these, to be conveyed by them to the minds and hearts of the greatest teachers the world ever had. It is a lesson to me that I should have my ears and heart ever open to receive what heavenly communications may come to me from any quarter, however unpromising. I may get my deepest and most gladsome knowledge of Divine things from those who seem to be the least likely to impart it.

Is it not very instructive, too, that this Gospel was committed to women? Does it not serve to indicate what is their special function in the Church, and to define the sphere of their ministry? They were not sent forth, as the apostles were, to preach the Gospel. They were not set apart as missionaries to the heathen. Their ministry was private and personal,—to speak in the ear that which they had heard, not to proclaim it from the house-top. Their sphere of labour lies more *within* the Church, for its edification, than *outside* of it, for the conversion of the world. Not, indeed, that such labour, in the innermost circle of mission-work, is exclusive of that which lies beyond it. God forbid that any one should be shut out from the joy of bringing a sinner to the Saviour. It is the property of every believer to give light, not within the house merely, but to those who have lost their way in the darkness. The candle which is shining within a cottage home, may be a guiding-star to the belated moorland wanderer. The domestic mission, in the fulness of its tide, overflows its banks, and irrigates the barren land on either side. The Home Mission has its complement and completeness in the Foreign Mission. The soul that cares for a needy believer, has compassion for him who is ignorant and out of the way. This charity of heaven droppeth as the rain from the clouds, and descends upon the evil as well as the good. It is a reflection of that light which shines from above upon the just and the unjust.

Hitherto, I have been speaking only of one part of that message with which the women were charged. The other part, though not less significant and important, does not demand much in the way of exposition and application. They were not only commissioned to tell the disciples and Peter that Jesus was risen, but moreover, to say that they would see Him in Galilee, whither

He was to precede them, and where they were again to hold converse with Him, in the first scenes of His ministry. This Gospel message thus contained the end and meaning of all gracious revelations from heaven. It not only contained a statement of fact, the enunciation of a doctrine pregnant with meaning, but it held out the promise and hope of personal fellowship with the Lord. We cannot doubt that this made the message doubly precious to the disciples; for, in truth, the real end and meaning of all religion is personal communion with the Lord. However important Divine truth may be, so long as it stands as mere doctrine, however thoroughly certified, it has but little influence over the life. The heart of religion is not so much doctrine, as re-union, living fellowship with the Lord. Of old, and now, this is true. The grand, permanently consoling fact was, not merely that the Lord had risen as He said, but that the disciples were to see Him, and hold converse with Him. If His resurrection had involved their separation from Him, it could not have brought such joy to their hearts, nor such strength of purpose. It would have put them very much on a level with those doctors who were teaching things hard to be believed, and would have gone far to convert the apostles into a mere school of mystic philosophers. But it was not merely, the fact of the resurrection, which was to be attested to them, but the promise of a real, living intercourse with the risen Saviour. His resurrection was not the termination of their communion with Him, but rather the beginning of a fellowship more intimate than that which they had hitherto enjoyed. For a brief period, they were to have the supreme joy of again seeing Jesus with the bodily eye, that they might grow into the capacity of beholding Him with the eye of faith,—of realising His unseen presence, and of walking with Him in newness of life.

And this is to us also the vital preciousness of the Gospel. It not only announces to us a doctrine, but brings us into living fellowship with a Person. It does not set before us historical facts only, but the actual presence of the Saviour. It brings us into converse, not only with the highest truths, but with Him who is the Way, the Truth, and the Life. We are invited, not merely to study what interests and exercises the understanding, but to hold converse with Him who is fairer than the sons of men, to speak to Him as a brother, and to listen to His loving voice. He not only brings near to us His righteousness, and His salvation, but is Himself with us always, even to the end of the

world, a Friend that sticketh closer than a brother, on whose arm
we lean as we go up through the wilderness, and who is a refuge
and strength, a very present help in trouble. Whither He invites
us to go, He goes before us, and at our journey's end we shall see
Him. We have, at every step, the benefit of His presence, and
counsel, and sustaining strength ; and, seeing Him with the eye
of faith, as we move onwards, we have the joyful assurance that
at last we shall be with Him to behold His glory.

GIVING THANKS

REMEMBRANCE OF GOD'S HOLINESS:

A SERMON.

BY THE LATE

Rev. JAMES SMELLIE,

UNITED ORIGINAL SECESSION CHURCH, EDINBURGH.

" Rejoice in the Lord, ye righteous ; and give thanks at the remembrance of His holiness."—Psalm xcvii. 12.

THIS command is addressed to the " righteous," not because they only *ought* to obey it, but because they only *can* obey it, and because, indeed, only they can understand it. The obligation of it rests on every human being as well as on them, but to all others it is impracticable, and deeply mysterious. Those who are unborn of the Spirit can see, in a measure, the propriety of thanking God for His *goodness*, but they cannot understand what it is to give thanks at the remembrance of His *holiness*. If there is one perfection of God which they fear and dislike more than another,— which surrounds Him with dread and unapproachable terror,—it it is that holiness of His which cannot tolerate sin, and which must ever lead Him to turn an eye of abhorrence and displeasure upon the wilful and obdurate sinner. They have a very imperfect and unworthy apprehension, as we shall see, of God's holiness; but, in so far as it *is* apprehended by them, it makes the thought of God intolerable, and leads them to banish Him wholly from their minds, saying,—" Depart from us, for we desire not the knowledge of thy ways." And, if one thing more than another can show the entire and radical change which the Spirit of God, in the hour of regeneration, works upon the hearts of sinners, it is, that after this change has passed upon them they are not merely *reconciled* to God's holiness—cannot merely *bear* the thought of it, even when apprehended far more clearly and powerfully than before—but regard it with complacency and delight; so that they are both able and disposed to obey the call of the text, and give thanks at the remembrance of His holiness.

The holiness of God, in its more general aspects, is not so much a *separate* attribute of His nature, as that which accompanies the exercise of *all* His attributes, and forms the crown and glory of the whole. It is that perfection by which He wills and acts in harmony with His own nature,—approving all that is in harmony with the excellence of this nature, abhorring, and visiting with consuming displeasure, all that is opposed to it. More particularly, it is that perfection by which He must always delight in moral purity and goodness, and abhor and punish all sin. As possessed of holiness, God is said to be Light,—incorruptibly pure and excellent as the light, and as essentially opposed to sin as the insufferable brightness of the sun is opposed to midnight darkness. In respect of it, God is said to be a consuming fire, for it is not more the nature of fire to burn up and destroy everything inflammable with which it comes in contact, than it is the nature of God to consume and destroy all sin. That God is 'thus essentially, incorruptibly, awfully holy,—of purer eyes than to behold evil, and who cannot look upon iniquity,—appears in every manifestation of Himself that He has given to His creatures. His holiness shines through all His Word. It is impressed on all His works. There is a witness for it in the conscience of every created being, even in fallen men and devils, who believe and tremble. It pervades His whole moral government of the universe; for He so orders things that, sooner or later, in one form or another, misery follows sin as surely as the shadow follows the substance, while in keeping His commandments there is just as surely great reward. Nor does the existence of sin in our world at all impugn His perfect holiness, seeing that, come how sin may, it exists only as the object of His infinite hatred and displeasure; seeing, too, that He has taken occasion from its existence to give a display of His holiness, in the work of human redemption, inconceivably brighter and more awful than could otherwise have been given. So far from the existence of sin casting discredit on God's holiness, He has only made it the occasion of more gloriously displaying His holiness, and enthroning it in the profounder reverence and adoration of all holy beings for ever.

In considering our text, two questions come up before us for meditation, — FIRST, *What is implied* in giving thanks at the remembrance of God's holiness; and, SECOND, *Why* God's saints may well give thanks when they remember His holiness; or, more briefly, the duty enjoined in the text, and the reasons for it.

I. *The duty enjoined.*

What is implied in this duty of giving thanks at the remembrance of God's holiness?

1. You will at once perceive that one thing presupposed in this duty is *our being in a state of reconciliation with God.* I have already hinted that the unrenewed sinner, so far as he does apprehend God's holiness at all, regards it with insuperable aversion and fear. And there is reason for this. It cannot, indeed, be otherwise. He feels in His conscience that God's holiness is *against* him. He feels that it arms God with the sword of consuming displeasure against him for sin. While he continues the sinner he is, God, because He is holy, can have no gracious dealings with him, nor be to him anything other than a consuming fire. How then can the sinner give thanks at the remembrance of Jehovah's holiness? Could the manslayer give thanks for the gleaming knife in the hand of the avenger of blood who was panting close upon his heels? Can the criminal give hearty thanks for the inexorable severity of the judge, who sentences him to life-long imprisonment or to death? Does the evil-doer delight in the strength and majesty of the law which is watching him with a sleepless eye, and is ready to lay hold of him with an unrelenting hand, the moment he incurs its penalty? Far less can the sinner, whose conscience tells him that he has still to do with an unappeased and angry God, delight in the holiness that kindles His displeasure, and renders it the most certain of all certainties, that "the soul that sinneth it shall die." Before we can delight in, and give thanks for the holiness of God, we must be at peace with Him,—we must believe that the flame of consuming wrath which His holiness kindled against us for sin has been quenched by the blood of His own Son poured forth on our behalf, —we must believe that His holiness, which was so awfully *against* us for sin, is now *for* us and on our side, because all its demands have been gloriously met by Him who was made "sin for us, who knew no sin, that we might be made the righteousness of God in Him "— in short, we must be persuaded that, pacified and propitiated toward us through the atonement of Jesus, God's holy eye no longer rests on us with the unpitying fury of an avenging Judge, but beams on us with the purest kindness and love of a merciful Father.

2. Another thing supposed in this duty is, that we have a *new* and *holy nature*; for otherwise, we can neither understand nor appreciate the holiness of God.

I say, without a new and holy nature, we cannot even *understand* the holiness of God. You cannot fail to have observed how ready men are to judge their neighbours by themselves, and how difficult it seems to them to recognise in others a goodness higher than their own. The deceitful person is constantly suspecting others of a disposition to deceive. The basely selfish person cannot understand a truly generous action, but is ever ready to account for it by the supposition of some base and selfish motive. As the jaundiced eye makes everything appear unlovely, so there is a tendency in the depraved heart to throw over every character—even the purest and noblest—the discolouring and loathsome hue of its own depravity. This blinding and perverting influence of depravity appears especially in the apprehension which sinners naturally have of the character of God. Utterly depraved themselves, they can no more form right conceptions of an absolutely holy God, than a man born blind can form an idea of the glory of the noonday sun. They think of God, but it is not the awfully holy God of the Bible; it is a God imagined very much according to the wishes of their own carnal hearts; such a God as they *would like* the Supreme Being to be,—weak, unstable, and imperfect like themselves,—easily imposed on by appearances, and very lenient toward their shortcomings and sins. Thus Paul tells how, when men knew God, they glorified Him not as God, but "became vain in their imaginations, and their foolish heart was darkened,"—"and changed the glory of the incorruptible God into an image made like to corruptible man, and to birds, and four-footed beasts, and creeping things" (Rom. I. 21, 23). And though you, my unregenerate hearers, have been delivered by the light of revelation from the folly and wickedness of heathen idolatry, I venture to say that the God of your habitual imagination is hardly less like the dread Being whom the Scriptures reveal, than the idols of the heathen. If your God were He before whom the seraphim cover their faces and their feet, could you, a sinful creature, rush into His presence in the most solemn acts of His worship with more thoughtlessness and unconcern than you would come before a titled or a sceptred fellow-worm? If your God were He who charges His angels with folly, and loathes all righteousness of man as filthy rags, could you feel so satisfied before Him, when you think you have prayed very

E

well, or have been very serious, or done some unusually good action, as though now He would be certain to be pleased with you? If your God were He who looketh on the heart, and judgeth the thought of foolishness to be sin, could you give up your heart without restraint to ungodliness, and pride, and vain and unholy feelings all the day and every day, and hope to cover all from God's sight by a few acts of outward worship on Sabbath? If your God were He whose wrath is revealed from heaven against *all* ungodliness and unrighteousness of men, could you venture to excuse this or that sin before Him, as not so bad as what is done by others,—as the result of your circumstances and the peculiar temptations that surround you,—or as what He may well spare, because it is a little one? Or, if your God were He who out of Christ is a consuming fire, could you venture to come near Him out of Christ,—could you rest out of Christ a single day? Be assured that your irreverence, and pride, and unbelief, and security, are the results of your having imagined a God who is an imperfect being like yourself, and not the unapproachable, holy God of the Bible. God is saying to you, "These things hast thou done, and I kept silence; *thou thoughtest that I was altogether such an one as thyself.*" You are alienated from the life of God through the ignorance that is in you, because of the blindness of your heart. You need a new nature wrought within you, before you can even *know* the holiness of God as His Word reveals it, far less give thanks at the remembrance of it.

And you must have this new nature, as I have said, before you can *appreciate or delight in God's holiness.* Though you did apprehend the holiness of Him with whom you have to do, yet, in your present state the more clearly and powerfully you apprehended it, it would only be the more intolerable to you. No sinner, while his heart is unchanged, while the love of the world and of sin is strong within him, can bear the thought of an all-holy God, searching him through by night and day,—marking his every act, and word, and thought, with the abhorrence and the displeasure which He must bear toward sin. To live in the presence of such a God would be an unbearable terror and restraint; and so, to get peace to pursue his worldliness and sin unchecked, the sinner shuts his eyes to the true knowledge of God,—imagines a God, as we have said, very much after the wishes of his own carnal heart, and even thinks of *Him* as little as possible. No! before you can take pleasure in the society even of a fellow-creature, you must have a character, disposition, and tastes, in some degree congenial to his. And much more, before you can take delight in God's holiness, you must have a new and holy nature like His,—a new and spiritual eye to see the reality and beauty of His holiness,—a new and spiritual heart to realise its transcendent amiableness and attraction. And such a new and holy nature has been wrought by God's own Spirit in all who have been born again. They "have put on the new man which, *after* God,"—that is, in the likeness of God,— "is created in righteousness and true holiness." They have been made "partakers of the Divine nature, having escaped the pollution that is in the world through lust." Possessed of this Divine nature, they begin, in their own finite and imperfect measure, to hate sin as God hates it; they begin, in their own finite and imperfect measure, to love holiness as God loves it; and therefore they remember God with supreme complacency and delight, because they see in Him the perfection of that which their nature loves and approves—the perfection of an absolute and ineffable holiness.

3. Once more: we remark that this duty consists in the *remembrance and contemplation of God's holiness as this is exhibited in the person and cross of His Son.* We have said that conscience testifies to the holiness of God: but conscience is darkened by the fall; it is perverted more or less by the deceitfulness of sin; it needs Divine revelation to enlighten and rectify it. We have said that God's moral government testifies to His holiness,—but only dimly and doubtfully. For, how often do we see under that government that the good are afflicted and oppressed, while the wicked flourish like a green bay tree. We need the light which revelation casts on the world beyond the grave, to see how the holiness of God will be glorified at last in swallowing up the afflictions of the one in endless joy, and the prosperity of the other in endless pain. It is in the glass of the Word,—that Word which God hath magnified above all His name,—that the spiritually enlightened eye discovers the glory of the Divine holiness, and that the spiritually renewed heart, full of admiration, is constrained to exclaim—"Who is like unto Thee, O Lord, glorious in holiness, fearful in praises, doing wonders?" There is a twofold revelation of God in the Word, through which we may discover the reality and perfection of His holiness.

First, there is the revelation of Him in the *law*, the revelation of Him as *Lawgiver and Judge*—declaring sin to be the abominable thing which He hates,—forbidding sin, even in the thought and wish of the heart, as a thing insufferable to Him,—threatening against all sin, and even every act of sin, everlasting destruction from His presence and from the glory of His power. In the light of that law,—to transgress which, in any case, is eternal ruin,—we discover how holy is the Being with whom we have to do. It is generally the law, applied with supernatural light and power to the sinner's conscience, that *first* opens his eyes to the consuming holiness of his Judge, and his own unspeakable vileness and guiltiness before Him. But the law worketh wrath; and the holiness of God, as seen in the law by sinful beings, worketh unmitigated terror. God spake, as Lawgiver, from amid the blackness and darkness and tempests of Sinai; and even Moses said, "I exceedingly fear and quake," while the terror-stricken people cried out, "Let not God speak with us, lest we die." The believer has seen God's holiness in the law, but it is not that which leads him to give thanks. It is another and, strange to say, a brighter and more impressive revelation of His holiness, that turns his terror into thanksgiving.

This is the revelation of Him in the *person and cross of His incarnate Son.* It is not in the law, with its far-reaching commands; it is not in the unquenchable flames of hell; it is in the sufferings of the Son of God, as the substitute for sinners, and the propitiation for sin, that we discover in its unapproachable light the glory of Jehovah's holiness. It is when we behold God subjecting Him who is the partner of His glory and throne, by whom also He made the worlds, to the awful humiliation of taking the nature and the place of His guilty creatures; it is when we behold God dealing with Him, the Holy One and the Just as a sinner, casting Him out of the light of His presence as one accursed, causing Him to drink of the wine of His wrath, poured out without mixture into the cup of His indignation, even when the cry of the Son's innocent, shrinking nature is, "Father, if it be possible, let this cup pass from Me;" it is when we survey the sufferings of the world's Creator and Lord under His Father's hand,—the sorrow unto death, the bloody sweat, the strong cryings and tears unto Him that was able to save Him from death, the slow death of shame and woe; and it is when we remember that such suffering, on the part of the Divine Sufferer, was all absolutely *necessary* ere God could pardon a single sin, or allow a single sinner to approach the footstool of His mercy :—I say, it is in this awful *necessity* for God's bruising and putting to grief the Son of His bosom, that we learn how holy, holy, holy is the Lord of Hosts. Those only have seen God's holiness aright, who with eyes opened by the Spirit have seen it in the cross of Christ; and while they behold it with adoring awe, they can behold it without slavish terror ; for its consuming splendours are softened, and tempered, and rendered safe and sweet as rays of morning light, by covenant mercy and love.

Now, it is the duty of such,—a duty to which they are called in the text,—to contemplate God's holiness much, as manifested in Jesus, to make it the theme of their daily remembrance and earnest and profound meditation, to pray for the Spirit to open their eyes to a clearer and more realising apprehension of its glory, that so they may give God the thanks and the glory for it that are His due.

II. *Let us now consider, in the second place, the grounds or reasons of this duty.*

Why may the righteous well give thanks at the remembrance of God's holiness ?

1. First of all, we reply,—if we may use the word " thanks" in the wider sense of admiration or praise,—they may well praise God for it, as that *which gives lustre and glory to all His other perfections.*

His holiness is the crown of all His perfections. It ensures, if we may so say, that they shall be exercised in a way worthy of Himself. But for it, the very infinitude of His perfections would render His government an infinite tyranny and terror to all His creatures, and Himself a Being to be infinitely dreaded, rather than, as now, to be infinitely loved and adored. Without it, as has been suggested, His patience would be a boundless indulgence to sin,—His mercy, a capricious fondness,—His anger, madness, — His power, oppression, — His wisdom, subtilty and cunning. But, as holiness attaches to all His attributes, it imparts an infinite moral splendour and glory to them all; this makes their exercise in the government of the universe supremely worthy of Himself, so that all holy beings are constrained to venerate and adore, and all wicked beings to bow and tremble. Holiness dwelling in infinite perfection in Jehovah, and characterising all His manifestations and all His dealings, is everywhere spoken of in Scripture as pre-eminently His glory, and as that which the glorified hosts of heaven chiefly and eternally adore; for the cry of the seraphim, ever sounding through the heavenly temple, is, "Holy, holy, holy is the Lord of hosts; the whole earth is full of His glory." And the new song of the multitudinous harpers, who stand on the sea of glass, having the harps of God, is, "Great and marvellous are Thy works, Lord God Almighty; just and true are Thy ways, Thou King of Saints; who shall not fear Thee and glorify Thy name? for *Thou only art holy*." O, when we think that our God is holy, that His wisdom is holy, that His power is holy, that His mercy is holy, that His providence is holy, that all His acts and manifestations of Himself in His government of the universe are, and ever must be, perfectly holy, and worthy of Himself,—well does it become us to join with every creature in heaven, and give *thanks* at the remembrance of His holiness.

2. Again, the righteous may well give thanks at the remembrance of God's holiness, because the *display and vindication of it in the work of their redemption pacify their conscience, and secure their everlasting safety.* When a sinner is truly awakened, his conscience pleads on the side of God's holiness. It declares God to be an awfully holy Being, who can by no means clear the guilty,—who must carry out the threatenings of His law in visiting sin with the penalty of death. And while conscience is thus pleading for the holiness and righteousness of God, it is not mere mercy that will satisfy the sinner. He sees God to be only holy and just; and to tell him that God is merciful, without showing him, at the same time, that God's holiness and justice have been fully satisfied for sin, would give him no abiding peace, but rather seem a cruel mockery of his woe. But we have seen that the holiness of God demanded and received glorious vindication from all the dishonour done to it by sin, in the suffering and blood of His incarnate Son. And when the sinner is enabled to believe that mercy and forgiveness are proclaimed and offered to him on the ground of the sacrifice of God's Son; when, moreover, he is enabled to receive the mercy and forgiveness of God as so proclaimed and offered,—then his conscience is at peace. His conscience is satisfied, fully and for ever, because He sees that God's holiness is satisfied; and not only satisfied, but glorified, in receiving vindication for all the dishonour he did it by sin, in the obedience unto the death of God's Son in his stead. Well, then, may he

give thanks at the remembrance of God's holiness, as glorified
in that sacrifice of Christ, which brings eternal peace and rest to
his conscience.

And God's holiness, as there vindicated and glorified, secures
the believer's eternal *safety.* For God has demanded and received overflowing satisfaction for sin at the hand of the believer's Surety; and, as a perfectly holy and just God, He
cannot demand that satisfaction over again, from the believer
himself. If He were not absolutely holy, I might well tremble
in perpetual terror, lest, after having punished sin in Christ, my
Surety, He should refuse to pardon it to me; and lest, having
received the price of my redemption from Christ, He should
yet deny some of its blessings to me. But well may I give
thanks at the remembrance of His holiness, when I think that
His absolute holiness is my security,—a security strong and
abiding as His own unchangeable nature,—that, having accepted
the price of my redemption at the hands of my glorious Surety,
He will assuredly bestow on me all its blessings, from the pardon
of my sin, to my full investiture with all the riches of glory.
Blessed and glorious holiness! It is indeed a wall of fire around
the soul of every believer.

3. Still farther: the righteous may well give thanks at the remembrance of God's holiness, when they remember that, *however
mysterious and trying God's dealings toward them may be, they
are all holy, and designed to promote their holiness.* When the
soul of the Saviour was surrounded with that mysterious darkness which enshrouded it on Calvary,—when He was wrapt in that
impenetrable gloom out of which He could only cry, "My God, my
God, why hast Thou forsaken Me ?"—this was the anchor of His
faith, that His Father, who was so awfully afflicting Him, was
holy; and hence he added, " but Thou art holy, O Thou that inhab-
itest the praises of Israel." And as it was with the Head, so it is
with the members ; when God's dealings toward them are full of
mystery and trial,—when His way is in the sea, and His path
in the mighty waters, and His footsteps are not known,—here
is a Rock on which they can always cast anchor with assuring
and consoling confidence, even that God is and must be holy in
all His dealings,—that, however mysteriously He may afflict
them, He can never act toward them but in a way that is holy
and worthy of Himself,—nay, that, being holy, He is chastening
them, not for His pleasure, but for their profit, that they may
be partakers of His holiness. Yes! this is their comfort, that,

while "clouds and darkness are round about Him, righteousness and judgment are the habitation of His throne."

4. In a word, the righteous may well give thanks at the remembrance of God's holiness, *because it is the security and pattern of their own ultimate holiness.* You hate sin, O Christian, and long to be delivered from it. Think, then, that the God of your salvation infinitely hates sin, and that His infinite abhorrence of sin is a pledge that He will destroy its power and its being in every soul whom He loves. Give thanks at the remembrance of His holiness; for it is your security that, ere He calls you from the earth into His own holy presence, He will have made you meet for that presence, by freeing you from every trace and vestige of your hateful and hated sin.

Again, you love holiness and long to be holy. But does not your covenant God love holiness infinitely more than you can do; and is not this a blissful security,—that He will not leave you, till He has transformed you into the likeness of His own perfect holiness? Your very love to holiness is a part of the image of God already impressed upon you; and as surely as He hath begun the good work in you, so surely will He perform it unto the day of the Lord Jesus; for His workmanship must, in every case, be worthy of Himself,—that is, it must be perfectly holy. O what comfort, amid your aspirations and struggles after holiness, to think that a holy God has implanted them; and that His holiness is your security that they shall reach their bright and glorious goal in likeness to His own nature! What comfort, when you are using the means of holiness,— often, as you fear, vainly, and with little success,—to think that this is the will of God, even your sanctification; and that, when your will is thus coinciding and co-working with the will of the Omnipotent God, it cannot fail to reach the summit of its highest endeavour! O then, give thanks at the remembrance of His holiness! It is the pledge of the progress and perfection of yours.

And not only so, but,—most elevating and ennobling thought of all,—it is the *pattern* of yours. Your duty is always your privilege; and God commands what He will certainly give, when He says, "As He who hath called you is holy, so be ye holy; because it is written, Be ye holy, for I am holy." Jesus Christ is the brightness of His Father's glory. He is the living manifestation of the brightness of the Father's holiness; and is it not said, "Ye shall be like *Him,* for ye shall see Him as He is?"

Amazing thought! to be like God in that holiness which is the crowning excellence and glory of His character. Most exalted destiny! to be the mirror in which angels shall see, with admiration and praise, the triumph of Divine holiness over sin. Well may you give thanks at the remembrance of God's holiness.

(1.) In closing, we may learn the *amazing wisdom of God* in so ordering it, that hell-deserving sinners have reason to give thanks at the remembrance of His holiness. What Divine wisdom is that great redemption-plan, which brings the brightest display of God's holiness out of sin,—not in punishing the sinner, but in pardoning him! How amazing, that God should never appear so gloriously holy, as in taking the vilest of His creatures into the very bosom of His love, and crowning them with all the blessings of His favour! Wondrous love of Christ, that makes the glory of holiness to lie in the forgiveness of sin, and the opening of heaven to the sinner! Wondrous blood of Christ, which, when applied to the conscience, enables the sinner, who once fled in fear from the very thought of God's holiness as ensuring his destruction, to give glad thanks for that very holiness, as the great security for His everlasting salvation! O, what a miracle of Divine wisdom, as well as love, in providing that blood as an atonement for sin! Out of the eater hath come forth meat, out of the strong hath come forth sweetness, —glory out of dishonour, gladsome thanks out of overwhelming fear. " O the depth of the riches, both of the wisdom and knowledge of God! How unsearchable are His judgments, and His ways past finding out !"

(2.) Learn also a test of *Christian character.* A hypocrite may have a kind of satisfaction in God's goodness, but he can have no delight in His holiness. He cannot bear that awful holiness, one ray of which, shot into his soul, would turn all his comeliness into corruption, and make him appear the vile, lost sinner that he is. Of all God's attributes, he shuns the thought of His sin-abhorring, sin-destroying holiness more than the thought of any other.

On the contrary, the Christian delights in God because He is holy. He would not have Him less holy than He is, for a thousand worlds. If the thought could enter his mind, that the God in whom he trusts were not absolutely and perfectly holy, it would fill him with inconsolable distress and dismay. The reason of the difference is this, that the hypocrite knows God out of Christ,—the Christian knows Him in Christ.

Brethren, how is it with you? Have you seen the glory of

God's holiness blending with that of His love, in the cross of His dying Son? Has the discovery that God is holy in pardoning sin through the blood of Christ, given peace to your conscience? Do you rejoice in His holiness as the security of your everlasting salvation in Christ? Is it your comfort and ground of thanksgiving, amid your darkest trials, that the hand of God, laid on you, is a holy hand, that can wrong neither you nor yours? And do you give thanks at the remembrance of His holiness, as the pledge and pattern of your own perfect holiness at last? By this you may know that God's Holy Spirit has given you a new and holy nature, if you are constrained to give thanks at the remembrance of God's holiness.

(3) If it is otherwise with you, then learn, from what has been said, the *need of regeneration*. Verily, you must be born again. If you dislike the thought of God's holiness now, how could you bear to dwell in the full light of that holiness for ever? If you see nothing attractive in God's holiness now, how could you join in, or even bear to hear, the everlasting song of the hosts of heaven, "Holy, holy, holy, is the Lord of Hosts?" A coward on the field of battle would not be so entirely out of his element as you would be in a holy heaven, where God's holiness fills all hearts, and praises for it are on every tongue. Heaven would be intolerable to you, though you were there. But, as you are, you can never be there. "Without holiness no man shall see the Lord." Without holiness, you would be consumed by the flash of Jehovah's displeasure. Without holiness, you must be banished for ever from the presence of this holy God, as abhorred and accursed. "Evil shall not dwell with Him, neither shall fools stand in His presence; He abhorreth all the workers of iniquity." No outward privileges will avail you. No outward perfections will veil your depravity from His eyes, which are as a flame of fire. *Ye must be born again.* "In Christ Jesus, neither circumcision availeth anything nor uncircumcision, but a new creature." Flee to the footstool of mercy, and in Christ's name plead for the Spirit to renew you. And here is a promise to take with you to plead, —the pleading of it has brought grace to others, it may to you. "I will sprinkle clean water upon you, and ye shall be clean: from all your filthiness, and from all your idols will I cleanse you. A new heart also will I give you, and a new spirit will I put within you; and I will take away the stony heart out of your flesh, and I will give you an heart of flesh.

And I will put My Spirit within you, and cause you to walk in My statutes, and ye shall keep My judgments and do them."

(4.) Last of all, learn how we have all sinned in *forgetting God's holiness*. This has been the cause of our irreverence and formality, in coming before God in the acts of His worship. This has been the cause of our pride, and self-righteousness, and self-satisfaction, in the presence of Him before whom the heavens are not clean. This has been the cause of our indulging sin, making light of sin, excusing sin, as if He, who, for imputed sin, bruised His holy Son in the winepress of Divine wrath, could bear with sin in us. This has been the cause of our undervaluing Christ, not sheltering ourselves daily and hourly under Christ's blood, nor making it our continual plea in coming before God's throne of holiness for mercy and grace.

Let us remember God's holiness. It will make us walk humbly and watchfully before Him. It will quicken our endeavours to be holy, as though we ever heard in our ears the solemn call, " Be ye holy for I am holy." By remembering it, we may hope to discover more of its glory, and to rise in admiration of its awful but sweet splendour, as that shines in the cross of Christ ; and thus we shall become more and more fit to join in the song of the living ones who rest not, day nor night, saying : " Holy, holy, holy, Lord God Almighty, who wast, and art, and art to come."

GOD'S PEOPLE COMFORTED:

A COMMUNION SERMON.

Rev. JAMES BEGG, D.D.,

NEWINGTON FREE CHURCH, EDINBURGH.

"In that day it shall be said to Jerusalem, Fear thou not : and to Zion, Let not thy hands be slack. The Lord thy God in the midst of thee is mighty ; He will save, He will rejoice over thee with joy ; He will rest in His love ; He will joy over thee with singing."—ZEPH. iii. 16, 17.

THESE interesting words, addressed originally to God's ancient people, were intended to apply to the true Israel of God in all ages. "Whatsoever things were written aforetime were written for our learning, that we, through patience and comfort of the Scriptures, might have hope." The words are the more remarkable, as coming after many sad denunciations against the Philistines, Moab, Ammon, Assyria, Ethiopia, and even Judah itself. All the more striking are they as contained in the very chapter in which the sins of Jerusalem are unsparingly unfolded and denounced. Jerusalem is here called the "filthy, polluted, and oppressing city," whose princes are "roaring lions, and her judges evening wolves," her "prophets light and treacherous persons," her priests men who "have polluted the sanctuary, and done violence to the law." But this is the manner of God. Just as the sound of condemnation had not ceased in Eden, till it was succeeded by the voice of mercy ; just as the Prophet Isaiah had no sooner, in his first chapter, exposed the wickedness of the Jews, than he said, in God's name, "Come and let us reason together ; though your sins be as scarlet they shall be white as snow :" so, no sooner had Zephaniah laid open the abounding wickedness of Judah, than he pointed forward to brighter scenes, —to the returning suppliants, under the power of the Spirit, ashamed of their doings,—to those who rejoiced in their pride removed,—to the power of sin destroyed by the omnipotence of Divine grace, and to the full flood of Divine eternal mercy going forth towards those who were redeemed, not with corruptible things, as silver and gold, but with the precious blood of Christ. " I will also leave in the midst of thee an afflicted and poor people, and they shall trust in the name of the Lord. The remnant of Israel shall not do iniquity, nor speak lies ; neither shall a deceitful tongue be found in their mouth ; for they shall feed and lie down, and none shall make them afraid." " In that day it shall be said to Jerusalem, Fear thou not; and to Zion, Let not thy hands be slack. The Lord thy God in the midst of thee is mighty ; He will save, He will rejoice over thee with joy ; He will rest in His love ; He will rejoice over thee with singing."

The text is consolatory. Its object is to bear up and establish the souls of true Christians in faith, hope, and joy ; and I trust the meditations to which it naturally leads may be found suitable on a day of high communion, when God brings His people into His banqueting-house, and says, " Come, eat of my bread, drink of the wine which I have mingled." Open the gates of righteousness, that my people may enter in and bless the Lord. The Stone which the builders rejected, the same is become the Head of the corner. Trust in the Lord for ever ; for in the Lord Jehovah is everlasting strength. He will not suffer thy foot to be moved. He will be thy sun and shield, giving thee grace and preparing thee for glory, and withholding no good thing from thee. Even in the wilderness a table is spread for thee in the presence of thine enemies ; and, seated around that table, thou shalt experience a foretaste of thy holy joy, when thou shalt see the King in His beauty, and the land that is a very far off,—when the wicked shall cease from troubling, and sorrow and sighing shall flee away for ever.

There are first, however, one or two points to be clearly apprehended and fixed in your minds.

This consolation is addressed only to true Christians. It is to " Jerusalem " that the admonition " not to fear " is addressed ; it is to " Zion " that it is said, " Let not thy hands be slack." No encouragement is therefore given here to open transgressors or persistent backsliders. " Unto the wicked God saith, What hast thou to do to declare My statutes, or that thou shouldest take My covenant in thy mouth ?" No encouragement is given to incorrigible hypocrites : " The sinners in Zion are afraid, and fearfulness hath surprised the hypocrites." No disguise can intercept the clear glance of Him who " searcheth the hearts and trieth the reins of the children of men." The encouragement is addressed only to such as have fled for refuge to lay hold on the hope set before them in the Gospel—who thus stand in the same relation to God, spiritually, in which the ancient Zion stood temporally. They are his peculiar people,—rescued from the spiritual Egypt, joined with Him in solemn covenant, and destined to dwell for ever in the Jerusalem above, " the mother of us all."

All the more necessary is it to make this clear distinction, because none are so prone to take to themselves the promises of the Gospel as those to whom they clearly do not belong. The natural blindness and foolish selfishness of man is strikingly illustrated in this. Just as the man who has evidently no righte-ousness at all is most prone to seek heaven as a reward of his obedience, so the man who has evidently no fear of God before his eyes is most prone to appropriate to himself the promises of the Gospel. " Thou sayest, I am rich, and increased in goods, and have need of nothing; and knowest not that thou art poor, and miserable, and blind, and naked," standing in need of all things. No! stand back, thou profane, from the sacred table; but still know that for you the Master calleth. His language is, " Let the wicked forsake his way, and the unrighteous man his thoughts; and let him return to the Lord, and He will have mercy upon him, and to our God, for He will abundantly pardon."

But not only is the text specially addressed to the people of God,—it is spoken *upon the supposition that they shall often be overwhelmed with anxiety*—that they shall " fear," and that " their hands shall be slack." No greater mistake can exist than that of supposing that a Christian's life is a period of continual sun-shine. It is more like one of the days of this world—sometimes fair, sometimes cloudy, the clouds returning after the rain. The rainbow in the cloud is an evidence that there shall be no deluge; but certainly not that there shall be no rain. Such is the power of unbelief, even in the best—so many are the trials, temptations, and sins, to which all believers are exposed—that it will gener-ally be found that those who have least cause for fear are most frequently under its dominion. David speaks of his heart as " overwhelmed and in perplexity." He tells us that he " looked on his right hand and beheld:" " refuge failed him, no man cared for his soul." Listen at the door of the closet of the daughter of Sion : " Zion saith, The Lord hath forsaken me, my

God hath forgotten me." The Church is represented as new enjoying all delight—again, in deep despondency ; as going about the streets of the city, and saying, Saw ye Him whom my soul loveth ! O Thou whom my soul loveth, tell me where Thou feedest, and where Thou causest Thy flock to lie down at noon. I opened to my beloved, but He was gone. My soul failed when He spake ; I sought him, but I could not find Him ; I called, but He gave no answer. Oh, that I were as in months past, when His candle shined upon my head. Such is the varying experience of the true members of the Christian Church. And if there is a time more than any other when Christians are apt to falter, it is when, amidst the solemnities of a communion table, they take the cup of salvation, and eat of the children's bread. Now, to those in such circumstances this admonition may most appropriately be addressed, "Ye are weak, of yesterday, crushed before the moth ; but the Lord thy God in the midst of thee is mighty. Ye are sinful dust and ashes ; but the Lord is a Saviour to the uttermost. All obstacles have been removed by Him. All the claims of justice satisfied, grace now reigns through His righteousness to the eternal life of the chief of sinners. Ye are sorrowful, but He rests in His love, which is, like Himself, eternal and unchangeable ; and rejoices over you, even with singing."

This brings me to the main object of this discourse—viz., to illustrate the grounds of confidence which all Christians may have in the unchanging love of their Almighty Redeemer. The whole scope of revelation is fitted to impress this truth upon our minds, as well as the whole past dealings of God with His people ; from which it appears that, insignificant and guilty as they are, there has been nothing too great for the Holy One and the Just to give, or to suffer on their behalf. Let us illustrate this.

I. *What are the marks of love ?*

Our love towards an object may be known *by the direction of our thoughts ;* for, on the beloved object our thoughts chiefly dwell. Time and space are annihilated, and distance only increases the flame. So the thoughts of Christ are turned towards His people, and have been from eternity : Before the depths were formed, when there were no fountains abounding with water, He was set up from everlasting, and rejoiced in the habitable parts of the earth, and His delights were with the children of men. During all the Old Testament economy, His thoughts were constantly towards His people, when, as the

Angel of the covenant, He accompanied the Israelites in all their wanderings; and when His Spirit, by the prophets, foretold His coming and sufferings, and the glory that should follow. When the appointed time of His advent came, His thoughts were upon His Church. He saw that there was no man; He wondered that there was no intercessor. "I know the thoughts I have towards you—thoughts of peace, and not of evil." "Save from going down to the pit, I have found out a ransom." "Lo, I come; in the volume of the book it is written of Me; to do Thy will I delight, O God; yea, Thy law is within my heart." I will go to yon distant world, and take the form of a servant, and pay the price, that these may go free. His thoughts were towards His Church, when on earth He went about continually doing good—gathering in the lost sheep of the House of Israel; when He said, "I ascend to My Father and your Father—to My God and your God;" when, in prayer, He cried, "Now, I am no more in the world, but these are in the world; and I come to Thee, Holy Father: keep, through Thine own name, those that Thou hast given me, for they are Thine." "Father, I will that they also whom Thou hast given Me be with Me where I am, that they may behold My glory." In the regions of heaven, His thoughts are still upon His people. There, He is preparing for them mansions of blessedness; thence is He continually sending the Holy Spirit to sanctify them, His angels to guard them, and making all the events of Providence to work together for their good. His unceasing occupation is to present their prayers, in the golden censer full of incense, perfumed with His infinite merits; whilst, throughout eternity, His thoughts will be on His redeemed and glorified Church. "The Lamb that is in the midst of the throne shall feed them and lead them unto living fountains of water; and God shall wipe away all tears from their eyes."

Our love towards an object may be manifested *by our anxiety in regard to its welfare.* "Deal gently," said David, "with the young man Absalom for my sake;" proving how intensely he loved that young man, wicked as he was. And so Christ overrules all events, and gives charge to His servants, the angels, that excel in glory and strength: "Are they not all ministering spirits sent forth to minister to them who shall be heirs of salvation?" Not only so, but He gives solemn charge even to wicked men: "Touch not Mine anointed, do My prophets no harm." He even charges Satan, binding him like

waves of the sea, and saying, " Hitherto shalt thou come, but
no farther." Satan himself was convinced of this in the case
of Job : "Hast Thou not hedged him about, and all that he
hath ?" Nay, we find God threatening those who meddle with
His saints : "It were better that a millstone were hanged about
his neck, and he cast into the sea, than that he should offend
one of these little ones." We find Him, in the days of old,
making the sun and moon stand still in the firmament for
them ; the sea stand up as an heap, that the ransomed of the
Lord should pass over. The solid rock gave forth streams of
water, and great laws of nature were reversed. We find Christ
identifying Himself with His people. " He that receiveth you,
receiveth Me." " He that giveth a cup of cold water to a disciple shall in no wise lose his reward." " Inasmuch as ye did it
to one of the least of these My brethren, ye did it unto Me."

Love may be known by *the extent of suffering which we
are willing to undergo for the person beloved.* Greater love
hath no man than this, that a man lay down his life for a
friend. Scarcely for a righteous man will one die ; "but God
commendeth His love toward us, in that while we were yet
sinners, Christ died for us." Jacob served seven years for Rachel,
and it seemed but a day, for the love he had for her ; although
the dews were upon him by night, and the sun by day. Now,
Christ hath endured inconceivable agony for His Church. We
may apply to Him the language of the prophet, " Behold, and
see, all ye that pass by, if there be any sorrow like to my sorrow,
wherewith the Lord hath afflicted me in the day of his fierce
anger." He suffered in His body, which was agonised and nailed
to the accursed tree ; in His soul, which was exceeding sorrowful and sore amazed ; and if we will come and see where he
bled, hear his groans, and behold the place where the Lord lay
after shedding that blood, every drop of which was infinitely
precious, we must be convinced that there never was love
like His. When Christ was about to be betrayed, He said
to those who came to take Him, " If, therefore, ye seek Me,
let these go their way "—a statement which will apply to His
whole Church. Cast Me, like Jonah, into the sea, that all
the rest may be saved ; nail Me to the accursed tree, spend
your malice on Me ; I am willing to tread the winepress alone,
and that of the people there shall be none with me—only let
these go. Thus Christ stood between His Church and danger—
He acted as the conductor upon which the lightning of Divine

F

vengeance might break and exhaust itself, that they might be untouched. He drank the bitter cup, that they might not taste it; He was wounded, that we might be healed; He bore away the curse, that we might carry away the blessing. There was no sorrow like His, nor any love to compare with it—I have loved thee, and given Myself for thee. Hence the apostle tries to measure this love, but his line is too short; he cannot find its height, and depth, and breadth, and length. He tries to speak of it, but language fails —it is unspeakable. He tries to know its extent, but the human mind, sustained by inspiration, breaks down in the attempt. "It passeth knowledge." Only, he infallibly concludes that the greatest evidence has been given of boundless love, and that God, who spared not His own Son, but gave Him up to the death for us, is, with Him also freely pleased to give us all things.

Our love is discerned *by the prominence given to the object beloved.* Solomon made a seat for his mother at his right hand. All men have some object on which they dwell with satisfaction — their wealth, their talents, their honours, their beauty. Now Christ regards the Church as the object of His chief love. That Church is His treasure. She is called "Hephzibah," for the Lord delighteth in her; she is Christ's inheritance, as it is written, "Ask of Me, and I will give thee the heathen for thine inheritance." In her he sees of the travail of His soul, and is satisfied. Her glory is the joy set before Him, for which He endured the cross, despising the shame. I gave Egypt for thy ransom — Ethiopia and Seba for thee. Nay, He has built a stately palace for this Church, of which this world, with its bright canopy of sun, moon, and stars, is only the porch. He gives that Church all the advantages of time and all the blessedness of eternity, so that we may well exclaim, "Who is like unto thee, O Israel: a people saved by the Lord, the Shield of thine help, and the Sword of thine excellency! All thine enemies shall be found liars unto thee, and thou shalt tread upon their high places."

II. Consider, again, *this love, and the relationships implied in it.*

If we come more closely to it, and examine into the nature of this love, the statement in the text will become more clear and wonderful. God is called, in the text, "thy God;" and He is said to be "in the midst of us," and to "rejoice over us, with singing." In other words, there is a close relationship between God and His people; He is their God, in a more peculiar sense than He was the God of the ancient Israelites. As he tabernacled of old amongst the Jews, so He dwells in them, and walks in them, and they are temples of the Holy Ghost. Nay, as the eagle fluttereth over her nest, carrieth her young upon her wings, so our Saviour God watches over His people, and rejoiceth to do them good.

Consider the names by which *He* is called. He is our *Surety* —that implies singular love. He has paid our debts hundreds of years before they were contracted—cast them behind His back, and into the depths of the sea, so that they shall never rise in remembrance against us. He is our *Mediator*. It was love that induced Him to undertake our otherwise desperate cause, and to stand between us and the offended majesty, justice, and truth of heaven. He is our *Advocate*,—not a hired intercessor, who may not care for the success of his client, or a poor, fallible earthly pleader; but One whose infinite wisdom, power, and love are spontaneously put forth in our defence, and are always prevalent. He is our *Captain*. Shall the Captain not love His soldiers, and feel a deep interest in their success and victory? He is our *Head*. Shall the Head say of any of the members of the body, I have no need of thee? No man hateth his own flesh, but nourisheth and cherisheth it. He is the *King* of *saints*. Their hearts are His throne, and love is the very sceptre by which He rules them. In a word, all the names of Christ in relation to His people prove that He rejoices over them, with singing. On the other hand, consider the names by which *they* are called. They are His *friends*. "Henceforth I call you not servants, but friends; for the servant knoweth not what his Lord doeth." It is in this capacity that we sit at His table, and hear the invitation, Eat, O friends; drink, yea, drink abundantly, O beloved. His is not the hollow friendship of this world, which changes like the varying sky; but Christ is "a friend that sticketh closeth than a brother," and is especially "a brother born for adversity." When even the dearest friends on earth forget and forsake us, we have a sure refuge in Him. "When my father and mother forsake me, the Lord will take me up." We are called His *children*—"being born again, not of corruptible seed, but of incorruptible; by the Word of God, which liveth and abideth for ever." We all know how strong a love is implied in the joy of parents. Yet this is the favourite image. Man, the prodigal son; God, eyeing him with pity amidst all his folly; hailing the first symptoms of his return, and saying, Bring forth the best robe, and put it on him; put a ring on his hand, and shoes on his feet. It was meet that we should make merry and rejoice, for this My son was dead, and is alive again—he was lost, and is found. How shall I give thee up, Ephraim? Is Ephraim a dear son, is he a pleasant child? We are the *spouse* of Christ. Thou shalt say, my Maker is my Husband, the Lord of Hosts is His name. All the splendours of Eastern imagery are lavished on this glorious bride. She is perfumed with myrrh, and aloes, and cassia, out of the ivory palaces. King's daughters are amongst her honourable women: on the right hand doth stand the queen, in gold of Ophir. O daughter, hearken and regard; forsake thy father's house and thine own people: so shall the King greatly desire thy beauty; for He is thy Lord, and worship thou Him. Thou art beautiful as Tirzah, comely as Jerusalem. Who is this that looketh forth as the morning—fair as the moon, clear as the sun, terrible as an army with banners. No greater mark of love can be imagined than this. He passes by all others, and chooses her to the most exalted place of honour, to the most endeared relationship. We are His *house*. Christ, as a Son in His own House, whose house are we, if we hold fast the beginning of our confidence stedfast unto the end. Now, every idea of happiness centres around our own home; humble though it may be, still it is ours, and all the objects of our most familiar and dearest affections are there. And so, when Christ called the Church His house, framed of living stones, in which are many vessels of gold and silver, but all meet for the Master's use,—He intended to intimate the intense and peculiar love with which He regards His people. We are His *sheep*. The shepherd defends His sheep, even at the risk of his own life, as David did against the lion and the bear. He knows them all by their names,—He makes them to lie down at noon in the green pastures, and beside the still waters. This great Shepherd of Israel, who slumbereth not nor sleepeth, drives away the wolves and birds of prey, gathers the lambs in His arms and carries them in His bosom, and gently leads those that are with young. His sheep know His voice and follow him, and will not follow a stranger; and He gives them eternal life, and they shall never perish, nor shall any be able to pluck them out of His hand. He is the Good Shepherd: the good shepherd giveth his life for the sheep. Above all, we are His *jewels*. "They shall be Mine, saith the Lord, in that day which I make up My jewels." Men chiefly value their jewels, and place them in the strongest hold of their dwelling-places. The jewels of a kingdom are especially precious. They are placed in a tower of safety, railed round with iron. And, as we look at them through the iron grating, the armed guards stand round to protect them from danger. When the ambassadors and princes of other lands assemble, and a grand display is to be made of the wealth and glory of a kingdom, these jewels are brought forth, and exhibited to dazzle the foreign eyes. So, in the vast dominions of the King of Kings, His redeemed children are His jewels—more precious than the topaz of Ethiopia or the fine wedge of Ophir. They are now hedged round, and all that they have. You may look on them, but, without Divine permission, you dare not touch them. Their place of defence is the munition of rocks; and when, at length, all the principalities and powers of darkness, and the kings of all lands are assembled with the mighty crowds of the judgment-day, these shall be brought forth, as the trophies of His power and wonders of His kingdom— enemies made friends,—souls once defiled and debased, but now elevated and made radiant as sons of the morning. Meantime is the statement true, "where your treasure is, there will your heart be also." The love of Christ is centred upon those who are His jewels.

III. Consider what *Christ has already done for His people.*

They are His by *choice.* He chose them from eternity. I have loved thee with an everlasting love; therefore, with loving-kindness have I drawn thee. We must look back, through a long flight of ages, to a period before the earth was made, before the morning stars sang together, and all the sons of God shouted for joy; and think of Christ, from the depths of eternity, choosing His people, and determining to secure their salvation. He saw us in ruin, and even then He passed by and said unto us, Live: yea, he said unto us, Live. His time was a time of love. These were the bosom-thoughts of God towards His people, this the love of that glorious sovereignty, out of which the whole plan of salvation arose. Love called the world into being, that it might be a theatre of redeeming grace: love triumphs over all difficulties, and the eternity of the future is only the full development of what was fixed and resolved upon in the eternity that is past.

They are His *purchase.* We love what is ours, especially what we have obtained with difficulty, especially what we have lost and then obtained again, as the poor woman rejoiced over her lost piece of money when found—as the shepherd rejoiced over his recovered sheep—as the father over the returning prodigal. Now,

all we like sheep had gone astray, and are bought back with an
unspeakable price—even the precious blood of Christ, as of a Lamb
without blemish and without spot.

Let us put the merits of the case thus :—The people of God
were cast out and condemned. A day's-man arose, but conditions
must be fulfilled—He must die that we might live ; He must
endure the curse, if we were to inherit the blessing--endure the
punishment of sin, if we were to live and reign. In a word, He
must buy us, or we cannot be His. He accepts the terms, finishes
transgression, brings in an everlasting righteousness, offers it to
us, sends ambassadors to urge it upon our acceptance, sends the
Holy Spirit to change our hearts. When it is accepted, the rebels
are set free,—the debtors bring their books, and the pen of heaven
is run through their debts, and thus God now sees no iniquity in
Jacob, nor perverseness in Israel. There is enough in reality, but
in them, clothed with Christ's righteousness, the Father sees none.
They are accepted in the beloved, and these clothed and justified
ones all the Trinity behold with a pleasant countenance,—whilst
Christ sees in them of the travail of His soul, and is satisfied.
Nay, strange though it may seem, the great delight of Christ is
here : He taketh pleasure in His people, and will beautify the
meek with His salvation ; He delights to see you, to be with you,
to converse with you—but for you the world would be only fit for
the fire. " Let me see Thy face, let me hear Thy voice : For sweet
is Thy voice, and Thy countenance is comely."

We are His *by a new creation*. David asks, " Wilt Thou show
wonders to the dead ? shall they rise and praise Thee ?"   The
question is answered in the experience of every Christian. For by
Him ye are created in Christ Jesus unto good works. At the
omnipotent command of Jesus, Lazarus comes forth, casts off his
grave clothes, and sings for joy. Man reckons it a great work to
raise the sick, greater to raise the dying, a still greater to raise the
actually dead—and it is the greatest of all to raise a soul " dead in
trespasses and sins." But the Almighty voice which called the
universe into existence and said, " Let there be light, and there
was light," can burst the barriers which shroud in darkness an
immortal spirit, can lift up the everlasting doors of the human
soul that the King of glory may enter in, can make the spiritual
lunatic come to himself, and appear clothed and in his right mind,
—in a word, can make a new creation rise from the ruins of the
Fall, radiant in new life and in the prospect of a blessed immortality. As God said of the first creation, it is all very good ; so He

regards with especial affection this new and wonderful workmanship, and "rejoices over it with singing."

We are *His by covenant*. We were by baptism solemnly
devoted to Him, and we have now devoted ourselves. On the day
when we received the truth in the love of it, our language was,
"Come, let us join ourselves unto the Lord in a perpetual covenant, that shall not be forgotten." Of old, there was a solemn
dedication of the Jews to God—Moses sprinkled the book and the
people, and said, "This is the blood of the covenant which the
Lord hath made with you;" and they said, "All that the Lord
hath said will we do." And year after year, as they observed the
Passover, their language was, "God is the Lord, who hath showed
us light: bind the sacrifice with cords to the horns of the altar."
Here are we—thine, O David, and on thy side, thou son of Jesse;
what wilt thou have us to do? We will take the cup of salvation,
and call upon the name of the Lord. Thus we have avouched the
Lord to be our God. ·Like wandering sheep, we have returned to
the eternal fold. The meaning of our communion is, that this God
shall be our God for ever and ever. Let us rest assured that He
never said to any of the seed of Jacob, "Seek my face in vain."
"Fear not, little flock; it is your Father's good pleasure to give you
the kingdom." "This is as the waters of Noah unto Me, saith the
Lord; for as I have sworn that the waters of Noah shall no more
go over the earth, so have I sworn that I will not be wroth with
thee, nor rebuke thee." "No weapon that is formed against thee
shall prosper, and every tongue that riseth in judgment against
thee shall I condemn." Affliction may depress, sorrows may cloud
our prospects, difficulties may perplex, but, amidst them all, "look
up, and lift up your heads, for your redemption draweth nigh."

We are aware that, notwithstanding all these powerful reasons, such is the insidious influence of unbelief, so many swarms
of "vain thoughts" not only enter, but "lodge" in our minds,
that we find God in His blessed Word seeking to drive them
out. "Comfort ye, comfort ye, my people, saith your God."
They are assured that a price is paid "double," though their sins
have been of the deepest dye. But this is not enough. Why
sayest thou, O Jacob, and speakest, O Israel, My way is hid from
the Lord? Hast thou not known that our God will abundantly
pardon all who truly repent? And if any are ready to object that
no man, no king, ever acted thus, God says, "My ways are not
your ways, neither are my thoughts your thoughts." Again: "He
shall dwell on high," like the eagle, beyond the reach of assault;

"his place of defence shall be the munition of rocks." But the hesitating soul may say, We may be starved there. No: your "bread shall be given." But, still, it may be argued, There is no water on the top of the rock. Yes: your "water shall be sure." Nor shall that be all: "You shall see the King in His beauty, and the land that is a very far off." It is added: There shall be a place of broad rivers and streams. But the hesitating soul may say, Ships may carry enemies. But this may not be: "no galley with oars nor gallant ship shall pass thereby." So, again, the apostle says, He hath blotted out the hand-writing of ordinances which was against us. This is not enough,—He hath taken it out of the way. Perhaps it may be found and read. Not at all: He hath nailed it to the cross. Nay, God not only gives His Son and His promise, but His oath: "That by two immutable things, in which it was impossible for God to lie, we might have strong consolation, who have fled for refuge to lay hold of the hope set before us." He heaps mountains on mountains of eternal strength; he lays heaven and earth at pledge, as it were, all to convince us. For the Word of God is the pillar of heaven, and the oath of God an eternal seal, which all creation cannot break—all to convince our doubting souls.

Above all, we have the whole past experience of the Christian Church to prove the truth of the text. We find Jacob using this argument from experience: " The God that led me and fed me all my life long until this day." When David fled from Saul, and came to the high-priest, he asked for a weapon with which to defend himself. The answer was: "There is none but the sword of Goliath the Philistine, whom thou slewest." " Give it me," said David, " for there is none like it ;" it is the trophy of past success and the pledge of future triumph. Thou hast been my helper, therefore will I put my trust under the shadow of thy wings. "They that know Thy name shall put their trust in Thee." Why? " For thou hast not forsaken them that trust in Thee." " Our Fathers trusted in thee : they trusted, and Thou didst deliver them." " To Him that divided the sea, and smote great kings, for His mercy endureth for ever," is the song of David. Awake, awake, O arm of the Lord. Art thou not it that hath cut Rahab, and wounded the Dragon ?

As often as the Passover was celebrated, it was part of the duty of him who presided to detail the wonders of the love of God, beginning with Abraham, and going on to the bondage of Egypt and Israel's marvellous deliverance. And so, when we observe our

New Testament Passover, we should look back over the past eternity,—and, especially, the six thousand years of the Christian Church—think of the millions who have drank at this fountain of redeeming love, an exceeding great multitude, which no man can number, all in glory, all singing the song of Moses and the Lamb, all monuments of eternal love. Do you doubt the Saviour's promise? Here He exposes anew the symbols of His death. Yonder are the trophies of His blessed triumph, whilst with one voice the ransomed in heaven exclaim, Thou hast redeemed us to God by Thy blood, out of every people, and kindred, and tongue, and nation.

In conclusion, the subject of our discourse is well fitted, under the power of the Spirit of God, to give an overwhelming sense of our own unworthiness, and to cast down all pride. Our language should be, We are ashamed and confounded, and will never lift up our mouths any more, since God is pacified towards us, notwithstanding all that we have done. It is fitted to banish all formality in worship, all unthankfulness, unfruitfulness, and hatred. "If God so loved us, we ought also to love one another." Let us seek, whilst clothed with humility and hating all sin, to be filled with love and joy. We may well say, "Let the children of Zion be joyful in their King." Why do ye, sons of a King, go mourning from day to day? Let us join in the glorious anthem of the Psalms: Praise Him, ye sun and moon; praise Him, ye stars of light; praise Him, ye heaven of heavens, for He spake, and ye were created. Who remembered us in our low estate; for His mercy endureth for ever. And hath redeemed us from our enemies; for His mercy endureth for ever. "And now, blessed be the Lord God, the God of Israel, who only doeth wondrous things. And blessed be His glorious name for ever: and let the whole earth be filled with His glory. Amen and Amen."

CHRIST'S UNSEARCHABLE RICHES:

A SERMON.

BY

ALEX. F. MITCHELL, D.D.,

PROFESSOR OF CHURCH HISTORY AND DIVINITY, ST ANDREWS.

" The unsearchable riches of Christ."—EPH. iii. 8.

THESE, my brethren, are very precious words, They disclose to us what the apostle thought of the Master for whose sake he counted all things but loss. They supply the reason why he delighted so constantly to speak and write about Him so devotedly, to spend and to be spent for Him. And they state nothing but sober truth respecting Him who, though He was rich, for our sakes became poor, that we, through his poverty, might be made rich. Yet, how often have we read them without feeling in any measure their intense reality, and turned away from that blessed One of whom they testify, as if there were no beauty nor riches in Him that we should desire Him, or, at least, none that were new or still unexplored by us. May that Holy and Almighty Spirit, whose it is to take of the things that are Christ's and show them unto us, open your understandings to understand and your wills and hearts to receive the truth in the love of it! May He enable me so to set before you the glory and riches of Christ, that you may discover Him to be indeed "the chiefest among ten thousand," and may be led personally to appropriate the freely offered riches of His grace.

The Apostle Paul, as one whose own soul was filled with a sense of the greatness of His Saviour's love, and the unspeakable blessings bestowed on him thereby, is wont to make use of the strongest epithets and most expressive figures in setting forth the glory of His person, and the all-sufficiency of His grace. In this very epistle, he dwells with rapture on the love of the Father and the Son, and the blessings that flow from it to sinners of mankind; he tells of the riches, and the exceeding riches of grace, and, in our text, of the unsearchable riches of Christ, and, in the immediate context, of the breadth and length, the depth and height of the love of Christ which passeth knowledge.

But how is Christ so rich? Who is He, that His riches should be unsearchable? He is, the apostle teaches, God, God over all, blessed for ever. He is rich, for he is "the image of the invisible God," who shares in all the perfections of the Divine nature, and is "infinite, eternal, and unchangeable, in His being, wisdom, power, holiness, justice, goodness, and truth." He is rich in the brightness of His Father's glory, sharing the worship paid by the most exalted of the heavenly hosts, and having obtained by inheritance a more excellent name than they. He is rich, for He has performed the mightiest works of Godhead, and manifested His glory by them; "for by Him were all things created that are in heaven, and that are on earth, . . . all things were created by Him and for Him;" He upholdeth all things by the word of His power, and "by Him all things consist." He thinks it "no robbery to be equal with God." He claims but His own when He claims divine perfections, and all that is implied in the possession and exercise of them.

Because Christ was so rich, and qualified for the work, He was appointed to be the Redeemer and Surety of sinful men. He became our kinsman that we might have right in Him, and that He might be such an High Priest as we need, able to sympathise with us, and to save unto the uttermost all them that come unto God by Him. The Word was made flesh and dwelt among us, full of grace and truth, that out of His fulness we might receive, even grace for grace. He took not on Him the nature of angels, but the seed of Abraham; and to redeem them that were under the law and under the curse of a broken covenant, He was made under the law, endured its penalty, and became obedient unto death, even the death of the cross. He is the Surety of a better covenant established on better promises, ratified by nobler blood. Travelling in the greatness of His strength, he has encountered and overcome the Adversary of our souls, purged away our sins, purchased back our forfeited inheritance, and obtained eternal redemption for us,—His manhood being sustained, in the mighty task, by its union with the Godhead, and His work itself owing its value and efficacy to that ineffable union. His riches, as Mediator and Surety, being de-

rived from, and only measured by, His riches as "the Mighty God,"
can never be fully told or known, but are, as the apostle teaches,
unsearchable.   Let me endeavour for a little to fix your thoughts
on this precious truth ; and the more fully to open it out to you,
let me observe in detail :—

I. That the riches of Christ's *pardoning mercy* are unsearchable.

As has just been said, He was the infinite God, who, for us
men, and for our salvation, took on Him our nature and became
obedient unto death, was approved and accepted in His vicarious
work, and raised to the right hand of the Majesty in the heavens
as a Prince and a Saviour, to give repentance and the remission
of sins.   And there can be no limit assigned to His ability to grant
these gifts, because there can be none to the value of His sufferings, or the merit of His obedience.   There can be no searching
out of the riches of His pardoning mercy, any more than of the
value of that mysterious work which secures our pardon, or of
the breadth and length, and depth and height of that love which
led Him to undertake and accomplish the work.   The Lord is
well pleased for His righteousness' sake, for He hath magnified
the law and made it honourable, yea, hath put more honour on it,
by His obedience unto death, than it could have had by the
eternal condemnation of every member of our guilty race.   By
His one obedience shall many be made righteous.   Yea, men and
brethren, by this Man is preached unto you the forgiveness of
sins, and by Him all that believe are justified from all that lay
to their charge.   The fountain of His mercy sends forth its
waters in such abundance and efficacy, that even the most
polluted may wash in it, and be cleansed from all their guilt.
The stream that issues from it, like that which Ezekiel saw in
vision, flows on till it expands into a river that cannot be passed
over,—waters to swim in,—an ocean whose vast extent we can
never traverse, whose hidden depths we can never sound.   In this
Gospel field, wherein lie hid unsearchable riches, He has opened
for the poor and needy an exhaustless mine of heavenly treasure.
We can bring you into those portions of it which have already
been opened up, and shew the treasures of mercy which have
been got in them, and have enriched others, once as impoverished
as you.   We can tell you of the riches of mercy found by a
Rahab, a David, a Manasseh, a Peter, a Paul, and even by some
of those who, with wicked hands, crucified and slew the merciful

One Himself. We can assure you, on the warrant of Him who cannot lie, that you may dig in this field and appropriate to yourselves as much of its precious treasure as you need, that from the Lord of mercy you may receive a full pardon and free justification, however guilty you may have been ; and if you only, in faith and penitence, accept His offered gifts, though you may have been chief of sinners, you may, by His mercy and grace, be made not a whit behind the chief of saints.

But we can give you no adequate conception of the treasures which are still untouched, still hidden from view. We can only assure you, on the authority of the God of truth, on the testimony of Christ and His apostles, that they are exceeding great, exhaustless, unsearchable ; that whosoever will, may take them freely, and that none who truly seek shall fail to find, or be sent empty away. "Here," to use the quaint expression of an old divine, "there is no man knows what, for no man knows whom." There is pardon, reconciliation, acceptance for a doubting Thomas, a murdering Saul, a dying thief, a Jerusalem sinner. It is a faithful saying, and worthy of all acceptation, that Christ Jesus came into the world to save sinners—even the chief. If only they turn unto the Lord, He will multiply His pardons, wash out their crimson sins, and shed abroad His love in their hearts. For His ways are not as our ways, nor His thoughts as our thoughts. But even as the heavens are higher than the earth, so are His ways than our ways, and His thoughts than our hard and narrow thoughts of Him. They who know most of the riches of His mercy are most deeply sensible how far short their conceptions fall of the reality, and most ready, with this chief of sinners, to gaze, with ever-deepening amazement, on its breadth and length, and depth, and height, and silently adore Him whose love passeth knowledge. Are not, then, the riches of Christ's pardoning mercy altogether unsearchable ? Let us now endeavour to explain :—

II. That the riches of Christ's *sanctifying grace* are unsearchable.

By His obedience unto death, our Lord Jesus Christ has fully merited for sinners, not only mercy to pardon, but grace to sanctify, and to help them in every time of need. He has condemned sin in the flesh, and set His people free from the law of sin and death—just that the righteousness of the law might be fulfilled in them, and that they might no longer walk after the flesh but after the spirit. He gave Himself for them for this very purpose, that He might redeem them from all iniquity, and purify them unto Himself—a peculiar people, zealous of good works. And He accomplishes this by the power of His risen life, working in all who accept His offered mercy, according to the working of the mighty power which was wrought in Him, when He was raised from the dead and exalted to the right hand of the Majesty in the heavens, that they may be raised to a holy and truly heavenly life, seeking the things which are above, where He is, and imitating His blessed example. He has been anointed with the Spirit above measure, that He may shed down His gifts and influences on them, and thus may bind up the broken-hearted, proclaim and give liberty to the captives of sin and Satan—give power to the faint, and increase strength to them that have no might; that He may comfort those who mourn, raise up those who have fallen, bring back those who have gone astray, and furnish them unto every good work. He is the infinite, almighty, and unchanging God, who has undertaken to carry on to perfection the good work which He has begun; who has purchased, chosen, and called His people, that they might be holy and without blame before Him; who has told them that this is His will and purpose in all His dealings with them—even their sanctification,—their deliverance from the love and practice of sin, and their conformation to His own holy and loving image; and who has promised to make His grace abound towards them, that they may have all-sufficiency in all things, and abound unto every good work. Hence, the riches of His sanctifying grace can no more be fully searched out or unfolded than the riches of His pardoning mercy and redeeming love. We can bring you into His garden, and point to many trees, now covered with the goodly foliage of a Christian profession, and glistening with golden fruits of righteousness, which once were planted on the banks of the burning lake, and yielded no fruit but the apples of Sodom or the grapes of Gomorrah. We can bring you to the "living temple," in which He is eternally to dwell and eternally to be glorified. We can point out the goodly stones, carved and polished, which now adorn its front or crown its pinnacles, but which once were as unsightly and unpromising as any in the rough quarry from which they were dug. We can tell of very monsters of iniquity who, by His marvellous grace, have been washed, justified, sanctified, and made patterns of all holy conversation and godliness. We can tell you of victims of debasing lusts, who, by the mighty power of His Spirit, have been set free from their bondage, and, exulting in the liberty with which Christ has made them free, have deemed it their highest privilege, no less than their bounden duty, to consecrate to Him their time, talents, influence, and opportunities—yea, their souls, bodies, and spirits—His costly purchase and rightful conquest. We can tell you of slaves of Satan, who have been brought back, as it were, from the very confines of hell, made more than conquerors over their oppressor,—yea, turned into chief instruments for thwarting his plans and overthrowing his rule. Such were Manasseh, Paul, Augustine, Bunyan, and John Newton,— who, being forgiven much, loved much, and proved their love by untiring obedience, and devoted, self-denying service. We can tell you that they are set forth as specimens to show you what, by the grace and Spirit of God, you also may become, and what abundance of blessing you may expect. We can assure you that the all-sufficient grace of Christ is as free to you as to them,—as abundant and effectual to supply your wants, to heal your diseases, and strengthen your weakness; to enrich your poverty, to subdue your enemies, root out your lusts, and mould anew your spiritual nature. We can assure you that it is as suited to your circumstances, whatever these may be, as able to quicken, sanctify, and comfort you; because it is the infinite grace of the Infinite God. We can assure you, with full warrant, that no one who has, in truth, applied to Him for sanctifying grace, has applied in vain, and that no one ever can apply in vain; for the faithful and true Witness hath said, "If ye, being evil, know how to give good gifts to your children, how much more shall your heavenly Father give the Holy Spirit to them that ask Him?" We cannot tell, brethren, how much more willing and able He is to do so, just because we cannot comprehend the greatness of that love wherewith He hath loved us, or the riches of pardoning mercy and sanctifying grace which He has treasured up for us in Christ. We can but partially describe them, imperfectly conceive of them, feebly commend them. Yet we can assure you, on the testimony of Him who cannot lie, that they are unexhausted and inexhaustible. "Sanctifying grace," to use the metaphor of an old divine, "shall fill every vessel of honour to the full; and, like the widow's oil, only be stayed when there is not a vessel more to contain it,"—when "all the ransomed Church of God are saved, to sin no more." Surely, then, the riches of Christ's sanctifying grace, as well as those of His pardoning mercy, are altogether unsearchable?

Let me now observe, very briefly :—

III. That the riches of His *rewarding glory* are unsearchable.

By His obedience unto death, our Lord Jesus Christ merited for His people, not only mercy to pardon and grace to sanctify in the life that now is, but a glorious reward, an exceeding weight of glory, in the life to come. Indeed, the latter is the end to which the former are the means,—or rather, it is the fulness and perfection of that higher life, of which the former are the earnests and first-fruits. The life of glory is the crown and complement of the life of grace. The end the Saviour had in view, in all His obedience and suffering, was just that He might entitle and fit them for it, and then bring many sons unto glory. He fulfilled the conditions of the covenant, that He might secure to His people the rewards and blessings promised under it. And having begotten them again to the hope of an inheritance which is incorruptible, and undefiled, and that fadeth not away; and having, by His own blood, opened a new way into the heavenly places for His people, He has entered and taken possession in their name; He now holds these for them, and in due season shall take them home to glory. He has power to give eternal life to as many as He will; and this is His will, and the will of the Father who hath sent Him,—that whosoever seeth the Son, and believeth on Him, should have everlasting life, and be raised up in glory. If, now, we believe in Him, we pass from death unto life, we receive power to become the sons of God; and, if sons, then heirs—heirs of God, and joint heirs with Christ. Though the world as yet acknowledge us not,—and it doth not to it appear what we shall be,—we know that, when He shall return in majesty, we shall appear with Him and share His glory. Eye hath not seen, nor ear heard, neither hath it entered into the heart of man to conceive the things which God hath prepared for them that love Him; but God hath revealed them unto us by His Spirit. He hath given us, in His indwelling, an earnest and foretaste of them; and, by images borrowed from things temporal and material, He hath dimly shadowed forth, in Holy Scripture, the glory of those new heavens and the new earth for which we look.

In those blessed abodes which Christ has gone to prepare, we are told, there is the broad river of the water of life, having on its banks the trees which yield their fruits every month, and the leaves of which are for the healing of the nations; there is a city with glorious foundations and streets of purest gold,— a temple in which God and the Lamb shall dwell, an inheritance that is incorruptible, and undefiled, and that fadeth not away, —yea, a kingdom that cannot be moved; a crown of life, and righteousness, and glory; a Father's house of many mansions, a table that shall never be drawn, a robe of spotless purity for every guest, a feast of fat things and of wines on the lees, of fat things full of marrow, and of wines on the lees well refined.

But these things, and all the unspeakable glory they faintly shadow forth, are the purchase of Immanuel's blood. Our forfeited inheritance, with all that belongs to it or has been added to it, was bought back by our Kinsman-Redeemer. Hence, the beloved disciple, to whom, in vision, the glories of the world to come were unveiled, describes the ransomed throng as casting their crowns at the feet of their blessed Redeemer, and saying, "Thou art worthy to take the book,"—that is, the title-deeds of the inheritance,—"and to open the seals thereof; for Thou wast slain, and hast redeemed us unto God by thy blood, out of every kindred, and tongue, and people, and nation; and hast made us unto our God, kings and priests." But the bliss of these kings and priests just consists in the glorifying and enjoying of God, and therefore in the perfection of that holy character which alone capacitates for glorifying and enjoying Him, in entire conformity to the moral image of Him who is at once our Redeemer and our Exemplar. And as He is the infinite, eternal, and unchangeable God, who is the Author and Finisher of our Faith, who is engaged to carry out and bring to perfection the good work He has begun in our souls; as it hath pleased the Father that all fulness of grace and blessing should dwell in Him, that out of His fulness we may receive unfailing supplies; as no giving can impoverish Him, or exhaust His divine fulness:— surely He is able to fill every vessel of honour to the full, and the riches of His rewarding glory, as well as of His sanctifying grace, are unsearchable.

Such, dear brethren, are the nature and extent of the riches of Christ,—your Saviour God,—which are all offered to you in His Gospel, and sealed over to worthy receivers in His holy sacraments. And now, in fulfilment of our commission, we would

G

preach them unto you,—declaring, in the name of the Master we serve, that these unsearchable riches are for you—for each of you,—to take, to use, to live on; for you, though poor and unworthy,—yea, just because you are poor, unworthy, and in need of all things; for you, as a free gift from the Father of mercies and His blessed Son. We say they are a free gift to you; for, though they are above all value, and have cost Him dear, the price has been fully paid, and you may now take them freely, and buy them without money and without price. In His name we offer these riches to you—to each of you. We entreat your acceptance of them,—as gold tried in the fire—the true-enduring, all-satisfying, inexhaustible riches—the treasures which neither moth nor rust can corrupt, nor thief steal, nor death part from you. The apostle declared the glad tidings respecting them to the Ephesians, who were, by nature, dead in trespasses and sins,—without God and without hope in the world. They listened, and believed, and received the offered boon, and they were raised from their low estate, to sit in heavenly places with Christ; they were brought nigh to God, blessed with all spiritual blessings in Christ, and set forth, as patterns, to show unto the ages to come the exceeding riches of His grace. Believing that it is only by the same Gospel—the same precious and life-giving truths respecting Christ and His fulness,—that the same blessed effects can be still produced, in our Master's name we declare the same glad tidings to you. We assure you, on His own faithful testimony, that He is as rich in mercy and full of grace now as then, and offers all His blessings as freely and lovingly to you as He did to them. We assure you, further, on His own warrant, that if ye will only be followers of their faith, ye too shall be pardoned, sanctified, and glorified; ye shall be no longer strangers and foreigners, but fellow-citizens with the saints, and of the household of God,—yea, heirs of God and joint-heirs with Christ,—monuments of the riches and efficacy of His unsearchable grace,—sharers in His unspeakable glory. Neglect not, then, His great salvation; spurn not His gracious offers. Hear, and your souls shall live; and He will make with you an everlasting covenant, and give unto you the sure mercies of David.

> " Act but the infant's gentle part,
>   Give up to love thy willing heart;
>   No fondest parent's melting breast
>   Yearns like thy God's to make thee blest."

In conclusion, let no one suppose that, in preaching thus, I have been preaching a different gospel from that which was believed and preached by the framers of those Confessions, which, in earlier and later times, have commanded the reverence of all the Scottish Churches. There are, as has been lately said, heights in these we cannot scale, and depths we cannot fathom ; but the highest of the heights, and the deepest of the depths, are found in the Word of God as well as in them, and can no more be eliminated from the epistles of Paul and Peter than from our symbolical books. While holding these mysterious truths in the sense in which they are meant to be held, and claiming the right, when occasion calls, to treat of them cautiously and reverently, I protest against all such caricatures of them as have been recently put into circulation.* I protest, with the Synod of Dort, that the Reformed Churches (and our own among the rest) do not hold, but, on the contrary, detest with all their hearts the opinion "that God, by His own absolute or arbitrary will, and without any respect of sin, hath foreordained or created any part of mankind to be damned, or that His decree is the cause of sin, or of final unbelief, in any such sense as it is the cause of faith and good works." I protest, with one of the most distinguished divines employed in drawing up the Westminster Confession, that "no man is created by God with a nature and quality fitting him for damnation. Yea, neither in the state of his innocency, nor in that of his fall and corruption, doth he receive anything from God which is a fit and proper means of bringing him to his damnation;" and with another, that "it is most certain that God is not the cause of any man's destruction; He found us sinners in Adam, but made none sinners;" and with a third, that "the just cause of a sinner's damnation is of and from himself; never lay it on God's decrees, or want of means and helps." And I claim it, as an act of barest justice to them, that the statements of the Confession be interpreted in the light of their own writings and teaching, and not by the travesties of caricaturists, who have never taken the trouble fairly to weigh it, or thoroughly to study it and them. Against the assertion that those who hold these opinions *cannot* preach a free Gospel, I am content to set the undeniable fact that they *did* preach a free Gospel, and that few ever did so with more winning tenderness than Arrowsmith,

* Preached to the United Presbyterian Congregation, St Andrews, shortly after one of these caricatures of Calvinism had been gratuitously circulated among ministers in this neighbourhood.

Calamy, Manton, and Sedgwick in the seventeenth century; or than Boston, Willison, and the Erskines, in the eighteenth; or than Chalmers, M'Cheyne, Bonar, Crawford, Macduff, and Nicholson, in the nineteenth. They all believed that God had a special purpose of mercy towards a people who were to be made willing in the day of His power, and that the stupendous plan of our redemption was not formed and executed at such a cost, to leave it absolutely dependent on the mere caprice of man, whether any fruit should come of it or not. But they also believed and taught, that, to all to whom the Gospel comes, the offer of salvation through Christ is really and sincerely made, and grace is tendered; and that the defect—to use again the language of the so-called grim Synod of Dort—" is not in the Gospel, nor in Christ offered in the Gospel, nor in God who calleth them, but in themselves, who reject the call, and refuse the offer." According to our Larger Catechism, " for their wilful contempt and neglect of the grace offered to them, being justly left to their unbelief, they do never truly come to Jesus Christ." This was unquestionably the teaching of the old Calvinists, and I hope it will never cease to be held and taught by their successors in the present day.

Plenteous grace with Thee is found,
Grace to cover all my sin;
Let the healing streams abound:
Make and keep me pure within!

Thou of life the Fountain art,
Freely let me take of Thee;
Spring Thou up within my heart,
Rise to all eternity.

PAUL SENT TO THE GENTILES:

A SERMON.

BY THE

REV. J. H. WILSON, M.A.,

BARCLAY CHURCH, EDINBURGH.

"And it came to pass, that, when I was come again to Jerusalem, even while I prayed in the temple, I was in a trance ; and saw Him saying unto me, Make haste, and get thee quickly out of Jerusalem : for they will not receive thy testimony concerning Me. And I said, Lord, they know that I imprisoned and beat in every synagogue them that believed on Thee : and when the blood of Thy martyr Stephen was shed, I was standing by, and consenting unto his death, and kept the raiment of them that slew him. And He said unto me, Depart : for I will thee far hence unto the Gentiles."
—Acts, xxii. 17-21.

THIS passage is possessed of an interest,—I might almost say, a *solemnity,* of a peculiar kind. In the account which Luke has previously given us of this never-to-be-forgotten event in the life of Paul and in the history of the Church, this further interview between the apostle and the Lord is not recorded ; and but for the special circumstances that now arose to call it forth, it might never have been mentioned at all. It had a very direct and weighty bearing on Paul's present position and argument, and might have availed—as, doubtless, he expected it would—to carry conviction to the hearts of his opponents, and disarm their further opposition, if it did not win them to the faith which he himself had been shut up thus wonderfully to receive. The account of any interview with the risen Christ, and especially one that was of such significance, and had such mighty issues dependent on it, may well be listened to with deepest awe.

The purpose for which it is introduced is manifest enough. Paul wished to convince his former co-religionists, that just as he had become a Christian and a Christian preacher because he could not help himself,—because the evidence was so irresistible, because, when he would fain have held back, he was carried forward by a Divine compulsion; so, when his heart was set upon labouring among and seeking the good of his people, he was obliged to surrender his own will, and undertake what otherwise he would have utterly shrunk back from, at the express and unmistakable command of his Divine Lord. Which of them, if they had been in his position, could have done anything else? Who would have dared to say, "No?"

Three remarks may suffice to bring out the gist of the passage.

I. THE REJECTION OF THE GOSPEL PREPARING THE WAY FOR THE WITHDRAWAL OF IT (ver. 17, 18).

At the time to which the narrative refers, Paul was paying his first visit to Jerusalem after his conversion. He must have returned with very strange and mingled feelings. He left the Holy City the proud champion of Judaism,—he came back to it the humble disciple of Christ. He left it the idol of the dominant party,—he came back the friend and companion of the despised Nazarenes. He left it with a heart full of hatred to the faith of Christ,—he came back wishing, above all things, to make that faith known to others, and ready to lay down his life in defence of it. And yet, as by a kind of instinct, he betook himself to the old place of prayer, and clung with a tender tenacity to the old ways. It does not surprise us to find him, on this his first visit, "*praying in the temple.*" In one respect, there was no reaction; and it was fitted to impress his Jewish hearers in his favour, that it was *in Jerusalem*, and *in the temple*, and *while praying there*, that he had this heavenly vision; and, in direct converse with his Lord, received the charge that had given its colour and direction to all his after life.

I can fancy his Jewish hearers speaking somewhat after this fashion:—"We can so far understand your own change of view and feeling, under such influences as you have described. We have nothing to say as to *that*. But what connection is there between that and separating yourself from your people, and making common cause with the despised Gentiles? *You* have been doing what even the great Nazarene Himself did not. *You* have been doing what even the other apostles of the new faith have not done." "I did it," says Paul, "by express

revelation—by express command. HE said to me, Hasten, and
go quickly out of Jerusalem, for they will not receive thy testimony about Me."

Much might have been said in favour of his remaining, besides
what we find him saying in the verses immediately following.
Had not his own people the first claim upon him? Were
their souls not as precious as *any?* Were conversions not
as important at Jerusalem as at Antioch and the towns and
cities of Asia Minor and of Europe? Should charity not
"begin at home?" Was it not time enough to think of *Foreign*
Missions, when the *Home* field should have had full justice
done to it? Was it not time enough to think of converting the heathen *abroad*, when they had got all the people converted *at home?* Why be carried away with the romance of
what is distant and strange and foreign? Had they no sinners
to save nearer hand, and was it not unchristian and even unnatural to leave these to their fate, in professed concern about
those who were further away? Does the fact of speaking the
same tongue as yourself, and wearing the same dress, and living
in the same street, or town, or country, dispel the charm that
gathers round what is called the "work of Christ?" Such considerations might have had weight *then*, as they have with
some *now*.

But not only was there a perishing world outside, *needing*,
if not *waiting for* the good news,—a world of immortal beings,
in countless numbers, in danger of eternal death, whose case the
Gospel entirely met, and whom it was designed to save, and who,
therefore, had a *right* to the one remedy for its deadly ailment,
—there was another reason for leaving the one and going to the
other. The Jewish people had enjoyed their opportunity—their
"day." They had been peculiarly privileged. For ages they
had possessed the knowledge of God, as no people on the face
of the earth ever did. They had direct communication with
heaven. They had a long line of saints and divinely accredited
teachers, stretching down almost to their own time. They had
the written Word, the honest and prayerful study of which
might have guided them into the light, and prepared them for
the coming of the promised Messiah. They had all these psalms,
and prophecies, and histories of God's dealings with men, which
we have now. And they had seen among them the Son of God
Himself, in human form. They had beheld, for once, a Perfect
Man—the image and reflection of God, the expression of the

mind and heart, of the grace and love, of the Father, in whose name He came. They had seen His holy life and miraculous working. They had heard His words of Divine wisdom. There had also taken place among them His mysterious death, and His wondrous resurrection, and His strange appearances during the forty days, and His ascension into heaven; they had startling proofs that He still lived and reigned as the ascended Christ. They had Him, too, all to themselves. He had said, "I am not sent but to the lost sheep of *the house of Israel.*" He had charged His servants, "Go not in the way of the Gentiles, and into any city of the Samaritans enter ye not." He had left behind Him the message, "beginning at Jerusalem." The rule for His servants was,—"To *the Jew first.*" And so it was. They had received the Pentecostal blessing. It was among them first that the Holy Ghost came down in Pentecostal power. They had seen the three thousand converts. They had heard the preaching of men who spoke in the power of the Holy Ghost. They had seen the holy lives of the first Christians. They had heard the dying testimony of the saintly Stephen.

Was all that not enough? What more could be thought of for them? If it could be said in Isaiah's time, surely much more might it have been said then, "What can I do for my vineyard more that I have not done in it?" But they would not have the Christ who was so marvellously authenticated,— they would not receive His Gospel. And now that a new and remarkable witness was raised up, the charge to him is, "Don't stay here. Jerusalem has had its day. It is wasting time to do any more here. Make haste, and get thee quickly away, for they will not receive thy testimony." It was a terrible message. No wonder that Paul, who loved his people so intensely, was loath to obey it, and in the words that follow, humbly argues against it.

And yet it is in keeping with what has been elsewhere, and at other times,—in the case alike of nations and individuals. You cannot read the history of the Church without being solemnly impressed with this. The light has shone brightly for a time among one people and another; and when they would not receive it, or violently extinguished it, they were left in the darkness which themselves had chosen, and are enveloped in it to this hour. One part and another of the dark continent of Africa is witness to this,—as are those lands in Syria, and Asia Minor, and the south of Europe, in which Paul himself once held up the lamp of truth. It seems to be God's way to give a people or an individual, the opportunity; and if it is not improved, to withdraw it. So it was, in more recent times, in France, in Hungary and Bohemia, in Italy and Spain. For a time, the door was opened. Distinguished instruments were raised up. The light blazed forth. Many were gathered in. But the body of the people refused to hear. They *allowed* the light to be put out, if they did not actually take part in the quenching of it. They expelled those who shone as stars of the first magnitude elsewhere; and you have but to look at these lands to-day, to see how disastrous such a course is, and how perilous it is to let the day of gracious opportunity slip. It *may* come back. It *has* come back. But it is also true, it may *not*,—in many cases, it has *not* returned.

Our own country and Germany seem now to be on their trial. They have both been highly privileged. The light of Reformation truth has shone, in both, with peculiar brilliance. But in spite of all that has been done, in the way of Christian effort, what multitudes in both lands are rejecting Christ, and abandoning themselves to carelessness and unbelief, to neglect of all divine things, and to open sin. We can hardly think of a Christian land like ours assuming such an attitude in regard to divine truth and Christian life, as has been assumed by some of the countries to which I have referred; and yet one of the most outstanding theologians of Holland said in my hearing, a few months ago, "We have had the tide of unbelief sweeping over the Continent. It is now coming to *you*. Within the next twenty years you will have it in full force, and all your Scotch theology will be unable to keep it out." We may well watch its advance with the utmost jealousy, and spare no endeavour to arrest it. It was once as unlikely that Jerusalem and the favoured land of which it was the renowned centre, should apostatise from God, and be abandoned by Him; and yet here you have Paul,—who was to be such a power elsewhere, and was to plant and foster the Church in so many other lands— receiving the charge, "Make haste, and get thee quickly out of Jerusalem, for they will not receive thy testimony concerning Me." And, as Hosea said in the Lord's name, at an earlier period of their history, "Yea, woe also unto them, when I depart from them!" there may be something analogous to this in our own case. But, short of this, there are some who think that there has been such an expenditure of effort in some parts of the home-field for more than a generation, often with very little in the way of result, that, without suicidally neglecting *home*, the stream of effort might now be fairly and legitimately diverted, in a more special way, to the great harvest-field *abroad*.

I shall not say much about the application of all this to *the individual*. But that it *has* such an application, of the most solemn kind, I need hardly say. That application may be found among ourselves. Are there not some here who have had every advantage of a spiritual kind that could well be ? They know all that can be told them. They have listened to every kind of appeal. They have had all sorts of helpful influences brought to bear upon them. And they have indolently or self-indulgently put off the great decision, or they have grown restive, and resisted, and made it next to impossible to venture on any further advances to them. It *may be*, that they have had their " day," that the voices that have spoken to them are henceforth to be addressed to others, and that the Divine word regarding them is, " Make haste, and get thee quickly away, for they will not receive thy testimony concerning Me." The very possibility of this, in the case of any of us, might well be the loudest voice of all.

II. The Divine call overriding our own views of duty (ver. 19, 20).

As we have seen, Paul could not silently acquiesce in this word, which took him so much by surprise. He may have felt, for the moment, as Moses and Aaron did, when, on the apostasy of Korah, the Lord said, " Separate yourselves from among the congregation, that I may consume them in a moment," and they fell upon their faces and pled for their people. Paul's appeal is a very touching one. He thought that what had convinced *him* would convince others. He thought his conversion was so wonderful, that it could not fail to tell on others. It seemed to him that he had been specially prepared for Jewish work. How could they resist the force of such evidence as he had to bring ? Did they not know his past life—how that, if there was one thing more than another remarkable about him, it was his intense and inextinguishable hatred of the name and people of Christ, and everything that had to do with Him ? Did they not remember what he was as a persecutor—how, even as a youth, he took the lead in the bloody crusade ; and how, on the memorable occasion of Stephen's martyrdom, that event—which must have awed and softened others—filled him with a kind of Satanic joy, and stirred him up to greater madness against the followers of Jesus ? And now that, after all this, he had become a Christian himself, how could he but be a power, wherever he went ? What did he need to do, but just to present himself, as *himself* the best argument he could use ?

But there was One who knew human nature better than he did, and HE said, "No. This experience and preparation has been for another purpose altogether. They will not receive thy testimony, wonderful though it be, and it must not be wasted on them. I have far other plans regarding thee." As He had once said to Ezekiel : "But the house of Israel will not hearken unto *thee*, for they will not hearken unto ME."

An analogous case is familiar to every one. When Melanchthon, the friend and companion in labour of Luther, had the truth opened up to him, and entered joyously into its blessed light and liberty, he thought he could not fail to commend it to others who were what he had been, but soon he had to make the confession that "*old Adam was too strong for young Melanchthon !*"

There may be some whom I address, who have had experience of this in a different way,—who have, at one time of their life, been under the power of unbelief, or of worldliness, or of some debasing sin. And when, by grace, they were emancipated, it seemed as if they had but to tell their story, and show the change they had undergone, to their old companions. Sometimes, indeed, this has been to purpose ; but often such have learned how they had miscalculated, how little they had taken into their reckoning the power of sin and the obstinacy of the unregenerate heart, and how the only course for them was, to *go out* from those whom they had hoped to carry by storm, and find their field of labour for Christ in altogether different lines.

III. THE IMPERATIVE CLAIMS OF THE HEATHEN WORLD ON THE CHURCH AND PEOPLE OF GOD (ver. 11).

I suppose one may say, without hesitation, that Paul stands at the head of the whole Christian army,—that he was the man and the minister of greatest power, of all whom the Church of Christ has ever had in its ranks. The place to which he was called, and the work which he did, are the vindication of such a statement. He was the Prince of ministers, taking the word in

its largest sense—not of preachers merely, but of Christian
workers of all kinds—servants of Christ and of His Church.
Such a man would, *of course*, be set apart to the work which the
Master regarded as most important.   Just as in a great warfare,
our best and bravest and most experienced general would be
despatched to occupy what was the key to the whole position,
the hinge upon which the entire campaign turned, so that we
should learn what that all-important point was, by the simple
knowledge of where the great leader was to be found ;—so, wherever we find PAUL, *there*, we may conclude, the Church's great
battle is to be fought, the Church's great work is to be done.

Now, to human eye, such a man seemed supremely desirable
at Jerusalem,—the cradle of the Church, the headquarters of
Christianity.   Reason would say, " Above everything, make sure
that the Church is strong at the centre—at the heart.   The best
you can do for the *extremities*, is to do the best that can be done
for the *heart*.   Do not, on any account, let Paul go.   He is worth
all the rest put together.   And he will do his best work *there*.
Anything will do for the *outposts*.   *Any one* will do for a *missionary*, especially to do evangelistic work among the ruder
tribes, and and among the ignorant and sunken masses of these
heathen cities.   At *Jerusalem*, you need culture, all the accomplishments you can get,—a man who knows Jews, and can meet
them on their own ground, who has acquaintance with rabbin-
ical literature and will command the respect of the learned.
And, having all these things in view, it is just as if Paul had
been *made* for the post, all the more with his clearly marked
conversion, the personal influence which he will carry into the
new sphere, and his love for his people, which amounts almost
to a passion."   Evidently Paul thought so himself.   What he
says is a most touching plea in favour of his remaining.   And
yet the authoritative and summary answer which he gets is—
" DEPART ; for I will send thee away TO THE GENTILES !"
There is no reason given.   There is no room left for expostula-
tion.   But the very form in which the charge is given, is enough
to show that the Church's greatest and most pressing work,
which must take precedence of all else, is the making known of
Christ AMONG THE HEATHEN.   And so, from that point, all
through his three successive missionary journeys, till he finished
his work and ended his days at Rome, his life was unceasingly
devoted to this end.

That was the great work of the Church *then*, and it is the

Church's great work no less to-day. Every reason might have been urged for keeping Paul in Jerusalem then, that could have been pleaded for retaining him in Christendom now. The Church in Jerusalem and in Judea was far more necessitous then, than the Church in this land is now. It needed training, and organising, and building up. The home-churches, in our case, are far stronger and more independent, and have far larger resources of every kind, than the home-church had *then*. It may, indeed, be said that Christianity was then in its infancy, and the circumstances were exceptional, inasmuch as the first proclamation of Christianity behoved to be made TO THE WORLD, otherwise the Gospel would never have been known at all, and it would have been all one as if Christ had never come. But that is just what may be said of the world as it now is. By far the greater part of it—as many as eight hundred millions, out of the twelve hundred millions of the world's population—is wholly uninfluenced by the Gospel. Say what you will, about the *needs* of home, and the *claims* of home, the fact is undeniable, that there are comparatively few at home who have not the opportunity, in some way, of knowing as much about Christ as may suffice for their salvation; while THREE-FOURTHS OF THE WHOLE PEOPLE OF THE WORLD are as ignorant of Christ and of the one way of life, as they were that day when the Lord declared His mind so commandingly to Paul! And the inevitable inference is, that the circumstances, in this respect, being the same, the greatness and urgency of the need the same, all the conditions the same, the Lord, to whom the souls of men, wherever they are found, are equally dear, because alike bought with His precious blood,—the Lord, who left the sheep that were safe in the fold, and went out after that which was lost,—is saying to His Church now, as He points to the great moral and spiritual wastes that are lying, and lying *open*, everywhere, " Depart: for I will send thee far hence *unto the heathen.*"

Has the Church been at all acting upon that conviction, either as a whole, or in its individual congregations and members ? What of the vast Empire of China, which has now been open for more than a generation, with its four hundred millions of people ? What of India? The Indian Mission of the Presbyterian Church in Scotland is now *fifty years old*. This is its Jubilee Year. As compared with what once was, wonderful progress has been made. And yet can the Church be said to be even half-awake ? What has been done for India's two hundred

and forty millions ?   What number in our congregations have
been stirred up to take a deep, living, personal interest in the
great enterprise ?   How much have we given, of thought,—or
heart,—or trouble,—or time,—or means,—or prayer, to the work
that lies nearest to the heart of Christ ?   What earnest effort are
we putting forth,—what real sacrifice are we making, for the
accomplishment of the great end for which our Divine Master
gave Himself ?   How many of us sympathise with a young
Christian lady, connected with one of our families, who, when
a friend remarked to her that it was a far way to go to Japan,
replied, " *Yes, very far*, if it was *only to make money;* but NOT
TOO FAR TO TELL THE HEATHEN ABOUT JESUS !"   How far are
we in sympathy with the Church's Head, when He said, and with
Paul, when he acted on the saying, " DEPART : FOR I WILL SEND
THEE FAR HENCE UNTO THE HEATHEN " ?

HABIT AND HOLINESS:

A SERMON.

JAMES RANKIN, D.D.,

MUTHILL.

" And He came to Nazareth, where He had been brought up : and, as His custom was, He went into the synagogue on the sabbath day, and stood up for to read."—LUKE iv. 16.

THE custom here referred to is a custom, on the part of Jesus, of going regularly to the synagogue, as often as the Sabbath day came round. And it is here mentioned in connection with Nazareth, where Jesus had been brought up. It was part of the pious training which He had received, in early days, under Joseph and Mary. It was also a feature in the training of all young people belonging to well-ordered, religious households. Such a custom would often secure attendance in the synagogue, when, otherwise, some obstacle or temptation might have led to absence,—some obstacle or temptation such as a wet day, or a headache, or previous fatigue, or the visit of a friend, or want of more fashionable clothes.

Here, in our text, is one case of Jesus conforming to a good common custom,—perhaps not only following the custom, but getting help from it to promote His own spiritual life. From this one well-authenticated custom of Jesus in regard to Sabbath observance, I purpose, in connection with the text, to set before you the value and use of habit, as an aid to holy life and character, placed by God's providence within our reach, and which we are bound, as wise men, to turn to account.

The capacity of forming habits is a very valuable part of human nature, as originally framed by God. By doing a thing often, we come to do it easily, and even to contract a liking and

craving to do it. Sometimes this facility and inclination grow
up before we are aware of it, in matters where we did not intend
it. Moreover, it is a power as ready for bad uses as for good, so
that it requires observation and guidance. It is by habit, by frequent exercise and use, that we learn to walk with firmness and
grace, as contrasted with the tottering steps of childhood. It is
by habit that we learn to write rapidly, neatly, and accurately,
as contrasted with the slow scrawling that goes on in the junior
classes of a school. It is by habit that we learn to read with
ease and pleasure. It is by habit and use that workmen in the
various arts and trades learn to manipulate skilfully the various
tools and materials which they employ. Similarly, by gradual
training, both animal and vegetable natures may be wonderfully
modified,—by more or less light, water, warmth, food, or motion.
It is the alteration of these conditions that determines life and
death, beauty and deformity, success and failure. Many of the
evils that give us the greatest annoyance in society, are largely
the result of neglected or misdirected habits or customs. Very
few men, if any, intend or wish to be drunkards; but the habit
of strong drink grows on them, till it masters them. So soon
as the inner craving for drink is stronger than a man's will, that
man is a drunkard. A large part of the profane swearing in the
world is the result of a bad habit, rather than of a deliberate intention to be irreverent; it becomes a way of speaking, a very stupid
and degraded way of speaking, rather than a deliberate disregard
of God's commandment. The same applies to a large part of the
lying and stealing that go on around us. Literally we speak of
thieves as being such by habit and repute. Repeated dishonesty
blunts the conscience or moral sense, and it is more easy to steal
the tenth time than the first time. By the tenth time, a man's
conscience has got weary, as it were, with finding fault. So with
falsehood. A first lie, or the few initial lies, are very painful
and shameful; they press heavily for days on a tender conscience.
But when once a habit of falsehood has been contracted, the conscience becomes hardened, like a macadamised road, and new lies
are told with very little temptation or remorse—often just to
give liveliness in the telling of a common story. Still, although
we can thus see into the interior and growth of evil habits, they
are not thereby excused. The sinner is responsible for them all
the same, the fiftieth time as the first time, in the eyes of both
God and man. This great fact makes it doubly important to
give attention to the subject,—on the one hand, to detect and

check all habits that are evil or dangerous; and, on the other hand, to mark and cultivate all habits that are fitted to help us in Christian virtue and Christian grace, by making these easier and more secure as our earthly pilgrimage advances.

It is no new thing to employ the force of habit in connection with piety; it has already been done very systematically in past ages. In fact, it is only in comparatively recent times, and in connection with Protestant Churches especially, that the power of habit has been neglected. Under the Romish system, there was both great use and abuse of habit and custom. At present, we are in the midst of a reaction and protest against former abuses. All the details of rule and discipline, as laid down for monks and nuns, had, for their aim, the utilising of habit on the side of virtue and holiness. But, in many cases, this was carried to excess, and rules became ridiculous when emphasised as important in themselves, whereas they were only means to an end. Such rules applied to dress, to hours of devotion, to repeating certain formulæ, to the period of sleep, to regulation of diet. When this was pushed beyond reasonable bounds, the system was open to ridicule, as an attempt to make virtue by machinery. But these ancient extravagancies of certain branches of the Christian Church are no reason why habit should not be studied and utilised, for the same purposes, within proper limits. Habit, in excess, is formalism or routine, and is near of kin to hypocrisy. This was the besetting sin of the old Pharisees. In the same way, habit or custom, in excess, becomes a system of ceremony, or ritualism, which is just old Pharisaism renewing its youth, but in adaptation to the Christian System.

Warned by these errors—but mindful that there is also, in habit, a mighty power for good—let us consider a few of those matters in which habit is desirable.

1. The instance in the text applicable to Jesus—the custom of being present at public worship every Sabbath. How great an aid is this to everything that is good! It puts us in the way of the chief means of grace; it puts us in the way of the best human companionship. Mere regular attendance at church may be overrated. Especially should we avoid the error of measuring profit by quantity of church attendance. It is not necessarily true that two services are better than one, and still less, that three are better than two. To be trotting to and from church three times each Sunday, is not a sign of a healthy spiritual appetite, but of spiritual dissipation and church gluttony. One

H

well-arranged service, properly attended to, may suffice for any
Christian, provided there be prefixed and added to the public
service suitable exercise in private, especially in our own day,
when wholesome religious literature, to be read at home is so
plentiful and cheap.   Probably, the best system for the Church
is a forenoon and an evening service, with an afternoon service
for children—*i.e.*, an afternoon Sunday school.

God Himself, in His wisdom and goodness, has provided for
this fundamental good habit in the ordinance of the Sabbath-
day, which returns at measured intervals, to call us away, from
worldly toil and care, to rest for body and soul, refreshing
fellowship with God.   If we neglect God's ordinance, or devote
it to mere idleness and mirth, we put ourselves recklessly in the
way of evil, and out of the way of good.   Wherever we be,
whether at home, or visiting friends, or travelling abroad, let
us be careful to keep the good custom of church-going every
Sunday.   It is a primary condition of all true blessing here on
earth.   Happy is that man to whom a churchless Sunday is a
weariness and disappointment.   Happy the man whom custom,
long and strong, ever urges to go to the house of God, while
going is at all practicable in point of health, and weather, and
distance.   In the Psalms, David's sweetest remembrances are of
Sabbaths in Zion; and his saddest regrets are of Sabbaths in
exile.   "When I remember these things, I pour out my soul in
me: for I had gone with the multitude; I went with them to
the house of God, with the voice of joy and praise, with a multitude that kept holiday."   "O, my God! my soul is cast down
within me: therefore will I remember Thee from the land of
Jordan, and of the Hermonites, for the hill Mizar."   "How amiable are Thy tabernacles, O Lord of hosts . . . a day in Thy
courts is better than a thousand."   Avoid, however, using the
Lord's day superstitiously as a Sabbatarian; worship not the
day itself, but welcome it as a chief help towards worship,—
recognising in it God's provision for one of the best of all good
customs.   "And Jesus came to Nazareth, where He had been
brought up, and *as His custom was*, He went into the synagogue
on the Sabbath-day, and stood up for to read."

2. A habit of prayer.   The prayer to which I refer specially
at present is family and personal prayer.   Public or common
prayer is implied in Sunday observance and church-going.   If
there is no habit of family prayer, the prayer is not likely to
be made at all.   All the details of family worship imply

arrangement—a certain hour—a fixed place—books at hand—
a person responsible for conducting the service. Family worship
thus becomes one of the most beautiful features of domestic
order in every house where it is duly attended to. Its omission
becomes at once a mark and cause of disorder. If children have
been brought up, from infancy, in connection with this good
custom, there is nothing so likely to lay a religious foundation
in their character. If servants have their place in such a household, then it is to be expected that the good custom will exercise
a beneficial influence in their case. If they change from a
prayerful house to a prayerless one, or from a prayerless to a
prayerful family, the difference between the two must make a
striking impression.

Personal prayer no less depends on habit and custom for its
maintenance. By a sort of natural consent, or religious instinct,
morning and evening—immediately before or after going to bed
and rising from bed—are the set times associated with private
prayer. If one is happily so accustomed, then the very act of
dressing and undressing the body, day by day, will come to
remind us of our duty of intercourse with the Father of spirits,
our duty to review, in a religious aspect, our conduct and conversation during the day, and our duty in the same aspect, to
prepare for behaving as becomes professed followers of the
Lord Jesus Christ. Unless one has a distinct plan, and makes
a special effort in the way of private prayer,—unless, in short,
one has a custom or habit of a short morning or evening prayer
in private,—how apt is the exercise to be altogether omitted.
At one time, you may be an hour or two later in going to bed,
or an hour or two earlier in rising, when fatigue or hurry may
present themselves as an excuse for omitting private prayer on
that occasion. A number of such omissions soon weakens the
perception of the propriety of morning and evening prayer
altogether, and one may fall into a habit of prayerlessness. And
if the two best times, most natural and most free for private
prayer, are thus neglected, is it to be reasonably expected that
much good will be made of other times that are more busy and
irregular? On the other hand, if a man is diligent and sincere
in his private devotions, morning and evening, is it not in the
highest degree likely that he will have private prayers at other
times, occasionally or frequently, in moments specially appropriate, or specially free, during the day or during the night?
The more that any man attends to and practises this exercise and

duty of secret, personal devotion, the more easy, and the more pleasant and profitable will it become, till it brings habitual fellowship with God,—a holy walking with God, after the pattern of Enoch, and Noah, and Abraham,—which is the true ideal of private prayer—a praying without ceasing, the cherishing of a constant remembrance and longing for God, which is the blessed realisation of that which was typified, of old, in those lamps and fires that were kept constantly burning in the temples. God Himself never, day or night, ceases from care of us; correspondingly ought He to be in our minds and hearts.

3. Labour may be the subject of another of those good habits, in a religious point of view. At first sight, it might seem as if a habit of labour, while good and useful in itself, had little to do with religion, This cannot have been the opinion of those ages when men held, as a motto, the words, *ora et labora* (pray and work). One of the fundamental conditions of a happy earthly life is to have plenty of work to do, and to do it with a will. This sound principle, like many other wholesome truths, has a fight for existence in modern times. Abridgment of the hours of labour is a mistake, unless the intention be, to occupy the hours, set free from a man's trade, in some other form of work that may be useful—*e.g.*, reading, to promote intelligence, or walking, or making of friendly or charitable calls, or cultivation of a garden, or some indoor occupation. Occasional *change* of occupation is the best of all forms of rest and recovery. Absolute idleness is an idiotic and unchristian state. One of the pitiable features of this generation is, the manufacturing of sports and games into separate existences and important pursuits. This is done with fishing, shooting, curling, skating, cricket. If simple, honest work had its proper place, alike with artizans and gentlemen, these pastimes would soon fall to their natural level, and innocent or wholesome use,—being left mainly, as before, to boys and semi-savages, and taken up by more reasonable persons now and then, in connection with suitable weather, or health, or holidays, without being idolised and made professional.

It is a more serious error, when, in their theory of life, people try to avoid regular employment from as early an age as possible. It is the ambition of many to retire early from business, and live at ease on their savings all the rest of their days. It is the ambition of others to possess a fortune, so that they may be able to travel about from country to country, sightseeing. These idle, aimless existences are the most unhappy condition possible for reasonable beings. Far better is it for a man to hold on steadily in his work to the end, and nobly wear out, than rust wearily and unprofitably. It is a calamity when a man cannot work, by reason of old age or sickness; it is a hardship, in dull times, when a man is willing to work, but fails to get employment; but it is a shame to see a strong man, with no serious or useful object in life, simply because he does not need to work for day's wages. Such a man's patrimony, or wealth, is essentially a curse to him: it hinders him from exercising and developing that, in himself, which is more precious than all wealth. The man who has acquired the habit of labour has got possession of that honest power which will advance him, alike in a worldly and moral point of view, and which will keep him out of many temptations.

4. A habit of learning may well form the sequel to a habit of labour. Work, done in a right spirit and method, leads to experience and intelligence in the line of the work so prosecuted. But the learning ought to be wider than a man's own work, and especially should have more of a religious direction than the average of ordinary work. It is in always aiming to learn something new that we secure for ourselves real improvement and progress, carrying the purposes of youth and early manhood into advanced years. There are various ways in which this habit of learning may develop itself. The simplest, perhaps, is observation for one's self; and the next in simplicity conversation with one's neighbours, so as to add their observation or information to one's own. But far more valuable are books and professed teachers, who have made a specialty of some subject. A habit of spending leisure time in careful, definite reading on matters useful in ordinary life, is one of the most noble exercises in which a man can train himself. But here our concern is with religious reading, in its mighty influence in enriching the thoughts and experience of the believer, as he goes on systematically devoting leisure hours to such occupation. Next to the habit of prayer itself is the blessed habit of reading the Word of God methodically, day by day, and especially Sunday by Sunday. There is perhaps no department of religious life in which modern times are so far ahead of previous generations as here, especially if care is taken to avoid the merely popular and sentimental class of religious books. In the department of Bible Commentaries, for example

many solid and scholarly books are quite available for nine-tenths of the ordinary members of any church, both in cost and style. The names of Ellicott and Perowne may specially be mentioned in illustration. In recent years, how many well-written biographies have we, of great men of God,—Arnold, Chalmers, Bunsen, Livingstone, Patteson, Norman Macleod. How many of our best old divines have recently been made available in good and cheap reprints,—as Bishop Hall, Archbishop Leighton, Jeremy Taylor, Thomas à Kempis. In the better class of our religious magazines, how much is there of real excellence, —only, unhappily the far larger half of our popular religious periodical literature is extremely deficient, by reason of superficiality and narrowness of view.

Yet another branch of the habit of learning, in a religious sense, is the occasional or regular use of the good old method of self-examination. It is to be feared that self-examination is neither so habitually nor so efficiently done as it used to be. The recurrence of one's birthday, the beginning of a year, entry on a new office, the death of a dear friend, and especially each return of the communion-season, once led many to this great means of self-inspection and self-knowledge, and still ought to lead us, if we would go on learning and improving in that which is most solemn and personal.

5. The last matter that I shall at present name, as a fit subject for a good habit, is charity. Charity I take here as equivalent to pecuniary liberality towards the Christian Church, Christian missions, the poor, and the sick. The four things previously recommended (Sunday observance,—prayer,—labour, —and learning) are matters of universal applicability. Charity, to which we now come, can, of course, be commended only to those who are themselves above immediate want. To expect charity from persons in debt, or those who are living beyond their income, or are themselves receiving charitable help, would be folly and sin. In recent business overturns in Glasgow and the neighbourhood, it came out that a number of church builders and church subscribers had been liberal out of other people's money,—in fact, contributed to religious objects, in order to gain a good name, to be employed in their career of swindling. These men were both hypocrites and thieves. A large number of people degrade charity by using it as a means of vanity, calculating on getting themselves advertised and be-praised in return for their gifts. True charity is shown when pecuniary help

is given to religious work, out of honest desire to promote the work for the good of man and the glory of God; or where aid is given to the poor and the sick, out of genuine compassion for their wants and sufferings, without reference to the vain-glory of printed lists of subscribers. It is one of the noblest incentives to labour and to economy, that a man should exert himself in his business, and, although prosperous, avoid luxury, in order to devote a good part of his savings to charitable purposes. St Paul's last word to the elders of Ephesus was this,—" I have showed you all things, how that so labouring ye ought to support the weak, and to remember the words of the Lord Jesus, how He said, It is more blessed to give than to receive." And in the epistle to the same Church, he says, " Let him that stole, steal no more; but rather let him labour, working with his hands the thing which is good, that he may have to give to him that needeth." Again, he inculcates method and forethought in giving, when he says to the Corinthians (1 Cor. xvi. 2), " Upon the first day of the week, let every one of you lay by him in store, as God hath prospered him, that there be no gatherings when I come." A second characteristic of true charity (besides that it come from a sympathetic heart), is that it be guided by *method*, or habit, and not be dependent on fits and starts of mere impulse. The habit of charity will lead a man to be liberal to the Gospel and the poor, in the proportion that he can afford to be so—*i.e.*, in the proportion in which God has prospered his lawful undertakings. Charity of this sort,—regulated, proportioned, sympathetic, unostentatious,—is one of the most perfect and Godlike outcomes of true piety. And observe how valuable and commanding is the element of custom in the matter: it is the very crown and climax of beneficence, showing that it comes from principle, and is persevered in, and is not regretted, not dependent on the urgency of canvassers, or flattering arts of the needy. A custom of this noble sort could not be formed or maintained, save by very deliberate effort and self-sacrifice. Yet, how many men have all this unconsciously within their reach, and reject it in favour of some custom of a wasteful or harmful character. Without countenancing asceticism, meanness, or tastelessness, there are many points wherein we may criticise our own habits and those of our neighbours, and discover undue expenditure. The particulars in question are wine, spirits, tobacco, sweetmeats, gloves, ribbons, too frequent new clothes, excessive sightseeing and travelling, luxury in food and jewellery. Many people hold extreme views with regard to one or more of these, and become tyrannical if they can; but, keeping strictly to reason and Scripture, and not yielding to the claptrap of mere popular movements, it is a clear fact that vast sums of money are spent on needlessly large quantities of some of these things, by persons of really excellent Christian character. Much more is such expenditure true of another class of persons, Christian still, but on the lower level of the Christian life. It is specially this class that forms the bulk of an average Christian congregation, to whom appeal is made for pecuniary help for religious and charitable objects, and from whom it is not easy to get very much as a response. How different might it be, if one-fifth part of the large and comparatively ungrudged stream that *habitually* goes to waste on the above-named luxuries (only the *excessive* part, and that moderately, and not ascetically judged) could be *habitually* turned to a pious and charitable use.

This is so very limited a suggestion or requirement, that it hardly reaches the edge of the great Christian virtue of self-denial,—a virtue which is of little value, unless it is genuinely spontaneous, and as much as possible concealed. Self-denial, however, is the main fountain of charity. We have all need of the *habit* of charity. Even a little of it would produce a mighty improvement both in the world and the Church. Of how few, even of professing Christians, can we say, in this connection, "as His custom was!"

Thus have we considered the place and utility of habit from a Christian point of view. A greater number and variety of good habits might easily have been specified by way of illustration. Yet the five which we have taken (church-going, prayer, labour, learning, and charity) are so wide, so fundamental, so practical, that they are enough to convince us of the mighty Christian force which they contain when rightly cultivated. They are no arts of man alone; their origin is in the nature which God has given us; their guidance is from that Holy Spirit of God who is the sole agent in conversion and sanctification. There is nothing startling or exciting in them, yet they are fitted, by God's blessing, to lead us far onward and upward in a holy career and holy character. If there is, on one side, a danger of habit degenerating into formalism and Pharisaism, that danger may be effectually avoided by remembering the sound principles that underlie all habit, and especially by keeping before our minds the ideal of Christian perfection, which never rests in any rut of routine, but is ever aiming at a higher and holier point. Thus is habit, when ennobled by Christian spirit and Christian principle, one of the best aids which the believer can possibly have to secure him in good, and to lead to greater attainments in it. It is an old method of holiness and grace, once abused and overdone, but in recent times too much neglected and forgotten. Let us revive it, and re-employ it, in so far as it is fitted to be a true spiritual friend and ally. There is, undoubtedly, a virtue in living by rule, whereby the path of holiness becomes a path of peace, pleasure, facility, and progress,—each good day, and week, and month, and year of Christian experience leading onward, to give smoothness and skill for all that are to follow. Amen.

WHAT IS THE "GIFT OF GOD?"

A SERMON.

BY THE

REV. JOHN J. BLACK, LL.D.,

FREE HIGH CHURCH, INVERNESS

"Jesus answered and said unto her, If thou knewest the gift of God, and who it is that saith to thee, Give Me to drink; thou wouldest have asked of Him, and He would have given thee living water."—JOHN iv. 10.

Two things must be noticed regarding this story, before we come to consider the words we have selected. The first point is—The value our Master puts upon a single soul. "He must needs go through Samaria," the "needs" being, that there, in Sychar, dwelt a sinner on whom He had set His love. So we find Him going far to the north-west, to put Himself in the way of the Syro-Phenician; and, once again, he crossed the Sea of Galilee, that He might still the storm in a maniac's breast, as He had hushed another storm "immediately" before upon the lake. Easily-wearied workers, take shame to yourselves for your excuses when you also mark that it was the *wearied* Jesus who, in each of these cases, won the poor sinner to His feet. "Being wearied"--"asleep on a pillow:" blessed words are these for the suffering and the seeking, but words having a sting in them for us who merely profess to follow His example.

But the second matter we would bring before your notice is the plan that our Lord adopts in bringing the Samaritan to Himself. She is a stranger, and separated from Him by the wide breach of political hate. This difficulty must be overcome, but not by making light of it, or fighting over it, as we often do. Our Lord stood loyally to His country's colours and His Church's principles. With no uncertain sound He rang out the rally-call

of the South, "Salvation is of the Jews." But He declined to
argue that question. That was not His business there. Her
soul was dearer to Him than His nationality. Everything must
be put aside till the work is done which His Father had here
given Him to do. "To seek and to save that which was lost,"
was the burden laid upon Him. He had sought her, and now
He must save. For this, He first attracts her attention,—" Give
me to drink." He then excites her wonder,—"If thou knewest
the gift of God, and who it is that saith to thee, Give Me to
drink, thou wouldst have asked of Him, and He would have
given thee living water." From wonder, He goes on to conviction,—" Go, call thy husband, and come hither." Having brought
her to the dust, He there can reveal Himself to her, and bid her be
a worshipper. Thus her Samaritan belief became strangely true.
At Gerizim's foot she worshipped,—now, to her joy however,
knowing "what" she worshipped. The worshipper is soon a
worker, and the chief, perhaps, of Sychar's sinners is away to
tell what a Saviour she had found. Thus it was that the Master
enlisted and educated His first Samaritan missionary.

The verse we have selected is the pivot of the passage. Let
us seek its meaning. Not elsewhere in the Word can we find
the marrow and mystery of the Gospel more beautifully shown
forth. May the Spirit of the living God enable each of us to
know experimentally this "gift of God!" Otherwise the mystery
is a mystery still.

I. What is "the gift of God?" is the question that naturally
rises first in our minds. Three answers have been given, which
appear to me not to contradict one another, but rather to fill up
and complete the interpretation of the Word. (a) "The truth,"
say some, "is what the Master means." Old Testament Scriptures
give this thought more than once. Isaiah, for example, cries,
"Ho, every one that thirsteth, come ye to the waters;" and,
previously, in the twelfth chapter, he speaks of drawing "water
out of the wells of salvation." In this way, it would seem that
Christ was not so much giving us a new thought here, as taking
an old illustration of the Fathers and applying it to His Gospel,
to show that the truth they taught was the message He was
commissioned to deliver. "The old, old story" is the story still;
but given in clearer light, and free from shadow and restraint.
We accept this interpretation, then. Truth—solid, eternal, satisfying truth—is the gift of God. We commonly call this gift
"revelation." Man could not discover, or purchase, or shape it.

Pilate but uttered the language of the disappointed investigators
of his day when he asked, in disgust, " What is truth ?" Man
was at his wit's end when the Son of God appeared to tell the
secret to the world. Let us test this truth on three points.

(1) First, let us consider its *realness*. In this, philosophy (so-
called) and idolatry fail. They deal with shadows and dreams.
In philosophy, we have men aiming at conclusions at which
they never arrive, and building on probabilities which fail
beneath the weight of stubborn certainties they are called to
bear. In idolatry, we find false gods propped up by superstition
and " old wives' fables." You cannot read their story, or visit
the ruins of their temples, without feeling how unreal they were.
How different is the truth of God ! It is no dream of the poet
—no fancy of the philosopher. It is *a fact*,—a stern, bold
reality. Test it for yourself, O, doubter ! It will bear any
strain. It will not sink under any burden. If it was a dream,
the Church would have awaked from it long ago. If it was a
delusion, the cheated crowd would have hooted it from the world.
But there it stands, rugged and real as ever,—as real as the
God who gave it.

(2) Its *finality* is another characteristic of gospel truth. The
Athenian, with his thousands of gods, confesses that yet there
is an " unknown God." The schoolmen have been dreaming
" since the world began," and they are dreaming still. The
world's cry is yet the same,—" Restful truth ! where, and what
is it ?" Like the ' waif ' of the London streets, I am weary of
the cry, ' Move on.' I want to reach some end,—some resting-
place. Like Ixion, I feel bound to an ever-revolving wheel ;
like the Danaids, I pour water into a cask full of holes." Weary
one ! become a scholar in the school of Christ. We have but
one text-book there. It is a tiny book. I can send it through
our post-office for one penny. It is God's book,—His truth. It
reveals the very rest you seek. It gives you " the conclusion of
the whole matter." What is said of the last portion of it is
true of the whole. " If any man shall add unto these things,
God shall add unto him the plagues that are written in this
book. And if any man shall take away from the words of the
book of this prophecy, God shall take away his part out of the
book of life." In the 14th verse of this chapter, Christ tells the
Samaritan that, "whosoever drinketh of the water that I shall
give him, shall never thirst." He has got his soul's desire, and
is at rest. All he wants is here, and now he has nothing to do

but "keep drinking," as the original suggests. Like some springs from nature's fountain, the more he draws, the sweeter and more refreshing the water becomes. No wonder it was said, "With joy shall ye draw water out of the wells of salvation."

(3) Its *dogmatic character* is the third mark of the truth of God. We know not how it is that dogma has got into disrepute of late. It may be that, in our pride, we wish to reason out and understand "things that are too high for us." Sure we are that God's dogmas are all axioms, if we had only power to comprehend them. They are so to Him,—perhaps they will only be so to us when we get home.

(b) "*Christ Himself*," say others, "is this gift of God." So Paul, in 1 Cor. x. 4, speaks of Christ as the antitype of the rock in the wilderness: "And they did all drink of the same spiritual drink, for they drank of that Spiritual Rock that followed them; and that Rock was Christ." Nor is this in opposition to the first interpretation, for Jesus is "the Truth,"—its secret, centre, and reality. Here, then, He teaches the woman what He had taught Nicodemus in the third chapter,—"God so loved the world, that He gave His only begotten Son, that whosoever believeth in Him should not perish, but have everlasting life." So, again, He says in the sixth chapter, "My Father giveth you the true Bread from heaven,"—"I am the Bread of life." Christ is preeminently *the* Gift of God. Not that God has given us no other gifts,—He is always giving, and His gifts are always good. But this gift stands out superior to all. Only let us speak of two out of many points. (1) Have we not all felt that other good things from our Father's hand, only met the wants of certain parts of our nature? Good though they be, they only lie on the surface. Our deepest nature is not touched,—the secret chamber is not occupied. But, if this Gift is ours, our innermost soul becomes His dwelling-place,—the water of life penetrates to the depths of our most hidden being. Yea, so thoroughly does it possess our every capacity, that there is an overflow; and out of the once-thirsty "flow rivers of living water." (2) The other point of superiority is—the thoroughly satisfying nature of this Gift. Other gifts are pleasant, and, *for the time*, meet our longings. At best, however, they but postpone the demands of our appetite. Soon, again, the hungerings and thirstings return, and cry with louder voice, "Give, give!" We must remain utter strangers to the "never" thirsting, if we only drink of God's nether springs. After we have taxed all our ingenuity, and worked up all our resources to meet the wants of our own souls, we have no alternative but to go and beg, as Christ represents the man in the eleventh of Luke,—"Friend, lend me three loaves; for a friend of mine, in his journey, is come to me, and *I have nothing to set before him.*' This man wisely went where there was "enough and to spare," and he got "*as many*" as he needed. "Precious promises" these,—"never thirst," "never hunger," "never die," "as many as he needed," etc.; but they are no exaggerations—they are literally, absolutely true. There is no postponement, no temporary hushing of desire. The demand is met, and satisfied. "O satisfy us early with Thy mercy," is the Psalmist's cry. "I will satisfy her poor with bread," is God's answer.

> " Who, with abundance of good things,
>   Doth satisfy thy mouth ;
> So that, ev'n as the eagle's age,
>   Renewed is thy youth."

(*c*) One other interpretation deserves our notice. Though we do not say it is the true interpretation of the expression, still it a most important truth, and not inconsistent with the other views we have put forward. A few sentences, then, to consider the "Gift of God" as the *present opportunity,*—the offer of salvation then and there. Every invitation given, and opportunity enjoyed, is a gift from God. Blind Bartimeus seized the opportunity, and got the blessing; the Gadarenes repudiated theirs, and Jesus "departed from their coasts." Never were more solemn words written than those of Isaiah, in his fifty-fifth chapter: "Seek ye the Lord *while* He may be found, call ye upon Him *while* He is near." There is a crisis in every man's history—a Hougomont in every battle of life. Many of the unbelieving children of Israel lived long after they were turned "back by the way of the Red Sea," but their doom was sealed—their day of grace was gone: "Your carcases, they shall fall in this wilderness." So Christ, in the end of His ministry, weeps over Jerusalem, saying, "If thou hadst known, even thou, at least in this thy day, the things which belong unto thy peace ! but now they are hid from thine eyes."

The story of Sychar, now before us, is an illustration of this. Jesus "must needs go through Samaria," because this sinner must have this offer of salvation. In God's electing love, it was decreed that she should get the opportunity, as well as the grace, to embrace it. When the cup of salvation was put to her lips,

the gift was hers, and on her was laid the responsibility of either
accepting, or putting it from her. By God's mercy, she did not
"let it slip." She opened her mouth wide, and it was filled.
Had she refused that present time, it is more than probable that
Jesus would never again have passed that way, and the water of
life would be for ever far out of her reach. Taking rank among
those described by Paul as "given up," and "given over," her
misery would be but intensified by the remembrance of that
strange interview, and that sweet invitation by the well. "O,
that men would consider" this! Unconverted sinner, we pray
you to remember that each time God speaks to you,—in His providence, in His Word, by His servants,—it is a gift offered you, and
each offer may be the last. The final offer is not distinguished
from any preceding. If you neglect your last opportunity, you
will not know till it is gone. Then, when despair comes, you
will seek, and knock, and cry,—but all in vain. "Because I
have called, and ye refused; I have stretched out My hand, and
no man regarded, but ye have set at nought all my counsel,
and would none of my reproof,—I also will laugh at your
calamity; I will mock when your fear cometh."

> " But if you still His call refuse,
>   And all His wondrous love abuse,
>   Soon will He sadly from you turn,
>   Your bitter prayer for pardon spurn :
> " Too late ! Too late ! " will be the cry,
> " Jesus of Nazareth *has passed by*."

II. Our second inquiry is regarding this gift, and how it deserves the name.

(1) To be a gift, it must be *free*. And so it is—free and
unmerited. For us, it would be useless, were it not so. We are
bankrupts. The Master photographs us in the words, "Having
nothing to pay." "All our righteousnesses are as filthy rags."
Our coin is base. Our labour is nought. Even let us suppose
that we could offer to God what would please Him. Some men
do not like the word "bankrupt." In its common use, we would
wish to see a greater number dislike and shun it. At present,
then, let it be put aside. We take the sinner at his own estimate, and assume that he has resources. But to whom do these
belong, good friend? Are you not, at best, but a steward in
charge? Does not every talent you possess bear the brand of
God upon it? Is there a power, or capacity, of your being that
you can call your own? You cannot offer to God, therefore, as

purchase-money, what is His own. Though you do your utmost, you are an unprofitable servant after all. The sooner this point is yielded the better. There can be no " transactions " in God's market till buyers come who are ready to do business on His own terms,—" He that hath *no money*, come, buy and eat : yea, come, buy wine and milk without money, and without price." We are quite aware of the difficulty that here stops the way, but there can be no compromise. Take salvation as a gift, and it is yours. It cannot be so on any other terms. " The free gift," Paul calls it. Once it is yours, the very fact that it has been of grace will make it all the more precious. Your present difficulty will then be your joy, and grace will be the burden of your song.

(2) That it is a gift, in the strictest sense of the word, appears also in the *eternity of the plan.* Sometimes we meet with what we may call spasmodic generosity. On the impulse of the moment, a man may bestow upon his neighbour some favour, which, perhaps, he will afterwards be sorry for. This we can scarcely call a gift. We are not very thankful, if we discover the disappointing secret. But God's generosity is shown by His eternal purpose. Before the foundations of the earth were laid, this gift and the plan of presenting it were decreed. What sweeter words can ring in sinner's ears than Peter's on the day of Pentecost ?—" Him, being delivered by the determinate counsel and foreknowledge of God." With the deepest reverence, yet with joyful praise, would we say that our God knew what He did when He gave His well-beloved Son. What a depth of meaning in that little word " so,"—" God *so* loved the world." " So loved," that He deliberately " gave Him up for us all." No wonder that the first burst of the angels' song at the nativity was, " Glory to God in the highest." We would not wonder if they had previously imagined that they knew all about the glory of their King,—now they find they are but beginning to know. May their first song be ours eternally.

(3) The fulness of the word, " The gift of God," appears again when we consider how it is *pressed upon our acceptance.* We are not told of it, and then left to seek it out, but, as Paul quotes in the tenth chapter of Romans, " The word is nigh thee." The gift is brought to our very door, and we are pressed, even entreated, to make it ours. The picture before us presents this very truth. *Christ* is here the Seeker. He had travelled from Judea, that He might place the gift within her reach. So He weariedly journeyed from town to town, and patiently pleaded,

and waited, and wept. So He commissioned His disciples to do when He was gone, and so He still stands at the door and knocks. "If any man hear my voice, and open the door, I will come in to him, and sup with him, and he with Me." Nothing seems to us to make the gift more precious than this, that the Lord still holds the right of presentation in His own hand, and claims the pleasure of bestowing it on "whom He will." If he had opened the fountain of living water in Samaria and left it there, the sinful daughter of Samaria might have doubted if it flowed for her; but when the Giver of the water is the personal Offerer of it, there can be no difficulty in appropriating it. By this personal offer, all questions about ability are silenced: for surely the Lord would not offer what He was not willing to help us to receive. Is not His pressing it upon our acceptance a promise that He will give the grace to receive? Sad mocking it would be, were He to hold before you that which He denied you strength to own. How dare any to say that our Lord but plays at pantomime, when He stands, and calls, and knocks, and weeps before a door that He refuses the occupant power to open! Let sinners seek to relieve themselves of their responsibility as they may, and conjure up excuses for not accepting an offered salvation, the position the Lord assumes, as well as the words He utters, takes from them every refuge of lies, and shuts them up to either accepting or rejecting the proffered grace.

(4) The truth of the title here given to the Living Water appears still more clearly, when we learn *how thoroughly it becomes ours on our accepting it*. It is absolutely bestowed. Indeed, in this sense, it deserves to be called a gift more fitly than anything else we can have, for it becomes ours irrevocably. What else can thus become mine? Property, power, influence, friends, health, capacity, life, I may have now; but all may be lost to me before the sun goes down. Here, however, God offers us a gift that even He (we write it reverently) cannot take from us when once we make Him ours. "Christ is mine," is no vain cry of the believing soul. The promised abiding is eternal. These "riches" never "make themselves wings," and "fly away." With what a triumphant rapture does Paul conclude the eighth chapter of Romans: "Who can separate us from the love of Christ?" "For I am persuaded that neither death, nor life, nor angels, nor principalities, nor powers, nor things present, nor things to come, nor height, nor depth, nor any other creature, shall be able to separate us from the love of God, which is in Christ Jesus our Lord."

I

This gift becomes indissolubly ours because it becomes a part of ourselves. Our heart becomes not a reservoir or cistern only, but a spring. The word translated a "well," in the 14th verse, should rather be a "springing fountain." Jesus is the Jacob of our New Testament, who sinks for springs of water. "He that believeth on Me, as the Scripture hath said, out of his belly shall flow rivers of living water." So it is that Paul can say, "Not I, but Christ in me." Christ had become in Paul the well-spring—the living, constraining power. If this be true, "Where is boasting, then?" "Without me ye can do nothing" is thus an axiom, a self-evident truth. "I in them, and thou in me." O, precious identification! What, then, is impossible for the believer? A Christ-pervaded being can sing of the future with as much assurance as of the past. He never despairs. He knows nothing of the way over which He must travel; but he knows most certainly the goal at which he must finally arrive. The Saviour's promise leaves no room for doubt: "I will come again, and receive you unto myself, that where I am, there ye may be also." His princely prayer is equally plain,—"Father, I will that they also, whom Thou hast given Me, be with Me where I am; that they may behold My glory, which Thou hast given Me." In no spirit of vain boasting, therefore, does the heir of glory sing—

> " Goodness and mercy all my life
> Shall surely follow me :
> And in God's house for evermore
> My dwelling-place shall be."

Absolute though our possession of the Living Water becomes, at the same time we must not forget that the inheritance of it brings *responsibility*. Springs of water do not burst forth merely to murmur music, and stripe the hillsides with silver; they have work to do, and they brightly and merrily go to do it: even so this new principle within us is a working power. Indeed, here is the great distinctive mark of the new life—the life of the worldling is an exhaustive life, the life of a Christian is a productive life. True, the Christian lives out his life; but he lives it out *into* his work. Paul says to the Corinthians, "Death worketh in us, but life in you." This well-sinker sinks his wells and dies, but the spring gushes forth as fresh as ever. Without Christ we are always "doing," but it is "*nothing*,"—that is the disappointing product; with Christ we "do" what lasts when we are gone. "Being dead, we yet speak." The elected

of Christ are "chosen and ordained, that they should go and
bring forth fruit, and that their fruit should remain."

Reality, abundance, permanence are the characteristics of
Christian fruit-bearing. We were impressed with this as we
walked among the ruins of the Roman Forum, and traced out
the remains of the palaces and temples of heathen heroes and
deities. We learn of Romulus and Numa, of Brutus and Cicero,
of the Cæsars and Septimius. But we read of and remember
them with a sigh. "Where are they, and what have they done ?"
"And he died also," is the closing sentence of each hero's history.
Our hearts burn within us, however, as we track out that "sacred
way," and tread, perhaps, the very pavements which "the apostle
of the Gentiles" trod as he was led a prisoner from Puteoli.
Haughty Romans despised, and persecuted, and slew him; yet
in their midst he uttered words, and from their city he sent forth
epistles that live and work as mightily as they did in his own
day. We go to our schools and libraries, and study the "dead
languages," to learn the achievements of kings, and consuls, and
emperors; but what Christ did, and is doing, by Paul, may be
seen in living epistles, all the world over. "I work for immortality," is no vain boast of the servant of Christ.

Nor is this reproductiveness a thing of constraint, except so
far as "the love of Christ constrains" us. It is the natural
springing of the living water,—the instinct of new life. Every
principle of the nature enters into the enterprise. Lovingly,
enthusiastically, heartily we seek to spread the tidings. As in
the East, when the traveller has pushed on and found the well,
after quenching his own thirst, his whole thought is how to
signal and encourage those that have fallen behind to come, and
drink, and be satisfied as he has been. Rejoicing in the benefits
he has received,

> " He loves to tell the story,
>   Because he knows it's true;
> It satisfies his longings
>   As nothing else can do."

"Therefore with joy shall ye draw water out of the wells of
salvation." How sad that there is so little of this joy in the
world ! Why is it that so few have received this living water ?
We fear we can only answer—Because they do not feel their
need, or do not realise its preciousness. Mark how the Master
says it must be asked for,—"thou wouldest have asked of Him."
But men will not ask for what they want not. The two prayers

which the Highland minister taught the Highland kitchenmaid, "Lord, show me myself,"—"Lord, show me Thyself," must be first offered and answered before we know the value of the water from the Smitten Rock. Then, no doctrine, however true,—no difficulty, however perplexing,—will keep the longing, thirsting, yearning soul from crying, "Give me this water." Can fancy picture a man, with a burning thirst upon him, putting away the cup of water from his lips till he had settled the question whether it was intended for him, or whether he had the strength to drink of it? Let him take and drink, and live. Then, and only then, will he fully know by the results that it was for him, and that the same Lord who put it to his lips gave the strength to partake of it.

Unconverted sinner, we want to have no controversy with you. We have never known an unsaved one argued into salvation. We would rather pray that God the Holy Ghost may deepen anxieties in your soul, and give you such views of Jesus that you shall be compelled to cast yourself at His feet, whatever may be the consequences. Then and there He will cause the well-spring in your soul to spring "up into everlasting life." Then you can know, as you never before could, that He loved you with "an everlasting love." Then you can join your testimony to that of thousands—

> " I heard the voice of Jesus say—
>   Behold I freely give
> The living water ; thirsty one,
>   Stoop down, and drink, and live.
> I came to Jesus, and I drank
>   Of that life-giving stream ;
> My thirst was quenched, my soul revived
>   And now I live in Him."

TRANSFORMATION:

A SERMON.

BY

THE REV. JOHN KAY,

ARGYLE PLACE UNITED PRESBYTERIAN CONGREGATION,
EDINBURGH.

"The wilderness and the solitary place shall be glad for them; and the desert shall rejoice, and blossom as the rose. It shall blossom abundantly, and rejoice even with joy and singing: the glory of Lebanon shall be given unto it, the excellency of Carmel and Sharon; they shall see the glory of the Lord, and the excellency of our God. . . . . And the parched ground shall become a pool, and the thirsty land springs of water: in the habitation of dragons, where each lay, shall be grass, with reeds and rushes."—ISAIAH xxxv. 1, 2, 7.

THE magnificent language of this prophecy, apart, even, from its spiritual significance, is calculated to arrest the attention, and to command the admiration of every reader. From the first sentence to the last, it breathes the spirit of truest and loftiest poetry. It is not one sentence here, and another there that has caught the sacred influence, but every sentence seems bathed in light and glory, till, at last, the triumphant shouts, and the glad songs, and the everlasting joy of Jehovah's ransomed ones, fittingly close the ever-swelling pæan, and all sorrow and all sighing flee away. The question, Who *are* these "ransomed ones of Jehovah?" demands that we look with some degree of minuteness into the context, if we would discover the true meaning and application of the passage.

This thirty-fifth chapter of Isaiah, be it observed, goes along with the thirty-fourth, as forming one prediction, divided into two parts. In the last-mentioned, the judgments of God are denounced upon the men of Edom, and the terrible doom of that guilty land is foretold. In the day of Judah's affliction, the descendents of Esau had rejoiced with an inhuman and unnatural joy over the daughter of Zion. When the men of Babylon might possibly have spared the city, whose inhabitants had been carried away into an apparently hopeless captivity, the Edomites had cried " Rase, rase it, even to the foundation." The account which is given by the prophet Obadiah of the malice shown by the hereditary foes of Israel, leaves no ground for wonder that the Almighty should threaten to pour out upon them the vials of His wrath. " The Lord hath a sacrifice in Bozrah, and a great slaughter in the land of Idumea." The transition from the thirty-fourth to the thirty-fifth chapter is, as if one passed out of the dark night, illuminated only by the fitful lightning-flash, into the clear light of a summer day, in which all nature seems to be in harmony with joy and with gladness. " The winter is past, the rain is over and gone, the flowers appear on the earth, the time of the singing of birds is come." The joy rises out of the fact that God has delivered His Israel ; that He has cast up for them a highway, and that they who were lately sitting in sadness by the streams of Babel, have returned to the Jerusalem which they " set above their chiefest joy."

Let any one, after reading the exegesis of the text, read once more the glowing words which stand at the head of this discourse, together with the other glorious things mentioned throughout the chapter, and say, if the mind feels satisfied by the statement, that the return of the Jews from the Captivity of Babylon is all that is brought before us by this magnificent prediction. Does it not seem as if the language were far in excess of such a meaning—as if it were too glowing and too highly wrought for an event which, however interesting to the Jewish nation, cannot be said to have the same interest for us ? The light hovers for a while round the City of David, with its reconstructed temple and its re-instituted worship. It projects upon the page of history the figure of one with a stout heart who says " I am doing a great work, and I cannot come down." But it does more : leaving all these in the background, it travels on through the centuries, and makes luminous the plain of Bethlehem, and shines like a halo round the head of One who is the glory of His people Israel, and who utters the word and performs the deed which " makes all things new." The prophecy before us is one of those in which the so-called secondary meaning is, in truth, the primary : here, if anywhere, " the first is last, and the last is first." The spiritual takes precedence of the natural, and the fulfilment is to be looked for, not in a remnant of Israel returning to the land of their fathers, but in those grand gospel times whose glory forms the woof of that marvellous web of prophecy whose spirit is the testimony of Jesus. It is, in fact, none other than the "old, old story" of humanity, cursed and blasted by sin, but, in the exercise of a compassion that is fathomless, blessed, and saved, and dignified by the Cross of Calvary. A nobler theme for poet's lyre never existed; and the words that seemed at first so full of glory, are all too feeble to tell of the Transformation into which the angels of God desire to look.

I.—*The sad condition of the localities on which the Gospel of Christ is intended to operate.*

Let us gather into one cluster all that is said of them. "A wilderness," "a solitary place," "parched ground," "thirsty land," "a habitation of dragons." With the exception of the last-mentioned, all the desolation seems to turn upon the absence of one element—*water*. The, wilderness and the solitary place are in this condition; for there is no refreshing stream, no spring, no well in the desert. The ground is parched and thirsty, because all water fails ; and as far as the eye can reach, there is nothing but one continuous expanse of arid sand. Neither vegetable nor animal life can exist amidst the dreary wastes: all is desolation and barrenness. What simile could so vividly depict the moral barrenness and desolation, whether of the individual breast, or of the world at large, apart from the glorious Gospel of the blessed God ? What a wilderness the heart is, that has not God dwelling in it ! How solitary the soul is that has no Christ for its inmate and its King ! You may surround it with all that might be supposed to give pleasure, and to add a charm to human life— wealth without stint, honours without number, influence without a challenge ; but still the desolateness remains unchanged, and life itself becomes a burden, and the sigh of the weary heart will ever be " vanity of vanities, all is vanity." The idea of " solitariness " may seem to disappear when this word " habitation " comes into view. But what an habitation it is ! " An habitation of dragons." That, and that only, was wanting to complete the picture—the foul serpent brood, with their huge encircling folds, prepared to crush the life out of every creature that may cross their dreaded path.

To a heart which has within it that " well of water springing

up into everlasting life," there is no sadder scene than the
unutterable desolateness of these moral wastes presented by
hearts that are unchanged. To know and to feel assured that it
needs only the presence of Jesus to make these hearts in-
expressibly happy, and to turn the wilderness into a smiling
garden of the Lord; and yet to mark how the Prince of Life is
kept standing without—what can be sadder than that? To
know that these dragons, lurking in the walls, are the only
inmates of what might be a splendid temple for the indwelling of
the Holy Spirit of God; to have the certainty that, unless they
be dispossessed, they will utterly devour the life of the soul in
which they have effected a lodgment—is it not enough to make
one take up the burden of the son of Hilkiah, and say, " O that
my head were waters, and mine eyes a fountain of tears, that I
might weep day and night for the slain of the daughter of my
people!" The hot blast of the simoom sweeps over the heart,
all solitary, all parched; and everything that has life droops, and
withers, and dies, and the wilderness becomes a region of death,
and the God of Life looks down upon a world of poor dead souls,
where reigns the " abomination of desolation."

What is true of the individual, is equally true of the aspect
presented by the world at large. Let one but think of the great
unreclaimed wastes of heathendom, and mark how all the higher
life for which man is fitted stagnates there. The sensual pleasures which engross the attention utterly sap all moral energy,
and cruelty of the most bloodthirsty kind reigns supreme. Far
as the eye can reach, the barrenness of spiritual death broods
over the scene. Nature may, with prodigal hand, have lavished
such store of external beauty upon these " desolate " parts of the
earth, that the contrast between the luxuriant life of the lower
orders of existence and that of man only becomes the more
marked. The feathery palm-tree waves above the scene, but
' the tree of life " is not known: the sun shines with unclouded
splendour, but " the Sun of Righteousness, with healing in His
wings," has never risen there: the stars stud the midnight sky
like jewels in dark ebony setting, but " the bright, the morning
star," nowhere appears: the rivers flow past banks of living
emerald, but " the river of the water of life " is wanting; and
hence, where everything is beautiful, while every scene charms
and ravishes the senses, man alone is vile.

It may perhaps be imagined that the one element which is
wanting to turn all this desolation into smiling fertility is—

Civilization. That, let me say, has been already weighed in the balances and has been found wanting. The civilisation of Greece and Rome did not effect anything in the way of changing spiritual death into spiritual life: it had no effect in changing barrenness into fertility. The utmost which it succeeded in effecting was, to cover the frightful corruption of death with a more beautiful funeral pall—to hide the naked hideousness of sin behind a veil spangled with silver, and gold, and precious stones. But death was there, none the less, and sin of such a kind that the foulest impurities of the most degraded heathen could not exceed the impurities of Athens and of Rome. The old lesson is being taught us, if we would but learn it, in our own day. It is not civilisation that can change the moral desolation of France, of Spain, of Austria. It is not civilisation, as understood by men of science, and doctrinaire philosophers, that can change the moral wilderness existing in our large cities, and among much of our rural population. It will only do what it did in Greece; it will cover the ghastliness of death with a more decent covering; but what the wilderness, and the solitary place, and the desert, and the parched ground, and the thirsty land require is—WATER, even the Water of Life, gushing from the smitten Rock, Christ Jesus.

II.—*The effects produced by the Kingdom of Jesus.*

There is no emblem in the whole range of language which can be compared with that which runs, by implication, throughout this magnificent prophecy, as descriptive of the Gospel of the Kingdom. Even to us, in a country where water is plentiful, the beauty and appropriateness of the image are at once apparent. What a charm it adds to the landscape, whether in the form of the great ocean, bearing on its bosom the treasures of the world, or of the river winding through the pleasant meadows, which drink in fertility and beauty from the living stream! The lake with its mirror-like surface basking in the sun, like to another sea of glass on which stand myriad harpers harping with their harps—that, too, suggests the theme of the prophet's song. But it was with an appreciation more intense, that the inhabitants of these eastern lands regarded this beautiful emblem of the life that is in Jesus Christ. Water spoke to them not of beauty only, but of deliverance from death. As the husbandman looked up to the skies and saw on the distant horizon the black cloud, the size of a man's hand, his heart leapt for joy, and his song of praise

ascended to the God of Israel; for rain meant life, and the
absence of it famine, and pestilence, and death. As the toil-worn
caravan passed over the desert, the fountain that met their
longing gaze spoke to them of deliverance from the most terrible
of deaths. Hence, wherever this glad gospel is spoken of, we
find this precious emblem employed to bring before the mind the
blessed and joy-giving results of the kingdom of Christ. Let us
note the results as these are brought before us in our text.

I. GLADNESS. "The wilderness and the solitary place shall
be glad for them," *i.e.*, on account of these blessings; "the desert
shall rejoice, ... it shall rejoice even with joy and with
singing."

It requires no great effort of imagination to realise the glad
aspect of nature refreshed by copious rains, after a heat that has
scorched the grass, and dwarfed the corn. The earth gave forth
no sound of music to the tread of the passer-by; the heavens
were as brass, and the earth was as iron. But lo! the windows
of heaven are opened, the groves are vocal with the liquid notes
of a thousand warblers, and the earth has doffed her robes of
mourning, and has put on her mantle of emerald, in which heart
and eye alike rejoice. "God has visited the earth, and has
watered it, and has greatly enriched it with the river of God,
which is full of water." Fitting emblem, this, of the great joy
which the gospel of Jesus brings with it to human hearts. For
the wilderness state is ever one of heavy, brooding sorrow. The
laughter of foolish hearts is not the laughter of true joy. The
song that rings out from above the brimming cup of this world's
pleasure is, in all cases, but a feeble effort to drown the wail of
real sorrow that lies underneath ; and the flowers that crown the
revellers have but to be touched by the finger of pain, or by the
hand of disease, when they wither and die. Do you wish to see
a glad heart? Then look on that one through which runs the
river of the water of life. *It* "rejoices even with joy and with
singing." The burden of the old life has been cast off; the
crushing load of condemnation, which the soul carried with it
day and night, has fallen, and the mourning is turned into gladness, and the sigh of sorrow into the song of joy. What our
eyes have seen of the joy of the new life, what our ears have
heard,—that declare we unto you. When the Lord had opened
the windows of heaven—when the Spirit, long prayed for, had
come—who has not seen a human countenance darkened by the
gloom of spiritual death; alarm, rising at times to terror; anxiety

deepened to anguish; the eyes filled with tears, and the wor ls
" O wretched that I am," hovering on lips that were parched and
pale ?   Twelve hours have passed, and the transformation was so
great that you almost questioned whether he with the beaming
eye, with the countenance from which a perfect love had cast
out fear, were the same who came to you and said " Sir, what
must I do to be saved ? "   It is the same, and yet another,—the
same, and yet a new man ; the darkness, the alarm, the anguish,
are gone, and the old prophecy has once more met its fulfilment ;
" the wilderness and the solitary place shall be glad for them."
In the depths of that heart is a deep well of water of life, which
no burning heat of trial or of sorrow can dry up : the waters, as
they rise to the surface of the man's life, run over, and gleam
and sparkle in the unchanging sunlight of the countenance of
God.   Hearken to the song as it rises, clear, and bold, and strong,
from lips that have been circumcised and touched with a live
coal from off the altar of God.   " Behold God is my salvation, I
will trust and will not be afraid ; for the Lord Jehovah is my
strength and my song, He also is become my salvation."   The joy
increases, and the song grows in volume and in power as the
waters flow through the whole nature of the man, till in heaven
it becomes *everlasting* joy, and the song becomes the same with
that sung by the hundred and forty and four thousand who
stand on the mount Zion—a new song that no man can learn,
save they that are redeemed from the earth, being the first-fruits
of God and the Lamb.   If there be on earth one man who has a
right to be glad, it is he who, having been as a wilderness and
desert, has drunk of the stream of life.   All the arid barrenness
has gone out of his nature, and the tree of life is laden with those
fruits which are to the praise and glory of God, by Jesus Christ.
He has One dwelling within him whose presence is an everlasting joy, and who, with a power and love which pass all
capacity of words to tell, can convert sorrow itself into gladness,
and death into life.

2. FERTILITY.   " It shall blossom : it shall blossom abundantly."   This fertility not only stands connected with life, it is
the outcome of its existence.   The desert is always barren.   If
men do not gather grapes from thorns, nor figs from thistles, still
less do they look for waving, luxuriant crops in the desert.   But
the mighty power of the gospel of Jesus converts this moral
wilderness into a fruit-bearing garden of the Lord.   The heart
under the sway of this blessed change is filled with the fruits of

righteousness; and not the heart alone, but the outer life as well. Indeed, the first intimation which the world receives of the transformation is from the presence of these precious fruits. Amidst the rich ripe clusters of Engedi, it is hard to say which should first occupy our thoughts. Shall it be the earnest, unceasing efforts put forth for the benefit of those who are still sitting in the "habitation of dragons?" The wilderness state was one of intense selfishness; all the thoughts were concentrated upon the one object, and that the narrowest and meanest which can possibly occupy the mind. But now, the heart through which flows this mighty fertilising stream, learns that it is not made blessed and happy for itself alone. It sees that the wants and the sorrows of others have a claim upon it; and it strives, with all the power of a deep love and an earnest faith, to deliver from darkness and death those who are hasting to the pit. The joy and peace which reign within, it desires—O how earnestly!—to share with others; while the prayer and the effort for the perishing are, that they may be saved. There is no fruit of the life that is made fruitful by the river of the water of life, which arrests the attention more than this. It prompts the collective church of God (and the church is simply a territory rescued from the wilderness and from desert barrenness, and made fruit-bearing by the power of Jehovah), to go forth and conquer more territory for Jesus, to endure the world's hate, to stand up against the world's evil, and to extend to the solitary places the fertility which reigns within itself.

See, too, how FAITH grows under the influence of this great stream. Day by day it becomes more simple, more unhesitating, more confiding, less staggered by difficulties, less beclouded by fears and doubts, till at last it reaches the full stature of the perfect man in Christ Jesus. It does not presume to measure itself with Jesus, but it prays to have Jesus near; and, with a heart that throbs with love, it sends out the invitation, " Let my beloved come into his garden, and eat His pleasant fruit." While the heart of faith is yet speaking, the voice of the Beloved says, " I *am* come into my garden, my sister, my spouse."

3. BEAUTY. " It shall blossom as the rose." Putting aside all questions as to whether the word here rendered " rose " indicates the same flower that receives the name among ourselves, we can have no doubt as to what is meant by the expression. One has only to picture to himself a part of this earth's surface, parched, desert, and barren, and to think of the marvellous change which

would be produced upon it were he, on revisiting the scene, to find it covered with the fairest flowers that our gardens know. The first and most striking impression made upon the mind would not be so much that of fertility, as of surpassing beauty. Even so is it with the marvellous moral transformation which the prophecy before us contemplates. We have only to contrast the state of a country before, with its condition after having received the gospel, and the force of the prediction becomes at once transparent. The glorious annals of missionary effort render it unnecessary to draw on the imagination. Think of what has been achieved in our day in Madagascar, in Samoa, in various islands of the Western Pacific! Have not the corruption and unrighteousness of spiritual death given place to the beauty of a life that is beyond life? Nor is the change one whit less striking within the narrower sphere of the individual life. What a beauty is unfolded in a holy, Christ-like life! Even the world itself, while either misapprehending or misjudging its source, is often forced to look with wondering and admiring gaze upon it. The light of heaven so streams on it; the sweet odours of an atmosphere loftier than that of this earth so flow forth from it; and the colours produced by the hand of the heavenly artist so glow in every part of it, that the eye of the beholder is ravished by the glorious sight. The voice of *one* beholder breaks forth into a stream of loving tenderness such as earth-born poetry has never approached—"thou art all fair, my love; there is no spot in thee."

4. GLORY AND MAJESTY. "The glory of Lebanon shall be given unto it, the excellency of Carmel." It is not necessary to enter here upon the geographical questions connected either with the site or the appearance of these two mountains. It is sufficient to know that they are (the first-mentioned more especially) the chosen symbols in Scripture of all that is majestic and glorious, and form a fit medium for conveying to the mind the exalted dignity of those on whom the transforming power of the gospel has wrought. To live under the power of Jesus is the true secret of a noble life. Whatever the sphere of life which the man occupies, however far it may be removed from the majesty of earth, he is in closest alliance with the majesty of heaven, and in virtue of that alliance is raised to regal dignity. In the Christian life, when rightly understood and faithfully followed, there is an essential nobility which raises it as much above the meanness of the unrenewed nature as Carmel towers

above the plain, or as Lebanon raises its cedar-girt crown above
the valleys of Palestine. The mountain-peaks catch and hold
the first rays of the sun; they are directed to heaven above, and
not to the earth beneath.

What a change the power of Jesus has effected! How it has
elevated and raised the character, and given dignity to the
pursuits of the man! It matters not that these pursuits may not
be among the higher departments of labour, whether in the
church, or state, or commerce; though they be confined to the
ordinary walks of every-day life, the *aim* that runs through
them all, even the glory of God, lends to them an elevation of
which the wilderness-state is utterly ignorant. Two men, for
instance, are engaged in business; they give themselves with
energy of spirit and fixity of purpose to it; whatsoever their
hands find to do, they do it with their might. Between the two,
however, there exists this vast difference—the one is bent on
acquiring wealth that he may hoard it up for himself, or that he
may gain influence and position among his fellow-men. His
ambition is of the most paltry kind,—that he may be spoken of
as worth so much; that he may have the satisfaction of seeing
those who are poorer humble themselves before him, and feed, by
their flatteries, an overweening vanity. The meanness of that
man's aims spreads itself over all his work, deprives it of all
claim to nobility, and drags himself down to the level of a mere
earth-worm. The other, with the noble end before him of con-
secrating himself, his work, and its results to the glory of God,
to the promotion of His cause on earth, to the helping of the
poor and needy, has, shining upon his path, a glory more grand
than that of Lebanon, an excellency greater than that of Carmel.
When we rise to the higher departments of Christian work—the
constant effort to attain a closer likeness to the image of the
risen Christ, the ceaseless striving after the lofty ideal of a life
that is hid with Christ in God, the untiring battle against sin,
and the aspirations after holiness—the man who doeth thus shall
not only never be moved, but his life has the glory of heaven
resting on it, and the excellency of that " mountain of the Lord's
house, which shall be established in the top of the mountains,
and which shall be exalted above the hills."

5. A VISION THAT EXTENDS INTO THE HOLY OF HOLIES.
" They shall see the glory of Jehovah, and the excellency of our
God." Further on in the prophecy, the effect of the Gospel is set
forth under the image of the opening of the eyes of the blind.

Had it been within the range of the present text, many things
might have been mentioned as coming within the scope of the
restored vision; but here we have to do simply with one point—
the glory and excellency of God. Nothing can let a man see
that, save the Gospel of the Lord Jesus Christ. In a certain
sense, the Great Jehovah has so scattered witnesses of Himself
over the face of nature, that His glory shines forth with lustrous
splendour; but not till we have by faith made the Christ of God
our Jesus, do we perceive Jehovah's excellency and glory. The
high priest of Israel beheld, within the holy of holies, a far
different sight from that which met his view amidst the hills and
valleys of Palestine. The Shekinah of the glory of God shone
forth there, from between the cherubim and above the blood-
sprinkled mercy-seat. It is that which every heart saved by
Jesus sees,—even Him who is " the express image of Jehovah's
person, and the brightness of His glory." Here, then, as in
everything else, all rises up to, and finds its glorious ending in
God. It began with joy, fertility, beauty, and nobility, and it
ends with the glory of the Most High, the excellency of our God.
Earth has no vision of beauty to compare with that which the
holy of holies unfolds. The world has no glory which may be
spoken of as compared with the glory of Jehovah. The universe
has no excellency like that on which the vision, unsealed by the
light-giving gospel, looks with enraptured gaze. Behold the
Glory of God, Him whom men on earth called by the name of
Jesus of Nazareth, the centre of the adoring praise of all the
heavenly host, and of all redeemed souls; the insignia of a King
resting on shoulder and on brow, and the priestly pectoral with
the names of His chosen ones engraved upon it. The crown on
all the glory is, that as we rise on the wings of faith, and soar
into the presence of the King of Kings, we are also able to say,
" He is our God, He will save us."

THE TOWER IN SILOAM:

A SERMON.

BY

THOMAS SMITH, D.D.,

COWGATE-HEAD CHURCH, EDINBURGH.

"Or those eighteen, upon whom the tower in Siloam fell, and slew them, think ye that they were sinners above all men that dwelt in Jerusalem? I tell you Nay: but, except ye repent, ye shall all likewise perish."—LUKE xiii. 4, 5.

THERE are few subjects on which it more concerns men to have clear and correct views and apprehensions, and yet there is perhaps no one on which erroneous and defective notions are more prevalent, than the subject of Divine Providence. It is perhaps not altogether to be wondered at that this should be the case, because there are undoubtedly difficulties connected with the subject which we cannot solve, and mysteries far too deep for any sounding-line of ours to fathom. We cannot, for example, comprehend, and probably shall never be able to comprehend, how the overruling providence of One who is omnipotent, and who doeth according to His will in the armies of heaven and the inhabitants of the earth, is consistent with that freedom of will which we are all conscious of possessing; and how the supreme and universal rule of a Being of infinite holiness is reconcilable with the great fact of the existence and prevalence of evil in the world. Such deep and mysterious questions as these we must be content to leave unanswered, in the confidence that if, in any future state of our being, it shall be essential to the discharge of the duties that may be imposed on us that we should understand them, God will undoubtedly furnish us with the means of doing so. In the meantime we have light enough to guide us in the path of duty that lies before us, in which we are required to walk at once under a sense of our own responsibility, and under a feeling of reverence and gratitude to Him who is over all, and who giveth us, out of His boundless liberality, all things richly to enjoy.

It is not, then, with our want of distinct conceptions or apprehensions respecting these mysterious subjects that any fault is to be found; but with habitual mistakes and misconceptions on the subject of God's providence, which must necessarily and directly influence the whole tone of our affections, and the decisions of our judgments on subjects very closely connected with our being and our well-being. It is, for example, we believe, far too much our habit to overlook and forget the providence of God in all the events of our lives that are of a joyous character, and to recognise it only in those which are of a painful and distressing kind. When some sore and grievous trial befals us, —when, it may be, we are laid prostrate upon a bed of sickness, and toss in weariness and pain from morning to night, and from night to morning, or when death enters into our dwelling and cuts down the desire of our eyes with a stroke,—then, very likely, we think of God as having to do with the matter, and regard the affliction that has befallen us as a visitation of His providence. And so it is; and it is very right that we should so regard and so acknowledge it. But it is not very right, but altogether very wrong, that we should forget, as we are so apt to do, or as at all events we are so apt not to acknowledge, that the sickness or bereavement with which we are visited is just as much, and not a whit more, traceable to God's providence, than is the health which, it may be, we have enjoyed unbroken for years, or the domestic comforts which have been long the joy of our hearts, to an extent which we never knew until we had lost them. It is not right to forget that the food which we eat, and the air which we breathe, and the light which gives all its beauty to the objects that please our sight, and the faculties by means of which we are capable of so much enjoyment, are the gifts of that God in whom we live, and move, and have our being.

It is probably in part the cause, and partly the effect, of the idea of gloom and sadness that we are far too apt to associate with religion, that we regard God so much as if He were only the sender of evil and not of good, as if He indeed sent the dark cloud that occasionally casts its shadow across our path, but had no concern with the bright and gladsome sunshine that habitually enlivens it. Judge for yourselves. Suppose that some being that knew nothing of God were to become an inmate of one of

K

our dwellings, and were to derive all his knowledge of Him from our conversation, is not the probability that he would first and oftenest hear His name mentioned in connection with some calamity, and that he would form the idea that we regarded Him as some mysterious power who had to do only with sickness, and death, and funerals? Now, it is doubtless well that we should recognise the hand of God in the evils that befal us; and a most blessed thing it is that we can resort to Him in the day of sore distress, when our hearts are ready to sink within us, and we feel that all others than He are miserable comforters; but surely it is not well that we should shut Him out from our thoughts when all goes well with us. We treat God very much as an unkind husband treats his wife, giving her the blame of all that goes amiss in the domestic affairs, forgetting that it is to her prudence and good management that he is indebted for innumerable and often unthought-of comforts.

Another misconception into which we habitually fall respecting the Divine Providence is to think of it as only having to do with the great and striking events of our lives, and not with the daily and hourly occurrences, which are individually small and scarcely thought of, but which, in the aggregate, make up very nearly the whole of our lives. It may have happened to some of us to be delivered from great and imminent danger, in circumstances in which it was almost impossible to avoid recognising the finger of God; and it is well if we have felt due gratitude for such a deliverance. But if we viewed the matter aright, ought we not constantly to be filled with gratitude to Him for keeping us from falling into danger? Is the continuance of health not as great and as special a blessing as the recovery from sickness? When some harrowing calamity occurs in our neighbourhood, we feel that those who have been in the midst of it, and who have escaped unscathed, have a loud call addressed to them for thankfulness and praise; but does it ever occur to us, that if there be any difference, the call is still louder to us for gratitude, because we have been kept out of the danger itself? To advert, for a moment, to the event that has occupied so large a share of all our thoughts during the past week.* We all feel that if there had been any left to tell the tale of the disaster, they would have had special cause of thankfulness and thanksgiving for their deliverance. Quite as much so those who in any way were prevented from carrying out their intention of travelling by the fated train.

* The " Tay-Bridge Disaster."

And why not we, who had no such intention? Depend upon it, that for one great event in our lives in which we see the hand of God's providence visibly at work, there are ten thousand small events in which it is not less really, though less manifestly, at work. It was a received maxim amongst a particular sect of the old heathen philosophers, that Jupiter had no leisure to attend to small affairs; but it is our blessed privilege to know regarding Jehovah, that, whilst He counts the number of the stars, and calls them all by their names, He superintends the fall of every rain-drop, and directs the course of every sun-ray, and clothes the lilies of the field with glory, and feeds the young ravens when they cry to Him; that, whilst He rules over the destinies of states and empires, He watches over the flight of every sparrow, and numbers the very hairs on the heads of His people.

We have been led to make these remarks by the text before us, because it refers to a mistake respecting God's providence, of not precisely the same, but still of a similar kind. We know the idea was very widely prevalent amongst the Jews, that there is a strict scheme of providential rewards and punishments in this life, in virtue of which every calamity is the direct punishment of some special sin, and every manifest blessing is the special reward of some good action. This idea prevailed so long ago as the time of Job, whose three friends argued, very cruelly, that since he was a greater sufferer than others, he must have been a greater sinner that others. There is little doubt that it was fostered in the corrupt heart and the perverted intellect of man by the peculiarities of the Jewish dispensation. Under that dispensation, God was pleased to assume a relation towards the people of Israel such as he never sustained towards any other people. He was not only their God, but also their king. From this it resulted that they were apt to confound the rewards and punishments which He bestowed or inflicted upon them, in the character of their temporal Sovereign, with those which He bestows or inflicts upon all men in His character of Supreme Providential Governor of the world. Certain sins, especially those relating to the public national worship, were, under that peculiar dispensation, crimes committed against the supreme authority in the state. Idolatry, for example, which in every place and in all circumstances is a great and grievous *sin*, became in that state, and in the peculiar circumstances to which we have referred, not only a sin, but also a *crime*. It was, in point of fact, rebellion against their king, and in that character God, as their King, frequently visited it with punishment. And so, in greater or less measure, with other sins. Now, this not unnaturally gave rise to the idea that all sin, as such, is punished in this life, and that signal providential visitations are always to be regarded as punishments for some notorious offences. We find this idea very distinctly stated by the disciples of our Lord, when, as we are told, they asked Him, respecting a man born blind, "Who did sin, this man or his parents, that he was born blind?" On that occasion Jesus answered them, "Neither hath this man sinned nor his parents." By which it is very evident that He did not mean to assert that this man and his parents were sinless, but only to intimate that it was not on account of any special or notorious sin on his part or theirs, that he was from his birth destitute of the blessing of sight. It was evidently with a similar view that, on the occasion to which our text refers, He was told of a massacre that had been committed by Pilate, who had fallen upon a body of Galileans while they were engaged in offering sacrifice, and had shed their blood close upon the altar, so that it was sprinkled over the victims which they were offering. They no doubt told it to Him with all the more zest, because the sufferers were Galileans, His own countrymen, whom they specially despised and hated. It seems to be as if they had said, What do you say of your countrymen now? See what a calamity has befallen them, at the very moment when they were engaged in the most solemn act of worship. God, instead of accepting their sacrifice, testified His abhorrence of them by suffering them to be cut off by a violent and horrible death Surely, in the face of this, you cannot maintain that we have not good reason for thinking ill of the Galileans, and of you as one of them. Can any good thing come out of Nazareth?

If this were the spirit in which they spoke—and we can scarcely doubt that it was—we cannot sufficiently admire the answer of our blessed Lord, who returned not railing for railing, nor reviling for reviling, but simply assured them that the fact of the worshippers' having been subjected to so dire a calamity was no certain proof of God's special displeasure; but that, in point of fact, they themselves were equally liable to the Divine displeasure, and, if they persisted in their present course, would certainly bring down that displeasure upon them. And this seems to be the proper place to remark that He seems especially to refer to their rejection of Him, and the destruction that was soon to come upon them and their nation in consequence. Repentance, in the language of John the Baptist (who was especially charged with the ministry of repentance), and in that of our blessed Lord, included that change of mind respecting the ceremonial law, and the dispensation which was about to pass away, which was necessary to prepare them for the acceptance of Him who was come to put away sin by the sacrifice of Himself. In this sense they refused to repent. They would not give heed to the things which belonged to their peace, and now they were about to be hid from their eyes. The time was near at hand when they were to be subjected to tribulations the most appalling that ever befel the sons of men; such tribulation as had not been from the beginning until then, nor were ever to be again, until the great day when the earth and the things that are therein shall be burnt up, and the elements shall melt with fervent heat.

But, as if He had feared lest exception should be taken to His treatment of this case, as if He had been afraid lest we, with our perverse ingenuity, might argue : "This might be so in the case specified. It was no doubt permitted by God, but at least the atrocity was perpetrated by a sinful, tyrannical, godless scoffer. It may be all true, therefore, that in such a case as that, the infliction of a grievous calamity does not authorize us to infer any specially atrocious sin; but the case is different with those calamities which are inflicted directly and immediately by the hand of God Himself." As if for the very purpose of answering by anticipation such an objection as this, He himself brings forward precisely such a case, and treats it precisely as he had done the other. It was a case, apparently, which had lately occurred, and which was fresh in the memory of his hearers, a case in which eighteen persons had been killed by the fall of a tower, and in which those whom our Lord addressed, doubtless, were ready to conclude that the victims of so dire a calamity were evidently the objects of God's special curse and displeasure. Now, it is most important to observe that, with respect to them, precisely as with respect to the Galileans, although the calamity came upon them by the immediate visitation of God, without the intervention of human agency at all, our Lord expressly declares that the speciality of the calamity was no indication that it was sent as a punishment for any special or specially enormous sin.

Now, then, with this Divine teaching before us, let us endeavour, with all humility, to inquire what we may, and what we may not infer respecting the punishment of sin in this life. And we would remark, *first* of all, that there are certain cases

in which temporal suffering is manifestly and directly the result
of sin. If a man ruin his health by drunkenness, or strike a dart
through his liver by going astray in the paths of her who hath
cast down many wounded, and by whom many strong men have
been slain, whose house is the way to hell, going down to the
chambers of death; if a man, by dishonesty, blast his reputation
and forfeit his credit; if the liar so bring his word into suspicion
that he will not be believed even if he speak the truth; if a man,
by extravagance or idleness, bring himself to poverty,—it were
altogether absurd to say that disease, and it may be death, in one
case, and dishonour and shame in another, and disgrace and suspicion in a third, and poverty and suffering in a fourth, are not
the *consequences* of the sin. To deny this were to abjure all
our common sense, and to shut our eyes to that connection be-
twixt causes and effects, which is the great foundation of the
greater part of our knowledge. Yet it were dangerous, even in
these cases, to say that the suffering is the *punishment* of the sin.
It is this idea, we believe, that gives a false and delusive peace to
many a sinner. The drunkard argues, Well, I have sinned, but I
have been sufficiently punished for it by the sickness, and the
poverty, and the disgrace that I have brought upon myself. No,
friend, these are but the punishments of your violation of God's
physical laws. You have swallowed a certain amount of poison,
and it has produced upon you the same physical effects that it
would have produced if you had swallowed it by accident or in
ignorance; but the moral guilt, the self-indulgence, the voluntary
degradation of yourself below the level of the beasts, the disregard of all God's invitations, warnings, and threatenings,—the
moral element of your transgression is yet unatoned for. You
have lived the drunkard's wretched life, and are going down to a
drunkard's unhonoured grave; but beyond all this, unless you
repent, and wash away your sins in the blood of Christ, there is
yet before you the drunkard's hell. That these results, although
the natural consequences of sin, are not to be regarded, in any
proper sense, as its punishment, is evident from the consideration that similar effects may be produced, and often are produced,
by courses of an opposite kind. One man is wounded in nobly
fighting the battles of his country, another in a drunken brawl ;
one man brings himself to an early grave by dissipation, and
another by exposing himself to a vitiated air in order to relieve
distress or minister to disease. The burglar falls from the ladder
which he is climbing for purposes of crime, the fireman falls from

that which he is climbing to rescue the shrieking woman or the sleeping child from the flames. Both violate physical laws, and bring upon themselves physical sufferings; yet how different is the moral character of the men, and of the courses of conduct which yet so far issue in similar results!

Then there is *another* class of evils which come upon men while they are actually pursuing sinful courses, but which have no direct or immediate connection with these courses, or with what is sinful in them. What shall we say with respect to these? As for example, with respect to those accidents, as they are called, which befal Sabbath excursion trains, and those fires which so frequently occur in places of sinful entertainment and ungodly revelry. We may not call them punishments of the sin, because similar accidents befal trains that are running on lawful occasions, and fires take place in churches as well as in theatres. But we do say it is a fearful thing to be hurried into eternity in the act of violating the command of God, profaning the day which He hath sanctified, or listening with complacency to those compositions in which that abominable thing which He hates is made a subject of jest and ridicule. Death is at all times a solemn and an awful thing; but O, it is tenfold more terrible when it comes to summon men, in the very midst of ungodliness and profanity, into the presence of their Judge!

What we have said is equally true, and more manifestly true, with reference to such calamities as those to which our text specially refers,—those which come upon men without any apparent connection with sins or faults of their own. With respect to these, one or two reflections may not be deemed unsuitable or unseasonable. In the first place, then, we would remark that there is no special reason to regard such calamities as indications of God's wrath. It is appointed to men once to die, and there is no reason to attach a notion of the Divine displeasure to one form of death rather than another. There are three circumstances connected with such forms of death that painfully affect our feelings, the suddenness, the violence, and the number of sufferers. Now, as to the first, we do not care to discuss the question whether sudden death be desirable or not. The fact is, that to the unconverted sinner death is terrible, in whatever form it comes, but to the man who habitually walks with God, who knows that death will be to him the entrance into a life of glory and blessedness, it is perhaps an object worthy of desire, if God's will should be so, that he should be spared all previous suffering, and the pain of parting with the

objects of his affection, and pass at once from the active service of
his Lord on earth to the enjoyment of his blessed presence in
heaven.   And certainly, however we may think of it, we cannot
believe that God regards sudden death as necessarily an evil, for
in this way he has called many of His most faithful servants
from their work on earth to their rest and their reward in heaven.
You remember, for example, how our own Chalmers, when he had
finished the work in which he was engaged, folded his arms, and,
like a tired child, fell softly and peacefully asleep.   And then,
perhaps, we should consider that all death is really sudden.   A
man in a long illness expects something which is called death,
but he can form no idea of what that thing is; and, when it comes
upon him, it is probably so different from what he expected it to
be, that it has really come upon him without any warning.   And
then, as to violent deaths, it is perhaps merely in our feelings
that there is any reason for deprecating them.   To our feelings,
it is no doubt repulsive that the body should be mangled or
crushed.   But we may be sure that this is nothing to the person
dying.   In fact, we may say that the most violent death is, generally speaking, the easiest.   And, at all events, we may say of this,
as we just said of the suddenness of death, God has permitted it
to befal the best and most honoured of all His servants ; and therefore it cannot be necessarily a token of His anger.   Those of the
children of men who cluster closest around the throne of the
Lamb once slain, are, doubtless, the martyrs who have sealed their
testimony with their blood, and, at the stake or on the scaffold,
have died under the hand of the executioner.

Lastly, as to the numbers who are sometimes hurried away at
once by some appalling calamity, this also is fitted to impress the
survivors, but probably is unknown or unthought of by those
who suffer.   We are horrified, and well we may, when we hear
of seventy or more of our fellow-citizens being swept, by one fell
crash, out of this world, into the presence of their Judge ; but we
see in the columns of some of our newspapers a not much shorter
list of those who die daily ; and we know that, in point of fact,
about one of the human race dies in every second, or, in every
hour two hundred times the number of those on whom the
tower in Siloam fell, or fifty times the number that perished
in the late catastrophe.   From these simple considerations, then,
regarding death without any reference to what is to follow, we
come to a conclusion in accordance with that of our text, that
such calamities as that to which it refers are not to be regarded

as special inflictions of God's wrath, but that they may equally
befal the righteous and the wicked.

Our next reflection connected with this subject is, that death
is not in itself either a good or an evil. It is a fearful evil
to those who are at enmity with God, and are still liable to His
wrath and curse. It is to them the termination of their day of
grace and opportunity,—the shutting up for ever against them of
that door of repentance and faith, by which they might have
escaped the curse and received the blessing,—the entrance into
that state of hopeless unchangeableness, when it shall be pronounced regarding them, " Let the unrighteous be unrighteous
still, and the filthy be filthy still." But, saith the Scripture, the
righteous hath hope in his death. To him to live is Christ, and
to die is gain. It may be that he hath a desire to depart and to
be with Christ, which is far better ; but if he have not, this is
owing to his infirmity and the weakness of his faith; and if,
through the weakness of the flesh, he cannot look forward to death
without alarm, we may be sure that, the instant it has passed
upon him, he looks back upon it with exultation. If doubts and
fears perplex him in the prospect, there is nought but unmingled
joy in the retrospect. If, with his last living voice, he be not able
to sing the song of triumph ; yet, the first feeling of his emancipated soul is in harmony with that song, "O death, where was
thy sting ? O grave, where was thy victory ?" The sting of
death was sin, but that was all washed away in the blood of
Christ; and the strength of sin was the law, but that was all fulfilled and satisfied by the work of Christ; and now, thanks, everlasting thanks be to God, which hath given me the victory
through my Lord Jesus Christ !

When death, then, to these two classes of persons, is so
entirely a different thing,—to the one, the king of terrors, to the
other, the messenger of peace; to the one, the end of all good and
the beginning of unmitigated evil, to the other, the end of all evil
and the introduction to unmingled blessedness,—how shall we
pronounce upon a calamity in which both these classes may be
involved ? When two are in the field, the one may be taken and
the other left; when two are grinding at the mill, the one may
be taken and the other left ; when two are in one bed, the one
may be taken and the other left.

Brethren, it does not need the allusions that we have already
made in various parts of this discourse, to tell you why we have
selected this subject for our consideration to-day. There pro-

bably never occurred amongst us an event of a more impressive
or solemnising character, or one that has more completely occupied and absorbed the thoughts of all classes of our people, than
that which occurred in our neighbourhood on the evening of this
day week, by which four times the number of those who were
slain under the tower of Siloam perished by a similar casualty.
We have been anxious to impress upon you the conviction that
their death in this way was no indication of their being greater
sinners than others, or of their being subjected to this form of
death as a special punishment for special wickedness. There
were amongst them both sexes, and all ages. The old, who, in
the course of nature, could not have long to live; the middle-
aged, who, doubtless, expected that they had long years of life
and work before them; young men and maidens, in the full flush
of joyous youth; and the little child, that scarcely had tasted
either the sweet or the bitter of life's cup. All these were speed-
ing on their way in health and happiness. No warning voice
informed them of the doom that awaited them. And when they
were counting the minutes that must pass before their journey
should end, without forewarning the great crash came, and the shat-
tered carriages were made their graves. Amongst those three score
and ten, we may well hope that some, but we dare scarcely venture
to hope that all, were ready for so sudden a summons into the
presence of their Judge. Perhaps there were some amongst them
who had put off, from year to year, the work of repentance, thinking that it would be time enough when laid on a deathbed. And
perhaps there may be some of you who are doing the same, quite
aware that if you repent not you must perish, but thinking that
it will be time enough before you come to die. O, friends, be
persuaded not thus to delude your souls! It may be unlikely
that death shall come to you precisely as it came to them; but
the delirium of a fever is as effectual a bar to repentance as the
sudden rush of waters, or the pressure of a load of cold iron.
Depend upon it, that the very worst of all places in the world
for repentance is a death-bed; and if you wilfully put off repentance now, the probability may be measured by a hair's-
breadth that you will ever repent at all. But perhaps there
were amongst those travellers some who had, through the grace
of God, been enabled to lay hold of the blessed offer which the
gospel holds out to all, of justification, and acceptance, and
eternal life, through the obedience and death of the Son of God.
To these, the sudden call was but like the announcement of some

joyous tidings, which is apt to confound us for a moment, but which, when we realise its import, fills us with unutterable joy. These were like those who, with their loins girded, and their lamps burning, were waiting the coming of the bridegroom; and the fearful crash,—for even to them, as flesh and blood, it was fearful and confounding,—was but the intimation that He had come,—come to receive them to Himself—come to wipe away all tears for ever from their eyes,—come to introduce them to those mansions of eternal glory which He had prepared in heaven for them. Brethren, be ye also ready, for in such an hour as ye think not, the Son of man cometh. As, day by day, you travel on to the end of your pilgrimage, see that, having been once washed in the blood of Jesus, you constantly wash your feet, with the tears of repentance, from the defilement which they are apt to sustain from contact with an evil world; and, night by night, commit yourselves to the keeping of Him who is the Shepherd of Israel, and who neither slumbers nor sleeps.

And now, let us conclude with a few reflections which may be suggested by the appalling calamity which has occupied so much of our thought during the past week.

1. First of all, let us think of the littleness of human greatness, the foolishness of human wisdom, the feebleness of human power. It is of our engineering skill, and the magnitude of our engineering works, that we, in this country, are in the habit of boasting, as beyond all comparison with those of all other nations; of the abundance of iron and coal beneath our soil; of the practical power with which these are turned to account in the construction of works which are beyond the reach of other nations; of the enormous wealth which makes the construction of these works possible to us on a scale of gigantic magnitude; of the union of scientific accuracy with practical skill, which brings the construction of these works to the border of absolute perfection,—of all these things we are never weary of boasting. A few months ago we gave voice to this boasting in trumpet tones: "Is not this bridge of ours the triumph of engineering skill? Could any other nation have produced its like? Must not all foreigners now see that competition with us is like the puffing up of the frog in the fable? Will not our children, in generations to come, be proud of the triumphs of their fathers?" Thus, and thus, and endlessly thus, on all our platforms, and through all our press. Thus might we have spoken, thus written eight days ago. Thus, probably, we did speak or write yester-

day week, for did we not do it every day and all day? But
when Monday morning came, and the newspapers brought their
usual tidings to our homes, and when we read of the dire catastrophe, where was our boasting then? And what was it that
converted this mighty structure into a miserable wreck? Not
some mighty earthquake, causing the earth to tremble to its
centre; but a puff of that same wind which converts the soap-
bubble of the little child, with its perfect form and it rainbow
hues, into a drop of dirty water! "The voice said, Cry. And he
said, What shall I cry? All flesh is grass, and all the goodliness
thereof is as the flower of the field: The grass withereth, the
flower fadeth, because the breath of the Lord bloweth upon it:
surely the people is grass."

2. I read in one of our newspapers that some of our ministers
had agreed not to make capital—such was the expression—of
this calamity in the controversy regarding Sabbath travelling.
Of course I know that this is an ordinary conversational expression, and I should be the last to make a man an offender for a
word. But I must say that such language I do not understand.
It is not for me to make capital of this, or of aught else, for the
purpose of any controversy, or for the purpose of inculcating any
duty, or reprobating any sin. It is my part, as God shall give
me grace, rightly to divide the word of truth. That, and only
that, is the capital committed to my stewardship, to be dispensed
for the advancement of His glory, and for the salvation of my
fellow-men. And, moreover, I neither need any capital which
such a calamity can furnish, nor can it increase what I possess.
If, on the one hand, every Sabbath train were wrecked, it would
add nothing to the authority of the Divine command. If all enjoyed an absolute immunity from disaster, it would not diminish
that authority. It is very likely, in a parallel case, that it might
be proved by extensive observation and experience that honesty
is the best policy; but a thousand instances of men obtaining
competency and wealth by honest industry would not increase,
as a thousand instances of the wicked spreading like the green
bay-tree would not detract from, the authority of the command,
"Thou shalt not steal," and "Let him that stole steal no more."

With respect to this matter, then, I say at once, and say frankly,
that it is not for me to judge the living—far less is it for me to
judge the dead. Whether they, all or any of them, were travelling on works of necessity or mercy, I cannot tell. One thing is
certain, that they must have *thought* their journey necessary, as

no one would have gone on such a night for pleasure. My belief is that the standard of ordinary public opinion as to what constitutes necessity in this matter is all too low. But those who act according to this standard are not more guilty than the other members of the community who hold that standard; and, therefore, it is literally true, that those whom this calamity has befallen were not sinners above all the men of Galilee or Judea. But there is an aspect of the matter on which I hope that this calamity will lead men to ponder. It was first suggested by the *Scotsman*, and seems to be generally accepted as the most likely explanation of the matter, that it was the train that wrecked the bridge, and not the bridge that wrecked the train. If this view be correct, then it follows, that if that train had not been run, that bridge might have been standing now. And that train was a Sabbath train. These are the simple facts of the case, and they have a special bearing upon the interests of those who run these trains for the sake of gain. It were simple absurdity to deny that while Sabbath trains may occasionally be made subservient by passengers to purposes of necessity or mercy, it is primarily gain that the Railway Companies seek from them. Now, simply in this view,—and I frankly admit that it is a low view, but men must be met on their own ground,—it is unquestionable that the tremendous pecuniary loss incurred in one night will swallow up all the gains of all their Sabbath trains for years past, and for years to come. Would that all our traders,—from our great railway companies, down to our humble shopkeepers, whose gain consists of the minute profits on penny-worths of confectionery —would learn to enter into their profit-and-loss account the not unimportant element of the blessing of God, which maketh rich, —would learn that in the keeping of God's commands there is great reward.

3. Let us think, this day, of hundreds of hearts over which a devastating flood of sorrow is rolling, deeper and darker than the material flood that has engulphed the bodies of their beloved ones. Let our hearts go out in earnest sympathy towards the darkened dwellings and the saddened hearts; and let our sympathy convert itself—as Christian sympathy ever will—into fervent intercession on their behalf. To God the Comforter we commend them—to Him and to the Word of His grace. May He, whose dealings now seem to them so terrible, make Himself known to them as a God rich in mercy; and make them know that, while He is mighty to smite, He is almighty to save.

THE
PROBLEM OF UNDESERVED SUFFERING:

A

SERMON PREACHED BEFORE THE
UNIVERSITY OF GLASGOW,

BY

DAVID HUNTER, B.D.,
KELSO.

" And David spake unto the Lord when he saw the angel that smote the people, and said, Lo, I have sinned and I have done wickedly ; but these sheep, what have they done ? Let thine hand, I pray thee, be against me and against my father's house."—2 SAMUEL xxiv. 17.

DAVID'S sin in numbering the people was want of confidence in God. He numbered them that he might know how many fighting men he could count on, forgetting that with the Lord of hosts on his side, it mattered little whether his armies were small or great. Perhaps, too, he had some desire to put his kingdom on the same footing with those of the heathen around him, and to order his own policy instead of looking to God for guidance. At any rate, it is certain that for a time he lost his faith, and was in open rebellion against God. Then came his punishment,—a grievous punishment for the king who has the welfare of his people at heart. The choice had been given him of seven years' famine, or three months' flight before the enemy, or three days' pestilence ; and he had preferred to fall into the hands of the Lord. But now, when he heard how many of the people were dying, when he saw around him so many wasting away with sudden sickness, all on account of *his* sin, his heart smote him. He could bear his own punishment, which lay in seeing the large numbers of his own subjects so wofully diminished ; but he could not bear to see the punishment fall also on those who, in this matter at least, had done no wrong. Innocent and helpless, they were falling around him like sheep; and so, with all right feeling, he prays to God that the punishment might no longer fall on them, but on himself and on his own. The plague was stayed, but we are not told that those who were already dead were restored to life. The simple facts of the case seem to be, that David sinned against God, that he was punished for his sin, and that a large share of the punishment fell on others, who, so far as we know, had not shared in his sin. One man sins; his sin is punished; but the punishment falls on the innocent—that is the strange problem which rises before us on reading this chapter, and it is a problem which very often presents itself in the facts of human life. We are not so wholly given over to philanthropy as to think that sin should not be punished at all. Our native sense of right and wrong demands that when a sin is committed, it should be punished; and we perhaps think that, if we had the ordering of the world, the punishment would follow quickly,—stern, and certain, so that no doubt could arise as to its meaning. But our native sense of right and wrong starts back at what it observes in human life. Sin punished! Apparently it is at times; at other times apparently it is not. As often as not, the man that sinned seems to go scot-free, while many who had no part in the sin groan under its severe retribution. As often as not, when the retribution does fall on the right man, it falls also on others who had no share in the offence in question. It seems to be a blundering, imperfect state of things amidst which we are placed, where there is no natural and right sequence of moral events, and where retribution is only a stone thrown into the air, sometimes falling on the head of the right man, but sometimes not.

The problem is forced on our notice every day we live. A careless shipwright does not send his bolt or rivet home properly, and, in a storm at sea, a gallant ship founders, carrying with it many precious lives. A man commits a great crime; he is found out and punished, but the punishment does not stop with himself: it falls also on his family, who have to bear the shame and the reverse of fortune. A husband and father becomes a drunkard; the sin brings its inevitable punishment; but the punishment is as heavy on the wife, who is never free from anxious care, and on the children, who grow up weakly, uneducated, and wilful, for the lack of parental guidance. Two or

three men combine in a gigantic fraud; they are detected and
punished, and utter ruin falls on them; but the consequences of
the fraud, in a thousand ramifications, affect the happiness and
prosperity of a whole nation. A sovereign does not feel himself
secure on his throne, and, in order to surround himself with mili-
tary glory and strengthen his position, declares war against a
neighbouring people. The punishment of his ambition is disastrous to himself; but still worse are the calamities which come
on thousands of his unoffending subjects. Is not the suffering of
the innocent with the guilty, and for the guilty, one of the most
familiar facts in human life?

But, look, again, at another abundant source of the same undeserved suffering—the great fact of hereditary evil. " Visiting
the sins of the fathers upon the children unto the third and
fourth generation." " The fathers have eaten sour grapes, and
the children's teeth have been set on edge." Even if no such
words as these were found in the Bible, they would soon be said
by some one who had an eye to see and a heart to feel. And
this form of innocent suffering seems more unjust than any other,
as it certainly arouses more the individual sense of wrong. How
many a young heart has been burdened by it, has cried out against
it with passionate upbraiding, has found it difficult to believe that
there is any moral government in a world where such a thing
exists! " My father, or some remote ancestor, had his full swing
of sensual indulgence; and here I am to-day, with a constitution
so feeble that my life is one long dying." Or, again: " My
mother sinned,—sinned through the very abundance of her love
and trustfulness; why should I be therefore all my days with an
opprobrious name?" It is not easy to give an answer to such
interrogations, made passionate by the sense of personal suffering.
It is not easy to say why one should be born with rude health,
with loving friends, with sufficient means for acquiring culture;
while another, through his parents' sin, spends his childhood in the
gutters, grows up without knowledge of human love and tenderness, and, so far from obtaining culture, finds it difficult to lead
an honest life.

We would think it fair and right that each one should start
in life with the same chance of good and evil, and should have it
in his power to carve out his fortunes as seemeth good to him;
but it is only too plain that such is not the case. Some are over-
weighted from the very first; some spend all their lives in reaching the point from which others start; some struggle on for a

few years, and die in the bloom of youth, through inherited
feebleness of constitution. And even if we did all start with
the same chances, it is evident that we do not work through life
freely and independently; our aims are defeated, our efforts
crushed by events over which we have but little influence.
There is no need to multiply examples; the facts are patent to
all; they lie, at all times, smouldering in the heart, until, stirred
by some individual wrong, they break out into a burning discon-
tent. Job, sitting among his comforters and bewailing his unhappy fate; Prometheus, chained to the rock and defying the
unjust power that chains him; Philoctetes, left behind in his
misery on the desert island—these present, in the highest flights
of tragic poetry, what many a one feels bitterly in his own
thoughts—the truth that wrong-doing and suffering do not
always go together; and to those who believe in a Governor of
the universe, they present also some apparent justification for
the complaint of mankind, which is most briefly expressed in the
words of Solon to Crœsus, King of Lydia, "The Deity is altogether envious and full of confusion.*

So long as the facts are put in this way, I do not think it
possible to explain or palliate them. It is of no use to say, that,
looking to the whole experience of human history, sin is punished
and righteousness prospers. The doctrine of averages, however
true and consoling to the philosophizing observer, does not make
the individual wrong lighter. Nor is it of much use, I fear, to
point out that suffering is not always a misfortune, nor prosperity a gain; for the man who has been ruined by others' guilt,
the wife who has been bereaved through another's folly, the
youth who finds himself cramped and fettered by the circumstances of his birth, does not cry out against the suffering so
much as against the seeming injustice and unfairness.

But let us look at all these facts from another point of view.
Our difficulty hitherto has been, that the innocent have often to
suffer for the guilty, that punishment often falls on those who
have not deserved it. But what are we to say about the *enjoyment
of benefits* for which we have not laboured, the reaping of reward
where there has been no desert on our part? Is there not such
a thing as receiving good where we had not earned it? And,
when we talk of the innocent suffering with or for the guilty,
should we not also speak of the undeserving being blessed with

* Herod. I. 32.

L

prosperity along with the deserving, or even instead of the deserving? We cry out passionately against receiving less than
justice in the arrangements of the universe; but do we not sometimes receive more than our just share? To go back to the case
from which we started: the people were suffering in Israel on
account of the sin of their king; but had they not derived great
benefit from the same king's good government, or success in
war? They were involved in the consequences of his wrong-
doing—which seems to us very unjust—but had they not also
become great through his greatness, honoured through his
honour? If they did not deserve to share in his punishment,
can we say that they deserved to share in his prosperity? But
the same is true of life generally. If we suffer where we have
not sinned, do we not also prosper where we have not proved
worthy? If, after all our toils and honest exertions, our hopes
are defeated through the fault of others, do we not also reap
where we have not sowed, and gather where we have not
strawed? If the wrong-doing of others sometimes brings an
undeserved retribution on our heads, is it not true that every
day some happiness is added to our lot, through the right-doing
of others? There are kind and sympathetic words which cheer
us amid our sorrows; there are generous acts which bring us
much-needed, but unexpected assistance in our difficulties; there
are upright, honourable men, whose lives sweeten the moral
atmosphere around us, and make our own lives more tolerable;—
can we say that any of these things come of our deserving?
The fraud of two or three men causes a notional calamity; but
the honest dealing of a thousand others, with their conscientious
discharge of duty, makes the nation prosperous, secures to very
many the advantages of an easy income with little trouble to
themselves, and preserves the country from bankruptcy, moral
and commercial; and if the calamity is undeserved, surely we
cannot say that we have deserved all the prosperity.

Just think, for a moment, how, in a hundred ways, we reap
the benefit of other men's labours; how our enormous material
prosperity during this century has been chiefly due to James
Watt's invention of the steam-engine, so that thousands have
now the opportunity of culture and refinement who otherwise
would have been toiling in the fields all day, with dulled senses
and faculties of thought disused. Think how many lives are
saved every year in our coal-mines by Sir Humphrey Davy's
lamp; think how much physical suffering has been spared us, in

the practice of surgery, by the discovery of nitrous oxide and chloroform; think how many pure and pleasant thoughts have come to us through the work of some great poet, or painter, or musician; think how much the Scottish people have owed for generations to those far-seeing ancestors who provided means of education, and founded such seats of learning as our own loved Alma Mater—and say, is it not emphatically true, that, if we suffer by the sins of our fellow-men, we benefit also by their virtues? Here, again, it would be easy to furnish examples; it is sufficient to observe the general principle, that the influence of other men on our fortunes is for good as well as for evil. If it be true that we sometimes suffer for others' evil deeds, then it is also true that we are sometimes the gainers by their good deeds. Already we begin to see that the passionate outcry against the arrangements of the universe proceeds from a very narrow and one-sided conception of things.

But look further at the problem of hereditary evil—"the sins of the fathers coming on the children"—is there not also such a thing as hereditary good? We have not all inherited feeble constitutions from our ancestors, or the race would come to an end; we are not all placed in circumstances where we cannot lead an honest life, otherwise, society would cease to exist. As an actual fact, hereditary evil is the exception; and what we have to consider, in most cases, is the great fact of hereditary good, which is as little deserved by us as the evil. Is it not the case with many of us that the patient industry, the upright conduct, and the virtuous lives of our fathers and forefathers, have surrounded us with advantages from the very moment of our birth,—advantages which they perhaps were morally bound to secure for us, but which we have in no sense earned by our own merit? If our fathers and forefathers were only discharging their duty, none the less have they, in such ways, conferred great blessings upon us. If the youth who begins the battle of life with a constitution enfeebled by hereditary disease, has just ground for complaint; if the man who, through his parents' sin, has been reared amid vice and crime, seems to have reason for inveighing against the harsh dealings of Providence; surely there are hundreds and thousands who have cause to be thankful for sound health, good upbringing, a liberal education, and the means of starting well in life. The sins of the fathers are indeed visited on the children; but no less truly must we say that the virtues of the fathers descend on the children in showers of blessing. Is it not plainer than ever, that the influence of others on our fate is for good quite as much as for evil ?

Thus far our considerations have involved no principle distinctively religious. We are dealing with facts which are facts to the Atheist or Agnostic quite as much as to the Christian. I have been trying to shew you that the problem has two sides; that there are two things, and not one, to be considered. There is undeserved good as well as undeserved evil. The truth is, that we too commonly approach such questions in the wrong way. We consider the constitution of the universe as if each human being in it were, or ought to be, free, independent, self-centred— a moral atom in short. Now, however useful the atomic theory may be in the natural sciences—and it may be useful in them, whether there really are such things as atoms or not—the theory has no place in morals or in human life. We do not stand towards each other as atoms acting freely and independently. Our interests, our fortunes, our happiness, even our life, are all affected by the conduct of others, whether we will it or not. If by freedom of the will is meant perfect independence of action, then we must say at once that no such thing exists; and, if it did exist, it would produce monsters and not men. Our freedom lies in the power of choosing, but the materials for the choice are not of our making; they come entirely from our relations with our fellow-men. We have, indeed, the liberty to carve out our own fortunes, but the stuff from which we are to carve them is not of our selecting, and in no two cases is it alike.

Up to this point, we have only reached this conclusion—that our weal and woe are indissolubly linked with the actions of our fellow-men, that from this connection there come to us both good and evil, and that we must be content to take the evil with the good. Now, how does the gospel of Christ stand to all this? Does it help us further in solving the problem ? It does give a complete solution, but in a very unexpected way. So far from regarding this problem of undeserved suffering as a part of the universe to be explained or defended, Christianity takes it up as the *starting-point* of its moral teaching. I take it, that, apart from the purely theological information regarding God and His dealings with man, the cardinal point in the practical teaching of Christianity is given in the words of Christ when he said, "This is my commandment, that ye love one another as I have loved you ;" and these words change what we have been considering as a painful fact into a plain and imperative duty. Love is the

SERMON BY DAVID HUNTER, B.D.   165

feeling which makes all our relations to our fellow-men tend to good—I mean, love in the highest and purest sense. Even in a lower sense, when the love is a preference for one fellow-creature over all others, its tendency is to good, for it creates the desire to promote that one's happiness and well-being in every way. The highest love—Christian love—is simply the same feeling extended to all our fellow-creatures alike; and when a man is fully possessed by it, he becomes a centre of good to all around him. We have hardly yet come to know what is meant by a man loving his neighbour as himself; but the progress of humanity is towards that truth, and it is the cardinal point in Christian morality.

Now, see how all this bears on our problem. The universe is so ordered that we live in the closest relations to one another; we exercise an immense influence over one another's fortunes, both for good and evil. We accept the good without acknowledging it with gratitude; we receive the evil with loud complainings against fate, and passionate upbraidings against Providence; but all the time we think only of ourselves. Christ bids us think of others. While we complain because we suffer from others' wrong-doing, Christ says to us, "Take heed that others do not suffer from your wrong-doing. You live in close relation with your fellow-man; then see to it that, from this relation, nothing but good flows to him; love even your enemies, bless even them that curse you, do good even to them that hate you; in all things strive to make your fellow-man better, happier, nobler, by loving him with all your heart." In short, while we cry out about our rights, Christ bids us think of our duties; while we think only of the claims we have on others, He calls us to consider also the claims which others have on us. In this there seems to me to lie the true solution of the problem. We must cease to look at it with purblind selfishness of vision; we must not continue to ask the one question, "Why should I suffer, being innocent?" but we must also ask, "Why should I receive benefit when I have neither laboured nor deserved?" and above all, we must ask, "How can I live and act, so that my life and actions shall bring good, and good only, to my fellow-men?"

It needs a very great deal to purify our thoughts from selfishness when we approach the consideration of any subject. Try as we may, self interferes, and at once our clear vision is dimmed, our large thoughts are contracted, our meditations on Providence and destiny are turned into weak, querulous complainings. The plain facts of the universe teach us that we cannot live our lives

apart from one another. A life of utter solitude would be the
death of all the higher faculties ; and, instead of being men with
large discourse of reason looking before and after, we would only
be animals fighting out a miserable and brutish existence. We
cannot live our lives freely and independently ; but, so far from
repining at this supposed hardship, we ought to welcome that community of suffering and prosperity which links our fortunes with
those of others, which merges our selfish individuality in the great
interests of the race, which gives us wider thoughts, warmer feelings, larger lives. We utter passionate complaints about our own
wrongs and woes, about the evil influences which our fellow-men
exercise on our fortunes ; but we should utter heartfelt acknow-
ledgments of boundless good received from the good offices of
those who went before, and those who are living now. We are
related to one another, not as Alpine peaks rising from a cold sea
of mist,—divided, solitary ; but as stones which help each other in
building up the great fabric of God's world. God has clearly
meant it to be so. Not one of us lives to himself or dies to himself ; the living or dying, even of the humblest man, has its influence on some other fellow-creature for evil or for good. What a
changed world it would be, if all such influence—if the influence
of every man's living and dying—were an unmixed good to
others ! Where, then, would be the undeserved suffering which
at present seems such a grievous wrong ? But Christ's command
has, for its practical result, the direction of every man's influence
for good ; and the whole essence of Christian morality lies in the
words of St John, " Little children, love one another." If we
could only adopt, in its entirety, the principle of Christ's commandment, we would be vexed no more by perplexing doubts
and anxious fears,—we would find, in this *solidarity* of the
human race, our greatest strength and our best educator. Suffering, whether deserved or undeserved, can always be traced to sin ;
and sin has its root in the selfishness of our thoughts, feelings and
actions. If love were to take the place of selfishness in every
human heart, sin would be unknown, its consequent suffering
unheard of, and earth be changed from a purgatory into a para-
dise. " A fanciful dream all this," it may be said ; but I humbly
think it is the consummation towards which our Christian faith
is striving : love everywhere ; love towards our neighbour, mani-
festing itself in unceasing kindliness and thoughtful benevolence ;
love towards God, expressing itself in the noblest aspirations to
become like Him whose love passeth knowledge.

In spite of the eighteen centuries and a half which are now nearly completed since Christ lived and died in the world, Christianity, as a moral force among men, is little more than in its infancy. Whatever power it may have had over individual hearts, in cleansing them from sin and widening them to some comprehension of God's love, the full significance of its teaching has been little felt on society as a whole. But more and more, as men become possessed by this intense feeling of sympathy with their fellows, this single-hearted desire to make all their influence on them tell for good, this death of all selfishness, this regenerator of the moral nature which Christ called forth, and which we denominate love,—more and more the evils under which the race of men now groan will disappear. We often speak of the triumphs of Christianity, but its triumphs have been small compared with what will be in the future. There will come a time when war will be no longer waged, because the angry passions from which it arose shall have disappeared : there will come a time when our pity for the misery of others will be so great that we shall not rest until we have removed all causes of their misery ; there will come a time when benevolence will not be stinted, because we fear to see it abused ; there will come a time when all the strifes and dissensions which attend our ignorance and our narrow views of God and His universe will be forgotten, and men will be able to differ on nice points of doctrine without consigning those who hold the opposite opinion to the pains of everlasting condemnation ; there will come a time when men will be no longer clamorous about their wrongs and their rights, charging Providence or destiny with their sufferings, but will be eager to learn how best they can discharge their duties ; there will come a time when the tumult and discord, which now rise before high Heaven, will pass into a grand harmony of love and concord ;—and then shall Christ, the Prince of Peace, indeed reign on earth. That time seems very far off to us now. The fervent love of our fellow-man, which alone can make its coming possible, seems to us a thing not to be attained. Only once has it been seen in perfect form on earth, and that was in Him who taught the truth and gave the commandment. He, at least, thought it possible to bind men together by the closest ties, to awaken the fervent love of humanity in every man, to purge every heart from its selfishness ; and His method was to cause all men to love Himself. Left in its simple form, the principle might have remained cold and lifeless, incapable of rousing enthusiasm, destitute of all kindling energy; and over many it would have had no power, through its vagueness and generality. But He summoned men to love one another through their love for Himself; He gave them an example of what that love should be; He endured undeserved suffering Himself, without a murmur; and, even at the point of an unjust death, thought nothing of his own wrongs, but much of others' welfare. And shall we say that he has done all this in vain? No, it has not been in vain. It has awakened, in return, a love which has been the strength and substance of many a noble life. The love of mankind towards the Son of man, the suffering Saviour, in spite of the blindness which has misconceived it, the intolerance which has made it a means of division, and the baseness which has degraded it by a canting profession, has made men purer, nobler, more Christ-like; and our earnest prayer should be, that, in the ages to come, that love may grow towards Him and towards our fellow-men, so that at last we may be able to abide for ever in the presence of God, whose very nature is love. "Unto Him that loved us and washed us from our sins in His own blood, and hath made us kings and priests unto God, His Father; to Him be glory and dominion, for ever and ever" Amen.

JACOB'S DEATHBED:

A SERMON.

BY

WILLIAM MARSHALL, D.D.,
COUPAR-ANGUS

"By faith, Jacob, when he was a-dying, blessed both the sons of Joseph ; and worshipped, *leaning* upon the top of his staff."—HEB. xi. 21.

"The chamber where the good man meets his fate,
Is privileged beyond the common walks
Of virtuous life, quite on the verge of heaven."

So the pious Cowper sweetly sang; and we are naturally reminded of the lines by such a passage of holy writ as this. The apostle had said of the patriarchs, in the thirteenth verse of this chapter, "These all died in faith." They lived by faith, and one after another of them died in faith ; and this he particularly exemplifies in the case of Jacob. It is into his dying chamber that the text conducts us. Let us enter it; let us tarry in it for a little, and contemplate the scene which it presents to us.

I. *See Jacob, when a-dying, leaning upon the top of his staff.*

Moses tells us in Gen. xlvii. 31, that "Israel bowed himself upon the bed's head;" and some have felt a difficulty about what they have termed the seeming discrepancy between Moses and Paul. There is no discrepancy between them. The occasions to which the historian and the apostle refer are different. When Moses says that "Israel bowed himself upon the bed's head," he refers to the visit which Joseph paid him, when he took an oath of him that he would carry up his remains to Canaan, and lay them in the sepulchre of his fathers. The whole paragraph runs thus: "And the time drew nigh that

Israel must die; and he called his son Joseph, and said unto him, If now I have found grace in thy sight, put, I pray thee, thy hand under my thigh, and deal kindly and truly with me; bury me not, I pray thee, in Egypt: but I will lie with my fathers; and thou shalt carry me out of Egypt, and bury me in their burying-place. And he said, I will do as thou hast said. And he said, Swear unto me. And he sware unto him. And Israel bowed himself upon the bed's head." When Paul says that "Israel leaned upon his staff," he refers to a subsequent visit which Joseph paid him, when he heard that sickness had overtaken him, in addition to the infirmities of age. "It came to pass after these things, that *one* told Joseph, Behold, thy father is sick: and he took with him his two sons, Manasseh and Ephraim," Gen. xlviii. 1.

It may be farther observed, that our best critics and commentators are agreed, that the statement of Moses, referring to the former of those occasions, "Israel bowed himself on the bed's head," would be better translated, "Israel worshipped upon his staff's head:" he worshipped, leaning on, or bending over the head of his staff. We are much inclined to think that Jacob did this on both the occasions referred to. If he required to do it when he was only infirm, much more must he have required to do it when he was also sick. That he did it on the first occasion, the historian expressly affirms; and it appears to us that the apostle affirms no less expressly that he did it on the second. Thus understood, there is no shadow of discrepancy between Moses and Paul: Paul only adding, as to the second visit, a very natural circumstance which Moses had not noted.

Jacob, when on his deathbed, "leaned upon the top of his staff." What a picture of human frailty! What an illustration of the touching words of the ninetieth psalm, that the very "strength" of old men "is labour and sorrow!" The days of the years of Jacob's pilgrimage had stretched out to a hundred forty and seven years, and exhausted nature was now ready to sink under the load. He, whose vigorous constitution had enabled him to bear so much travel and labour, and so much exposure by day and by night, was now reduced to a state of the utmost feebleness; and if he is to be raised for a little from his recumbent posture, he must be propped with his staff. "The glory of young men is their strength;" but they have need to consider and lay to heart, that in extreme age "the keepers of the house tremble," and even "the grasshopper is a burden."

But we have more here than the patriarch's bodily frailty. He was worshipping; and he had put his body—he had studiously put his body, though in his feebleness it required no small effort to do so—into the best posture for that solemn work.   He assumed the attitude which might best help and best express his heart's devotion.   "Bodily exercise profiteth little."   In worship, bodily attitude profiteth little.   But it is not, therefore, a matter of absolute indifference.   God is to be glorified in our bodies as well as in our spirits.   The seraphim are represented as covering their faces and their feet with their wings when they adore in His presence.   Our blessed Lord himself, in the days of His flesh, kneeled when He prayed: He kneeled three times in the garden, and poured out the agony of His soul with strong crying and tears.   So Jacob, sinking, as he was, under the debility of approaching dissolution, when he would worship, rose on the bed on which he lay: he "strengthened himself, and sat upon the bed;" though he had to support himself in that posture by leaning upon his staff.

We may add, that in this he sustained to the last, and very beautifully sustained, the confession which he had made all his life long.   He had "confessed that he was a stranger and a pilgrim in the earth."   Wherever we see him in his sojournings, we see him with the pilgrim's staff in his hand; and, lo! he has it in his hand still, he is grasping it, and leaning on it, on his dying bed.

May not this staff, too, have been the very same staff with which he had passed over the Jordan long, long ago, when he was fleeing to Padan-aram from the wrath of Esau ?   And if so, what a train of most thrilling associations would cluster around it! Many a year had it been the companion of his wanderings; and now that he was about to lay it aside for ever, what memories, what moving and melting memories, the very touch of it would awaken in his breast!

II. *See Jacob, when a-dying, worshipping.*

He "worshipped, leaning upon the top of his staff."   He "worshipped."   Men generally die as they live; and Jacob's death-bed exercise was in fine keeping with his life.   He had his infirmities, as every one has; but he was a man who, with all his infirmities, had led a devout life, a life of worship.   He raised his altar to God wherever he went; he lived near the throne; he breathed much of the atmosphere of that "better country," the ceaseless employ of which is worship; and now that he was on the verge of it, we behold him worshipping.

There is no reason to think that there has been left on record a full account of his worship, when he was on his beathbed. But piety is essentially the same in all its subjects, and in all ages of the world. This is an axiom; and, proceeding on it, we are at no loss to conceive what the worship of the dying patriarch was. It doubtless included *confession*—humble self-denying, self-abasing confession. Some persons talk much of looking back from a deathbed on a well-spent life. The good man, in so far as he has differed from others, knows who made him to differ. But in the review of the past, O how little he sees that he can contemplate with satisfaction; and how much to lay him in the dust, and to strip him of all confidence in the flesh! He feels that he has been an unprofitable servant; and in his last approaches on earth to the throne, even more than on all previous occasions, he says. " If thou, Lord, shouldest mark iniquities, O Lord, who shall stand? I come, trusting not in anything in myself, or done by myself, but in the mercies and in the plenteous redemption that are with thee. I come, desiring only to win Christ, and to be found in Him."

> " Not in mine innocence I trust ;
> I bow before thee in the dust ;
> And through my Saviour's blood alone
> I look for mercy at the throne."

Again, Jacob's deathbed worship doubtless included *thanksgiving*. What grateful emotions must have fired his bosom, as he thought of all the way in which the Lord had led him, so signally fulfilling the promises made to him, "I will surely do thee good "—" Behold, I am with thee, and will keep thee in all places whither thou goest, and will not leave thee till I have done that which I have spoken to thee of!" Bethel and its vision; his safe arrival, after a journey of several hundred miles, much of it through trackless deserts, at the house of the churlish Laban; the building up of his family and his fortune during his exile there; his return to Canaan; Mahanaim and its vision; Peniel and its vision; his peaceful and happy meeting with his brother Esau; the wonderful issue of the sorrows that had wrung from his heart these words of anguish, "Joseph is not, and Simeon is not, and ye will take Benjamin away. All these things are against me;" his going down into Egypt; Beersheba and its vision; the ecstacy with which he embraced his long-lost Joseph, and said, "Now let me die, since I have seen thy face, because thou art yet alive;" his comfort, and happiness, and honour, for the seventeen years that he and his family had dwelt in Goshen —how the memories of these, and of many such things, would now crowd upon him! And as they crowded upon him, how he would say, in low and tremulous, but fervent tones, "Bless the Lord, O my soul; and all that is within me, bless his holy name. Bless the Lord, O my soul, and forget not all his benefits!"

Yet again, Jacob's deathbed worship doubtless included prayer, properly so called, that is, *petition*, supplication. He had yet to die. He had yet to take the solemn and awful step into eternity. And we may be sure that, in view of it, he implored dying grace, with all the importunity and power of "a prince with God." "O God, be not far from me; O my God, make haste to help me. O God, thou hast taught me from my youth, and hitherto I have declared thy wondrous works; and now, Lord, leave me not, when I am old and gray-headed, and when flesh and heart are failing me. Into thine hand I commit my my spirit: thou hast redeemed me, O Lord God of truth. Into thine hand I commit my dust, that in the grave it may be in thy keeping, and that in my flesh I may see God. I have waited for thy salvation, O Lord; help me to glorify thee in the death by which I am now to pass to the full and eternal enjoyment of it."

III. *See Jacob, when a-dying, blessing the sons of Joseph.*

"Jacob, when he was a-dying, blessed both the sons of Joseph." We have the history referred to in Gen. xlviii., and in the narrative of Moses there is a simplicity and pathos which no words of ours could approach. Hearing of his father's illness in Goshen, Joseph hastened to visit him. It might be, it turned out to be, his last illness on earth; and all Joseph's honours and engagements in his exalted station must not prevent the performance of this last act of filial piety. His two sons, Manasseh and Ephraim, who had been born to him in Egypt, and brought up amid all the splendours of Pharaoh's court, he took with him, that they might receive the patriarch's blessing, and that the scene they were likely to witness might make a deep and lasting impression on their minds. Ushered into the dying chamber, Jacob broke silence, beginning with the Lord's appearance, and blessing, and promise to him at Luz, and with the double interest which Joseph's family had in that promise. Then—

"Israel beheld Joseph's sons, and said, Who are these? And Joseph said unto his father, They are my sons, whom God hath given me in this place. And he said, Bring them, I pray thee, unto me, and I will bless them. (Now the eyes of Israel were dim for age, so that he could not see.) And he brought them near unto him; and he kissed them and embraced them. And Israel said unto Joseph, I had not thought to see thy face; and, lo, God hath shewed me also thy seed. And Joseph brought them out from between his knees, and he bowed himself with his face to the earth. And Joseph took them both, Ephraim in his right hand toward Israel's left hand, and Manasseh in his left hand toward Israel's right hand, and brought them near unto him. And Israel stretched out his right hand, and laid it upon Ephraim's head, who was the younger, and his left hand upon Manasseh's head, guiding his hands wittingly; for Manasseh was the first-born. And he blessed Joseph, and said, God, before whom my fathers Abraham and Isaac did walk, the God which fed me all my life long unto this day, the Angel which redeemed me from all evil, bless the lads; and let my name be named on them, and the name of my fathers Abraham and Isaac; and let them grow into a multitude in the midst of the earth. And when Joseph saw that his father laid his right hand upon the head of Ephraim, it displeased him: and he he held up his father's hand, to remove it from Ephraim's head unto Manasseh's head. And Joseph said unto his father, Not so, my father, for this is the first-born; put thy right hand upon his head. And his father refused, and said, I know it, my son, I know it: he also shall become a people, and he also shall be great; but truly his younger brother shall be greater than he, and his seed shall become a multitude of nations. And he blessed them that day saying, In thee shall Israel bless, saying, God make thee as Ephraim, and as Manasseh. And he set Ephraim before Manasseh."

Thus "Jacob, when a-dying, blessed both the sons of Joseph." He blessed them as a dying saint, and a dying grandfather, invoking on them the blessing of Jacob's God, the blessing of Him who blesses and no man can curse; the blessing of Him whose covenant with His people is, "I will be a God unto thee, and to thy seed after thee." But he blessed them also as a dying prophet. Under the influence of the Spirit of prophecy, he foresaw and foretold the blessing that would descend and rest upon them. And, it did so, as their subsequent history shows. The best commentary on the patriarch's prophetic benediction is the record we have of the tribes of Ephraim and Manasseh in the historic books of Scripture.

Jacob, on his deathbed, blessed the sons of Joseph ; and what is that to us ? Much, in many ways : in particular, it reads to us one great lesson. It says to us, Be ye useful to the last. Be ambitious to do good, be ambitious to bless, not only living, but dying. And what means of usefulness, what opportunities of good-doing, does a deathbed like Jacob's furnish ? If it shall be our lot to be laid on such a deathbed ; if we shall have the possession of our reason ; if we shall have freedom from agonising pain ; if we shall have the requisite strength of body ; if we shall be surrounded by dear friends eager to catch every syllable that shall fall from our lips :—O, will it not be well that our words be words of blessing ? Will it not be well that they hear them rising to the throne for a blessing on them ; and directing, entreating, and charging them to walk in the way in which the blessing runs ? Parting words, words uttered in death's parting, how peculiarly impressive and memorable they are, and what a blessing has often been in them ! Even children, who had trampled on the living counsels of fathers and grandfathers, have not seldom followed their dying admonitions. The commendations of religion by dying saints ; the comforts of the Holy Ghost experienced by them ; the prayers they have breathed, and the charges they have left behind them : how many will have to bless God for ever and ever for being eye-witnesses and ear-witnesses of such things as these ! The scene has bequeathed to pious survivors a comfort which they would not part with for a thousand worlds. It has encouraged the fearful. It has awakened the careless. It has softened the obdurate. It has convinced the unbelieving. It has constrained even the Balaams of the world to do homage to religion, by crying, " Let me die the death of the righteous, and let my last end be like his ! "

IV. *See Jacob, when a-dying, exemplifying the power of faith.*

" By faith Jacob, when he was a-dying, blessed both the sons of Joseph ; and worshipped, leaning upon the top of his staff." It was faith that made his deathbed the scene which we have been contemplating for a little. It was faith which gave it all that renders it so instructive and so impressive to us. In all that we have now been looking at, we have been witnessing the working, the solace, the joy, the victory, of faith. And a great sight it verily is, to see faith not only enduring to the end, but supporting and cheering the heart when "the earthly house of this tabernacle" is falling, and triumphing in the last and solemn hour.

It was so with Jacob's faith. Did he, when a-dying, bless the sons of Joseph? It was by faith. It was in the faith of what God had revealed to him concerning them. And, on his death-bed, his faith had manifold other exercises. Did he, for ex-ample, command his sons to carry him up, and bury him in the cave of Machpelah? It was by faith that he did this. It was in the confidence that God would surely visit them, and restore them to their own land. The burial of his dust in it would be as it were, taking infeftment of it. Did he, when a-dying, take a retrospect of the leading passages in his pilgrimage? He did so by faith; tracing all that had entered into his lot to the mercy and the faithfulness of the "God who had fed him all his life long, of the Angel of the covenant who had redeemed him from all evil." Did he, when a-dying, descry among his posterity the Messiah, the Hope of Israel and the Saviour thereof? He descried and hailed Him by faith. Did he, when a-dying, look beyond the boundaries of time and sense, and recognise the earthly Canaan as the type of the heavenly, and his death as his entrance into it? All this he did by faith,—that faith which, resting on the word of God, resting on the promises of God, "is the substance of things hoped for, the evidence of things not seen."

And the same faith we shall all need, when, like Jacob, we are a-dying. Men may contrive to live without faith; but how shall they die without it? Dying, as has been truly said, "is hard work;" and, ah! the faithless will find it to be hard work. "I have provided," said one of them, "in the course of my life, for everything except death; and now, alas! I am to die, although entirely unprepared." But faith can make dying work easy work. "I can smile on death," said a believer, as he faced it, "because my Saviour smiles on me." Simeon, with the babe in the arms of his flesh, and the Consolation of Israel in the arms of his faith, could say,—and many like him, with the same Jesus in the embrace of faith, have said,—"Now, lettest thou thy ser-vant depart in peace, for mine eyes have seen thy salvation." Who does not instinctively cry out, "O that I may die thus! O, Thou God of all grace, inspire my soul with this divine prin-ciple, with this precious faith!"

We conclude with a single reflection. This subject brings before us, with much prominence and power, one unspeakable

advantage of a life of religion. It ends well. It always ends
well. " Mark the perfect man, and behold the upright ; for the
end of that man is peace." Look forward to the end, Christians,
and let the prospect of it sustain and animate you amid all the
troubles of the way. These will soon be over, and they will be
richly compensated at last. You will not regret them when you
are a-dying. Though the voyage may be often stormy, and even
tempestuous, you will not repent of the choice you had made,
when you are entering the haven of eternal rest. You will bless
the Lord for all the way He had led you through the wilderness ;
finding that all that entered into it was blessing, though much,
very much of it, may have been " blessing in disguise."

And, fellow-sinners, will you not be at length persuaded to
be wise ? We have been already saying, that you may contrive
to live without faith ; but how shall you die without it ? It is
only repeating the same thing in other words, to say that you
may contrive to live without religion ; but how shall you die
without it ? When your immortal spirits are struggling to burst
the tenement of clay ; when it can contain them no longer ; when
you are on the brink of eternity ; when the gloomy vale stretches
out before you, and you have the immediate prospect of standing
at the judgment-seat ; how, O how will you then bear up, if you
are strangers to religion ?

> " How shocking must thy summons be, O Death !
> To him that is at ease in his possessions ;
> Who, counting on long years of pleasure here,
> Is quite unfurnished for the world to come !
>   In that dread moment, how the frantic soul
> Raves round the walls of her clay tenement,
> Runs to each avenue, and shrieks for help,
> But shrieks in vain ! How wishfully she locks
> On all she's leaving, now no longer hers !
> O, might she stay to wash away her stains,
> And fit her for the passage ! Mournful sight !
> Her very eyes weep blood, and every groan
> She breathes is big with sorrow. But the Foe,
> Like a staunch murderer, steady to his purpose,
> Pursues her close through every lane of life,
> Nor misses once the track, but presses on,
> Till, forced at last to the tremendous verge,
> At once she sinks to everlasting ruin ! "

Fellow-sinners, this is what your deathbed will be to you,
continuing what you are ! But why should you ? Be persuaded,
O be persuaded to seek Jacob's faith. If you live without it,

M

there is tremendous hazard of your dying without it; for, as we have said already, men do generally die as they live. Seek faith, and seek it now. It cannot be gotten too soon, and you cannot be too sure that you have it. It is a matter of life and death ; a matter of eternal life and eternal death. "Hear instruction, and be wise, and refuse it not." "Forsake the foolish, and live ; and go in the way of understanding." "How long, ye simple ones, will ye love simplicity, and the scorners delight in their scorning, and fools hate knowledge ? Turn ye at my reproof : behold, I will pour out my Spirit unto you, I will make known my words unto you."

THE VOICE FROM THE EXCELLENT GLORY:

A SERMON.

BY

ROBERT ELDER, D. D.,

WEST FREE CHURCH, ROTHESAY.

"And behold, a voice out of the cloud, which said, This is my beloved Son, in whom I am well pleased; hear ye Him."—MATTHEW xvii. 5.

THE Lord of Glory lived in this world,—"despised and rejected of men; a man of sorrows, and acquainted with grief." But, besides the testimony of His glorious miracles, there were glimpses of His Divine Majesty given in His times of deepest humiliation. One of the most notable of these we have in the narrative before us.

We learn from the chapter preceding, that, about this period of His public ministry, Jesus began to forewarn the disciples of His approaching sufferings and death. But immediately thereafter came this great event of His transfiguration, narrated by three of the Evangelists with historic calmness and precision, and bearing the full stamp of Divine reality. It is, beyond doubt, an incident of great spiritual significance, designed to cheer the holy human soul of the Redeemer in the prospect of His agonies; to manifest to the disciples, for their encouragement, the glory of that death which they deprecated; to transfigure, if I may so speak, the cross itself; to proclaim Him Lord and Lawgiver of His Church; and to foreshadow His future glorified condition.

It is not my intention to speak of the facts and circumstances in detail, but, while adverting to these, to fix your minds *specially* on this sublime statement of the fifth verse, "And behold, a voice out of the cloud which said, This is my beloved Son, in whom I am well pleased; hear ye Him." May the Lord teach us by His Spirit, giving "the light of the knowledge of the glory of God, in the face of Jesus Christ."

I. *Let us consider whose voice it was that spake.*

We are told that, while Peter was uttering his rash proposal mentioned in the verse preceding,—" behold, a bright (or luminous) cloud overshadowed them" (namely, the three glorified ones, Jesus, Moses, and Elias), separating them from the three disciples; and that then a voice was heard by the disciples, proceeding out of the cloud, and uttering the testimony which is here recorded. It is significantly added in the next verse—" And when the disciples heard it, they fell on their face and were sore afraid."

Looking at the whole facts mentioned, we cannot reasonably suppose that this cloud was some mere natural phenomenon, or any other than the glorious *Shechinah* cloud, the symbol of the Divine presence all through the old dispensation. We read of it at the setting up of the tabernacle, and again at the consecration of the temple, when, as it is written, "the cloud filled the house of the Lord, so that the priests could not stand to minister because of the cloud: for the glory of the Lord had filled the house of the Lord" (1 Kings viii. 10, 11). Hence it is called by Peter, who was one of the three eye-witnesses on this occasion, "*the excellent glory;*" and he casts the light of inspiration on the question before us by this clear, definite statement,—" He re-received from *God the Father* honour and glory, when there came such a voice to Him from the excellent glory, This is my beloved Son in whom I am well pleased" (2 Peter i. 17). Beyond all question it was the voice of God the Father.

But these facts, on which I need not dwell, convey to us important practical lessons. In our present state, even when spiritually enlightened, we are not fit to bear the manifestation of heavenly glory, with its blissful fellowships and enjoyments. The symbol-cloud also teaches us that here we cannot see to the end of the things that are revealed; while the *voice* from the cloud reminds us that, in this world, Christ's people must "walk by faith, not by sight." It is the same great and solemn lesson which the Lord taught Israel of old by Moses,—"Take ye, therefore, good heed unto yourselves; for ye saw no manner of similitude on the day that the Lord spake unto you in Horeb, out of the midst of the fire" (Deut. iv. 15). May the Lord teach us, by

His spirit, to stand in awe before Him, and, restraining vain curiosity and and daring speculation in things spiritual and Divine, to say from the heart, with true humility, "I will hear what God the Lord will speak."

II. *Of whom did the voice testify—"This is my beloved Son?"*

The narrative informs us that there were *three* glorified persons there, and Luke particularly states, concerning *Moses* and *Elias*, that they "appeared in glory." These two glorified saints were unquestionably *sons of God*, having of old received "the adoption of sons," having been born again and sanctified by the Spirit, and having long before entered on the heavenly inheritance of sons. They were beloved of God, and pleasing in His sight, having served Him faithfully on earth, and now serving Him in perfect purity day and night in His temple above.

But no doubt was left in the minds of the disciples that this Divine testimony from the cloud had reference to *Jesus* only. There seems to have been something peculiar in the radiance which shone, as from within, on His countenance and person, and also in the attitude of the others towards Him, which marked Him as exclusively the object of the testimony. To this, Peter evidently alludes when, speaking of the scene in the passage above quoted, he says, "We were eye-witnesses of His majesty." We have the same significant utterance, accompanied by still clearer evidence, at the baptism of the Lord Jesus by John, when, "lo, the heavens were opened unto Him, and he saw the Spirit of God descending like a dove and resting upon Him; and lo, a voice from heaven saying, This is my beloved Son in whom I am well pleased" (Matt. iii. 16). You remember how John speaks of the meaning and effect of this testimony, "And I saw and bare record that this is the Son of God" (John i. 34).

The design obviously was to separate, in their estimation and in ours, between Jesus and all others, whether in heaven or on earth. This is *my own* beloved Son, says Jehovah, in a sense peculiar, unparalleled, Divine. And so the Apostle John, another of these three chosen witnesses, declares, "We beheld His glory, the glory as of the only begotten of the Father" (John i. 14). It is, in short, a Divine testimony to the supreme divinity and eternal Sonship of the Lord Jesus Christ, that, as it is written, "all men should honour the Son, even as they honour the

Father" (John v. 23). It is also written that "no man knoweth the Son but the Father;" and here the Father comes forth to declare Him.

But let us not overlook the fact that this testimony was given to the Son of God *incarnate*. The veil which hid His Divine glory was drawn aside for a moment, and God the Father bore witness to Him, and to these chosen disciples, and through them to us and to the world, that this same Jesus is very God. "Without controversy, great is the mystery of godliness, God was manifest in the flesh" (1 Tim. iii. 16). O, to have a clear apprehension, by faith, of the truth and spiritual significance of this great mystery,—Jesus, our Brother and kinsman-Redeemer, and yet "the brightness of the Father's glory, and the express image of His person!" This is the grand foundation of our hope, the secret of His people's peace. "Yea, doubtless, and I count all things but loss, for the excellency of the knowledge of Christ Jesus my Lord" (Phil. iii. 8).

III. *Consider the scope or burden of the testimony, " This is my beloved Son in whom I am well pleased."*

There are two parts in this Divine testimony. The one pointing to Jesus, *personally*, and the other, mainly, though not wholly, to His *offices and work*.

1. As to the *former*, the Father says,—"This is my beloved Son," or literally, "*my Son, the beloved.*" This word of Jehovah expresses infinite, eternal, and unchangeable love, illustrating not only the Divine glory of Christ, but the unfathomable depths of Divine grace towards sinners in and through Him. From eternity He was the Beloved of the Father, "the only begotten Son who is in the bosom of the Father," "daily His delight, rejoicing always before Him," one with the Father in nature, counsel, and working. Like the Father himself, He was infinitely worthy to be loved, and was, therefore, infinitely beloved of the Father and the Holy Ghost. But, as mediator now incarnate, we are here specially called to regard Him as the object of the Father's love. "Behold my servant whom I uphold; mine elect, in whom my soul delighteth" (Isaiah xlii. 1). God the Father loved Him (if we may say so) with a peculiar love, for consenting to the scheme of redemption, and freely entering as Surety into covenant bonds, in His zeal for the Father's glory, and in love and pity for the sinful and perishing, given Him by the Father. He loved Him when he mixed for Him that cup of

wrath which the people had deserved to drink, and laid on Him the awful chastisement of their peace. "Awake, O sword, against my shepherd, and against the man that is my fellow, saith the Lord of hosts." "*Therefore*," said the Lord Jesus, "doth My Father love Me, because I lay down My life that I might take it again" (John x. 17). So now, the Father proclaims it to the joy of the Redeemer's soul, and for strengthening the faith and hope of His people.

But what an affecting view is thus presented of the marvellous grace of God in the redemption and salvation of sinners! "God so loved the world that He gave His only begotten Son." "He spared not His own Son, but delivered Him up for us all." "Herein is love, not that we loved God, but that He loved us, and sent His Son to be the propitiation for our sins." How blessed to be partakers of this love of God in Christ, and, by living faith uniting us to Christ, to be "made accepted in the Beloved!" How heinous the sin, and how aggravated the condemnation, where this glorious exhibition of God's love is treated with indifference, and this rich provision of His grace is refused in unbelief!

2. The second part of this Divine testimony says, "*in whom I am well pleased;*" and this I apply mainly, though not solely, to the offices and work of Christ. The Father is "*well pleased*" or divinely satisfied with the *person* of Christ as the God-man, the grandest manifestation of His glory to the world. He rests also with supreme delight in His entire quaification for all that is implied in His mediatorial work,—His *Divine* sufficiency combined with perfect *human* sympathy, together with the crowning fact that "God giveth not the Spirit by measure unto Him." Here is found one to whom God can confidently entrust the interests of His cause and glory, and to whom poor, perishing sinners can look with assured hope for the salvation of their souls. Accordingly, when this great device of Divine grace and wisdom was revealed, the heavenly host praised God saying, "Glory to God in the highest, on earth peace, goodwill toward men" (Luke ii. 14).

But again, and specially, God is "*well pleased*," because, in and through Him, all the conditions of the covenant of grace, and all its promises, are gloriously fulfilled. The eternal Son of God came, and assumed man's nature into union with the Divine, that, as the Surety and Substitute of His people, He might "make His soul an offering for sin" and "fulfil all righteousness," that

God "might be just and the Justifier of him which believeth in Jesus." "When the fulness of the time was come, God sent forth His Son, made of a woman, made under the law, to redeem them that were under the law, that we might receive the adoption of sons," (Gal. iv. 4); and the Father, anticipating the glorious success of the undertaking, here proclaims, "This is My beloved Son in whom I am well pleased." In *Him* I see My holy law fulfilled in all its just demands and threatenings; in Him I recognise the substance and fulfilment of all My gracious promises. In witness of this, Moses, the great lawgiver under God, and Elijah, the great prophet of Israel, appear with Him in glory, and, as Luke informs us, "speak of His decease which He should accomplish at Jerusalem" (Luke xi. 31). That great event, they testify, is the perfect fulfilment of all the law and the prophets. They proclaim the fact of a suffering, dying Messiah to be the grand, fundamental doctrine of the Old Testament, as well as of the New. They honour Him as their own Saviour and Lord, and, with adoring gratitude, declare that His cross is their crown. It is as if they hereby joined in the testimony of His forerunner, "Behold the Lamb of God, which taketh away the sin of the world." A bright and heavenly illustration this, of the truth, "that God was in Christ, reconciling the world unto Himself" (2 Cor. v. 19).

And, once more, God is "*well pleased*," because, in and through Him, the richest revenue of glory redounds to Jehovah's name. There never was, so far as revealed to us, so grand a display of the moral attributes of God, all in harmonious exercise. Never was there such service rendered, nor such a sacrifice presented on God's altar. And then, what glorious fruits, in the justifying of sinners by God's grace, through the redemption that is in Christ Jesus,—the coming forth of the Holy Ghost to quicken dead souls, to sanctify believers, and to prepare those who had been heirs of *hell* for *heavenly and eternal glory!* God is well pleased, not only *with* but *in* Christ, and therefore in all who, by living faith, are found in Him; and He rejoices in and over them for ever, as His purchased possession and peculiar treasure.

IV. *Consider the Command annexed to this Divine testimony, —" Hear ye Him."*

There seems here an allusion to the prophecy delivered by Moses, and applied to Christ by Peter,—"The Lord thy God will raise up unto thee a Prophet, from the midst of thee, of thy brethren, like unto me; unto Him ye shall hearken" (Deut xviii.

15) ; or, as the Holy Ghost by Peter puts it,—" Him shall ye hear in all things whatsoever He shall say unto you " (Acts iii. 22).

1. Consider briefly the *general import* of this command. It proclaims and holds up the Lord Jesus Christ, the great High-Priest and Fulfiller of the law, as also the great *Prophet*, and the *Lawgiver* and Head of His Church and people. " One is your Master, even Christ " (Matt. xxiii. 10). You must hear Christ as He speaks in His holy Word, and not " the wisdom of this world, nor of the princes of this world, that come to nought." You must hear *Him*, and not merely Moses and Elias. They gave forth great testimonies for God and His truth in their day, and for ages after ; but these lesser lights must disappear, now that the Sun of righteousness has arisen. " He must increase, but I must decrease." " God, who at sundry times and in divers manners spake in time past unto the fathers by the prophets, hath in these last days spoken to us by His Son " (Heb. i. 1, 2). Nay, if you hear their testimony in faith and with spiritual understanding, they will bring you to the feet and the cross of Christ ; for the law and the prophets are fulfilled in Him. And further, while you hear those who speak to you in the name of Christ, you are called ever to remember that only so far as Christ's own truth is in them, and as Christ speaks by them, will there be any true light or blessing to your souls. In a word, you must hear *Himself*, or all other hearing and knowledge will be vain, and utterly worthless for your souls' salvation.

But this leads us to inquire—2. *What kind of hearing* is meant by this Divine injunction ? Our Lord follows up the parable of the sower with that word of warning,—" Take heed therefore *how* ye hear." Many, alas ! hear Christ's word, prac-tically to refuse and disobey it, or to treat his warnings and counsels with indifference. Others listen only to speculate and criticise, as if man's imperfect reasonings and conclusions, and not Christ's Divine revelations, were the standard of truth and right. *This* hearing in the text is what Moses calls " *hearkening*," add-ing these words of solemn warning (ver. 19), " And it shall come to pass, that whosoever will not hearken unto my words which he shall speak in My name, I will require it of him." It is to hear in the sense of giving " earnest heed,"—of " believing with the heart unto righteousness." It is to commit ourselves wholly to *Him*, cheerfully and practically to realise and own His autho-rity, when He warns, or invites, or promises, or commands. It is, in short, to embrace and follow Him as our Prophet, Priest, and

King, with the trustful, loving, entire obedience of faith. Thus Paul, by the Spirit, writes—" For this cause also thank we God without ceasing, because, when ye received the Word of God which ye heard of us, ye received it, not as the Word of men, but, as it is in truth, the Word of God, which effectually worketh also in you that believe " (1 Thess. ii. 13). This is that living faith, which, by the grace of the Holy Ghost, dwells and operates in every man who is savingly united to Christ, and which, God's word declares, is essential to salvation. So the Lord Jesus Himself testified, " He that believeth on Him is not condemned : but he that believeth not is condemned already, because he hath not believed in the name of the only-begotten Son of God " (John iii. 18).

In conclusion, let us solemnly ask ourselves, What think *we* of Christ ? Have our consciences been awakened to a true sense of our sinful and perishing condition, and have our eyes been opened to see His glory, as the Divine Surety and Substitute, the all-sufficient Saviour of sinners ? Have we been brought to the conclusion that our only hope of acceptance and salvation is bound up in the great fact proclaimed in our text, that the Father was " *well pleased in Him*," when he stood in the breach and finished the work given Him to do ? Have we, therefore, being " renewed in the Spirit of our mind," embraced Him in our hearts ; and are we cleaving to Him with that true " faith which worketh by love ?" Are we now seeking to sit at His feet and learn of Him, and to honour and obey Him as our Lord and King ? O, to have the " Beloved " of the Father as *our Beloved*, to find our souls' rest and satisfaction where the Father is " well-pleased," to be hearing and following Jesus,—this is assuredly the way of life !

Again, let me earnestly exhort those who have truly embraced Christ, to ponder and lay to heart their holy calling, as summed up in these words of my text—"*hear ye Him.*" He has redeemed you with His precious blood, and has quickened and renewed you by His Spirit, that He might " purify you unto Himself a peculiar people, zealous of good works." Now, therefore, you are called to hearken to His word, to watch for the intimations of His will, and, hearing with the obedience of faith, to " follow the Lamb whithersoever He goeth." " I will hear what God the Lord will speak." " O Lord, truly I am thy servant ; I am thy servant, and the son of thine handmaid : Thou hast loosed my bonds." This is a high and holy calling, beset with

many difficulties in this world of sin and temptation. In yourselves you have no sufficiency for it. But surely there is Divine
encouragement in the first word spoken by the Lord to His
trembling disciples, after the voice from the cloud charged them
to "hear Him." We read (verse 7) that "Jesus came and touched
them and said, Arise, and be not afraid." So He says to every
believer, truly bent on hearing and following Him—"My grace
is sufficient for thee; for my strength is made perfect in
weakness."

Again, how woeful the state of those who, ignorant and insensible as to their lost condition, are blind to the glory of
Christ, and indifferent to the great things of Gospel salvation!
Perhaps you make no profession, and are living only for the
world. Or, if you do make mention of His name, you have no
ear for His counsel, and no heart to follow Him. It may be that
you have some vague purpose, at a future and more convenient
season, to deal seriously with Him and His truth, but meantime
there is no disposition to hearken, and no obedience of faith. O,
be assured, whatever may be your outward character, that, thus
living, you are in the way of darkness and death! Ponder, I
earnestly beseech you, that solemn version which Peter, by the
Holy Ghost, gives of the word to Moses; "And it shall come to
pass, that every soul which will not hear that Prophet shall be
destroyed from among the people" (Acts iii. 23).

And finally, I press this gracious call on all to whom this
word comes. "*Hear ye Him;*" for there is no other refuge for a
sinner, no other Saviour of souls; but, as the Lord Himself testified to the Jews, "if ye believe not that I am He, ye shall die in
your sins." "Knowing, therefore, the terror of the Lord, we
persuade men." "To-day, if ye will hear His voice, harden not
your hearts." "See that ye refuse not Him that speaketh; for
if they escaped not who refused Him that spake on earth, much
more shall not we escape, if we turn away from Him that
speaketh from heaven" (Heb. xii. 25). Yea, rather, "I beseech
you, brethren, by the mercies of God," praying that the word
may come home to you "in demonstration of the Spirit and of
power,—"Incline your ear, and come unto me, hear and your
soul shall live; and I will make an everlasting covenant with
you, even the sure mercies of David" (Isaiah lv. 3).

THE CHURCH'S MISSIONARY PSALM:

A SERMON.

ANDREW THOMSON, D.D.,

BROUGHTON PLACE UNITED PRESBYTERIAN CHURCH, EDINBURGH.*

"God be merciful unto us, and bless us ; and cause His face to shine upon us. That Thy way may be known upon earth, Thy saving health among all nations."—Ps. lxxii. 1, 2.

THIS prayer of the ancient Church consists in part of the benediction which the High Priest was accustomed to pronounce upon the assembled tribes of Israel. The people here lay hold of the sublime benediction, send it up in united supplication to heaven, and beseech God Himself to make it His own blessing upon His own people,—"God be merciful unto us, and bless us ; and cause His face to shine upon us." Whatever other thoughts there may be in this comprehensive prayer, we cannot be mistaken in regarding the following as standing prominent among the blessings which it implores :—the continued enjoyment of God's forgiveness and friendship, and especially the increased experience of His love in quickened graces and enlarged spiritual strength ; that the spring of His Church might ripen into summer ; that the dawn might brighten unto the perfect day ; that, having life already, His people might have it more abundantly ; and all this the effect of mercy, free and unforced, far-reaching as the firmament, and fathomless as the sea.

It is remarkable, however, that as this prayer of the Church proceeds, its desires are not restricted to itself, but extended to the vast Gentile world that is "sitting in darkness and in the region and shadow of death." It seeks to have the heavenly benediction spread over the whole race of man. And more than than this, it supplicates a higher spiritual life for itself, partly in

* Preached during a season of revival.

order that it may become a qualified instrument for proclaiming and extending the true religion over the entire world, in all its nations, and kindreds, and peoples, and tongues,—" that Thy way," by restoring men to Thy favour and renewing them after Thy likeness, " may be known upon earth ; Thy saving health,"—thy salvation,—" among all nations," proclaimed to all and possessed by all.

It is scarcely possible for us to determine, with any certainty, whether this prayer, when it was first spoken, had reference to any single period or event. Perhaps it may have pointed forward to more than one great era of enlargement and blessing, for there are germinant prayers as well as germinant prophecies. We shall not, however, be mistaken, in supposing that there was a special reference, at all events, to the advent of the Messiah, when the glory of the Lord was to arise upon the ancient Church, and " Gentiles were to come to her light, and kings to the brightness of her coming,"—a period for which holy Jews, for many an age, waited and prayed with longing eyes. The fact therefore stands out, distinct and clear, from such a prayer as this, that the Jews, in their purer and better times, did not think of themselves as the monopolists of the Divine favour, or regard the people of other countries with proud and arrogant exclusiveness. It belonged to an age of corruption and formalism to do this, for charity to man always decays and dies out with the decay of piety to God. The devout Hebrew of David's times anticipated the period when the Gentile should become a common partaker of his light and privileges, as the true golden age of the Church of God. It was a false and vitiated Judaism which grudged those highest benefits to other nations, as unlike the Judaism of the Psalms and the Prophets, as the Christianity of the twelfth century was unlike the Christianity of the first.

Proceeding now to consider the text a little more in detail, there are three things in it to which I invite your special attention, and which are not unsuitable to our present circumstances. I. There is a prayer for the Revival of the Church. II. There is a prayer for the Increase of the Church. III. The connection between the revived life of the Church and its beneficent influence upon the world is indicated in the words, " *That* Thy way may be known upon earth, thy saving health among all nations."

I. *The Church is here represented as praying for Revival,*— that is, for a higher state of spiritual life, for eminence in holy

character, " God be merciful unto us and bless us, and cause His
face to shine upon us."

Whatever other desires may be contained in the words, this
at least stands prominent in them. What are some of the signs
of this advanced religion in an individual, in a congregation, or
in a fellowship of Churches ? What are some of the tokens, when
they unmistakably present themselves, that, in this truest and
most blessed sense, a people have " put on strength " ? Increased
knowledge of Divine truth; a firmer grasp of its Divine realities,
and a living upon it daily as the very nutriment of the soul ; a
glow of Christian love that burns against sin, that delights in
God and in every creature that is Christ-like,—that makes Christian obedience easy, and lightens the cross of heavy trials,—that
causes the mouth to speak out of the abundance of the heart the
the praises of Christ, and that yearns, with the intensity of a
commanding passion, for the conversion of souls. There will also
appear, in such a case, an abounding and delighting in prayer
that will no longer be confined to the stated times of devotion,
but, mingling itself even with common duties and engagements,
will many a time overflow its banks, like Jordan in the time of
harvest. There will be a growing weanedness from the world
and indifference to the pleasures of sense, because the heart has
found satisfaction in a conscious salvation, in holy affections, and
heavenly hopes. There will be a growing spirit of thankfulness
and praise, a sense of divine sonship, and, in the midst even of
trying providences, an inward peace, a sweet undertone of joy.
These are signs of God's blessing a people, and causing His face
to shine upon them, as distinct and certain as the tongues of fire
resting on the first Christian disciples. Many of them have
appeared in our congregations during the past months, reminding
us of the power that wrought so wondrously at Pentecost, carrying our thoughts upward to the enthroned Redeemer, from whom
the power has come ; showing us the working of spiritual forces
that could transform the world; and giving us glimpses of a state
of things which, on an immensely greater scale, is to bring in the
glories of the latter day. It is a state of things which every
Church should seek to reach and to retain, like the continued
spring and summer of the tropics, and for which we are taught
in the text constantly and universally to pray, " God be merciful
unto us and bless us, and cause His face to shine upon us."

There are various considerations which, in addition to that
which we are afterwards more particularly to specify, indicate

the duty and the supreme importance of our seeking to have this eminence in spiritual life as the normal state of our Churches. Thus, we are struck with the fact that this is the principal request —I had almost said, the sublime refrain—of our Lord's intercessory prayer in the seventeenth chapter of John's Gospel. There is scarcely an epistle of Paul in which his argument or exhortation does not, at some point, kindle into prayer; and in every prayer, however varied the phraseology, the central and absorbing desire which gathers everything into itself, is the greater holiness of the Church. And in that grand symbolic picture in which the ascended Saviour is represented as continually moving in the midst of the seven golden candlesticks which are the seven Churches, and, with those eyes which are as a flame of fire, taking infallible note of the condition of each, it is again the question of holy character and attainment that is the supreme inquiry. What amount of holy radiance are those light-bearers, which were originally kindled from heaven, continuing to shed around them? How He remonstrates with one Church because of its little strength, and because the things which remain are ready to die; and how He rejoices over another, because of its purity, its fidelity to the truth, its service in action, and its yet higher service in suffering! His representation, coming before us in many a form, is that it is only where there is vigorous and abounding life in a people, that they fulfil their mission and design as churches, and that His Father receives glory from them, and that He Himself delights in them. "Herein is my Father glorified, that ye bear much fruit; so shall ye be my disciples." Our religion, in order to influence others, must be visible; and in order to be visible, it must be strong and deep. Our Lord declares, in one place, that He would have preferred even to see the Laodicean Church extinguished, rather than continue to misrepresent His religion and dishonour His name by its state of living death. Should not such considerations as these send us back in thought upon our own history as individuals and as a Church? Measuring from some point in the past not very remote, has ours been a history of progress or of decay? What our Lord in heaven requires of us is, a religion so pronounced, so self-consistent, so all-pervading, that, like Himself when on earth, it cannot be hidden, and that, when seen, it cannot fail to proclaim its own divinity to the world. But let us remember that this blessed condition cannot be reached, and, after it has been reached, cannot be retained, except through a constant, living, communion with Christ, and a daily drawing, by faith and prayer, out of His fulness. Each one must be going habitually with His own vessel to the Divine fountain. We cannot live upon traditions. We cannot, as Churches, live upon a history however noble and honourable, even though we had prophets and martyrs for our fathers. Even our denominational flag cannot be held high by a palsied hand. Our history itself will prove a condemnation and a snare to us, if in any degree we make it a substitute for present, glowing life. The words of our text must be assimilated into our every-day thought and prayer, " God be merciful unto us, and bless us, and cause His face to shine upon us."

II. *The Church comes before us in the text as not only praying for Revival, but for increase.*

After supplicating for itself, it pleads for the world, that the Gospel of heaven's love may both be universally proclaimed and actually received by the whole family of man,—" God's way known upon earth, and His saving health among the nations." The very fact that such a prayer has been placed in the inspired psalter of the Church, as teaching it how to pray, implies that this was to be the Church's predominent desire and constant aim, and that its eye, looking down through the ages, was ever to be fixed on this as its mission and its goal. Even the Jewish Church to whom this psalm was first given, and by whose congregated tribes it was first sung around the ark of the tabernacle, was to have this vision ever before it, though it could only be realised by a change in its form and framework, more perfectly adapting it for this end. Its system was one of preservation rather than of propagation,—receiving those who came to it rather than going out into the highways and hedges of the world to seek them and to bring them in. Its emblem was the stationary lighthouse, rather than the glorious sun moving in majesty across the firmament, and shedding down its light and its heat upon every land. But if even this ancient Church, with its lofty wall of ceremonial and of local institute and observance, was divinely taught to desire and anticipate the universal subjection of the world to that Divine faith of which it was for a time the chosen guardian, and to incorporate this desire with its synagogue and temple prayers, how much more is this the case with the Christian Church, with its completed revelation, and its whole system and agency adapting it to propagation, and with the renewed commission resting ever upon its heart and conscience, to " go into all the world and

preach the Gospel to every creature." The missionary motive
has acquired a mightily increased momentum under Christianity.
Whatever other work may be taken up at times by the Church,
this is a service which is never to be forgotten, or suspended, or
slackened, " That God's name may be known upon all the earth."
This is always to be the work af the Church, and of every part of
the Church. The sublime commission stands unrevoked and irre-
vocable, while there is a single rebel hand among all the tribes of
earth that is held up against Christ and His kingdom. The
Church must not only protest but proselytize. Christianity is
essentially a religion of conquest, which will make no compromise with false philosophies, or with false gods. The dream of
universal empire which kings, maddened by ambition, have
attempted to realise through sword and fire, is to be achieved by
the Gospel of God's mighty love, blessed by the Spirit, and bringing in the reign of righteousness, purity, and peace.

How the soul of Paul was ennobled and fired by this conception ! Hence we find him, in his successive missionary circuits,
ever widening the sphere of his operations, and never forgetting
that his field was the world. Wherever he planted his standard,
—at Antioch, at Corinth, or at Rome,—he was still thinking of
" the regions beyond." Every year he was lighting up one orb of
truth after another, in wider and still wider orbits, till the whole
heaven glowed with the radiance. And though the Church has
sometimes allowed herself to be engrossed by controversy, or to
be made indifferent by worldliness, or torpid through unbelief,
or inactive because of discouraging obstructions, so as almost
to forget her work and her destiny ; still, whenever there has
come a baptism of new spiritual life, there has also come a revival of this spirit of benignant proselytism. And therefore,
while we are humbled by the fitfulness of our efforts, and by
their sad disproportion to our ability and opportunity, let us
beware of ungratefully undervaluing the actual results. Take
this very missionary psalm, which was sung by the tribes of
Israel alone for so many centuries, and think in how many parts
of the world it is now sung every Sabbath-day by gathering multitudes, and to what a great extent its prayer has already been
transmuted into accomplished prophecy. Not only by myriads
in so many of the great cities and centres of civilization, but
beneath the bread-fruit trees of the Polynesian isles, among the
cinnamon groves of Ceylon, on the banks of the many rivers of
India, among the mountains of Madagascar, amid the snows of

N

Greenland, on the steppes of Siberia, and beneath the shadows of the pagodas and heathen temples of China, there is going up, from hearts that have tasted the salvation of God, the prayer that "God's saving health may be known among all nations."—It is a happy word, "God's saving health,"—that which alone can give true health to the soul of man, and breathe a Divine life into a dying world,—the enlightener of the darkened mind, the healer of the guilty conscience, the purifier of depraved affections. It is itself the most precious of all good things, and it gives a new excellence and value to all other blessings, — the sanctifier of literature, the sanction of law, the safe-guard of liberty, the sweetener of sorrow, the lamp that guides along the way to immortality and heaven. This prayer seems to gather into itself the very notes of that song of angels on the plains of Bethlehem, "Glory to God in the highest, peace on earth, and goodwill towards men."

III. *The text brings under our particular notice, in the third place, the connection between revived religion in a Church and its influence upon the world.*

We must first be blessed ourselves, in order to our becoming the means of extensively blessing others. The prayers in this text are based on this very principle, that eminent piety among a people is the condition of eminent usefulness—"God be merciful unto us, and bless us, and cause His face to shine upon us ; *That* Thy way may be known upon earth, Thy saving health among all nations." When a Church is in a low state of religious life, it is wanting in the very elements that qualify it for doing great religious good to others. Nay, it sometimes operates rather in an opposite direction. Suppose a young convert, for example, with all the glow and ardour of first love about him, to connect himself with a congregation in the hope that he shall find the union favourable to his Christian progress, that there shall be sympathy with him in his religious affections and new-found joys, and encouragement in his every effort to do good ; and that, instead of this, he finds little prayer, or love, or zeal, or holy gladness,—is not the connection likely to operate upon him with a moral chill ? Will he not feel that, instead of entering a congenial home, he has come into a winter-palace or a desert ?

But, on the other hand, let there be a strong and pervading religious life among a people, and two results may be expected to follow. *First*, the members of such a church will be in the best position for withstanding the assults of surrounding error and unbelief. It is not in churches that are shining with holy graces and have much of heaven's dew resting on them, that rationalism finds its ready disciples. Heresies usually spring from arid soils. It is when men have never had the actual, living experience of Divine truth in their own hearts, but keep it merely outside of them in their creed, that they are in danger of "giving heed to instruction which causeth to err." But let a man have had daily experience of the Gospel in his own heart, and a consciousness of the blessed change it has wrought within him, and he has the testimony to its divinity within himself. He can say, " we know and are sure." He is divinely guarded and garrisoned against all the assaults of unbelief. *Secondly,* it is the individual or the church that is distinguished by the vigour and constancy of its Christian life that God chooses and employs for the extension of of His kingdom. And He does this, not only on the principle of honouring them that honour Him, but also because such a church is qualified for telling with beneficent influence upon the world, in a manner in which it would not be qualified were it in a lower state of religious temperature. It is "a vessel fit for the Master's use."

There is something kindred to this principle, if not, indeed, identical with it, in the answer which our Lord gave to some of His disciples when they met Him on His descent from the mount of transfiguration, and enquired of Him why they had not been been able, during his absence, to expel the demon from the possessed youth. "Because of your unbelief," was the immediate reply. "Nevertheless, this kind goeth not out but by prayer and fasting." Their comparatively little faith was the explanation of their failure. We have a glimpse of the same spiritual law, in the direction of Joshua to the Israelites when they were about to be carried, by a wondrous miracle, across the Jordan. "Sanctify yourselves, for to-morrow the Lord will do wonders among you,"—get yourselves into a higher state of moral preparation for being at once the subjects and the witnesses of so stupendous a blessing. And so it is, in like manner, that when God intends largely to bless the world through the Church, he begins by qualifying the Church for the honour and the service. And when he revives and quickens a congregation, or a whole fellowship of churches, he is about to use it for making His way known upon the earth. According to the beautiful image of Leighton, when a father goes to awaken his children, you may be sure that it is near to sunrise. How utterly unfit were our Lord's disciples, while he was yet with them, for going forth as the messengers of His gospel to the world. They needed the knowledge that came with His death, and resurrection, and ascension, the season of united and prolonged prayer in the upper room, the purifying fires of pentecost, and the enlarged effusion of the Holy Spirit, to qualify them for the mighty enterprise of a world's evangelisation. But after this, they were prepared and panoplied for the glorious service, and those one hundred and twenty disciples in the upper chamber began to hold in their hands the highest destinies of the world.

To illustrate our principle, let us glance for a moment, as we bring our discourse to a close, at some of the qualities by which a revived church will be certain to be distinguished.

1. *One of these will be a spirit of dependence leading to abounding prayer.* Self-emptiness is of the very essence of deep religion, and this brings us with our empty vessels to God, that we may supply our need out of His fulness. It is individuals and churches in this state of mind that are singled out for special honour. Was it not this temper in the young Jerusalem church that drew down the showers of Pentecost? And many a pentecostal blessing it has attracted since. When a church has begun to pray earnestly and continuously, it has already begun to be revived, and is on the first steps of the ascending ladder that leads up to heaven's gates. When man's weakness thus lays hold of Christ's omnipotence, it becomes itself omnipotent. A praying church goes forth to do battle in Christ's name with the powers of evil, uniting in itself the meekness of a child with the might of an angel.

2. *Then there is great moral power in a church with strong religious life,* which specially qualifies it for hopeful Christian action. Doubters are poor evangelists. But revived Christians speak to others out of their own experience. They have known the new life and the holy gladness which the gospel has carried into their own heart, and this gives them confidence and courage in speaking of it, and commending it to their fellow-men, just as a recovered patient can speak with fervour of the medicine that has healed him. Besides, the message of heaven receives a new momentum when it is spoken from a heart that is in loving sympathy with it. It is like an arrow shot from a bow that is fully bent. There is a charm in an earnestness which is the outcome of deep conviction. Then, further, think of the influ-

ence of holy character and moral consistency upon an onlooking multitude. We need not wish for miracles or lambent tongues of fire, where there are these stars of God shining as lights in the world. The beautiful vision of the Jerusalem church standing in its virgin-beauty, conquered the prejudices and won the attachment of many whom miracle had left unconvinced. The argument of a single Christian life shining in its holy beauty, has been mighty over a whole community; what must be the influence of multitudes of kindred excellence united in a congregation, and sending out a constant stream of moral influence on their neighbourhood? Paul testifies of the church of Thessalonica that its example was felt for good, not only in all Macedonia and Achaia, but in regions far beyond. What centres of spiritual force must have been such congregations as those of Rutherford at Anwoth, or of Baxter at Kidderminster, or Boston at Ettrick, or Ebenezer Erskine at Portmoak!

3. Then, when a church is in a state of strong religious life, *it will be distinguished by the prevalence of brotherly love among its members*, and this will produce and maintain union and united action in its society. Alienations, jealousies, discords, and divisions will disappear before this heavenly temper, as wild beasts and foul creatures hide themselves in their caves and dens before the risen sun. It is astonishing how much good of the highest kind can be accomplished by a church, when its members are thus knit together in love, and the multitude of them that believe are of one heart and one soul. No one can read, with even average intelligence, the thrilling story of Nehemiah building the ruined wall of Jerusalem, without seeing that it was not a mere work of common patriotism, but of revived religion. And how did this pervading life from heaven give vigour to the weak, inspirit the faint-hearted, bind them together in one compact unity, drive away the fear of man, turn every common man into a hero, and build the wall to its copestone, while the enemy was still mocking and prophesying failure.

4. Then a revived religion in a church is certain to manifest its presence and influence *in a spirit of unreserved self-consecration*. It is a whole burnt-offering which those hearts on which new fire from heaven has descended, offer to God. Strong love keeps nothing back. We have seen it operating in this very manner in the number of young men who have recently devoted themselves to the work of the Christian ministry at home, or to missions abroad, making it evident that in a state of flourishing

piety in our congregations, it would be easy to double the staff of
our missionaries in a single year. And as the church which had
put on spiritual strength, would never need to be anxious about
the supply of missionaries, it would have as little occasion for
fear about the obtaining of ample funds for the support of our
missionary enterprises. Piety reigning in a heart makes a man
the steward of his wealth, and leads him to value it principally
as the means of doing good. This open-handed, unwearied giving
comes within the sphere of self-consecration. Give us a higher
and more generally diffused religious life, and all our present
charities will be dwarfed in comparison with the munificent gifts
that shall begin to flow into the treasury of the Lord, and that
shall flow out again to the ends of the earth. The giving will
become as universal as the working was, when Nehemiah built
his wall. And the liberality of such men as the Thorntons and
Howards of other days, will become as common things.

And now, in conclusion, what we have to seek first, and above
all things, is a mighty increase of religious life in our pulpits, in
our sessions, in our presbyteries, in our synods, in our families,
and in our congregations. We must give up the tone of self-
complacency, and no longer be reconciled to our faults. We must
no longer measure ourselves by ourselves, or compare ourselves
with one another, but earnestly and perseveringly aim at a state of
things in our churches, in respect to which an apostle like Paul
could say, "I do you to wit of the grace of God bestowed on
them," and the sight of which would make a Barnabas glad. It
is here that we must begin, if good is to be obtained by us on a
large scale. This one thing would rid us of a hundred evils, and
bring with it a hundred benefits, just as the flowing, deepening
tide sweeps before it the weeds and the wreck, and floats the
stranded vessels that lay motionless in the shallows, out into the
deep and sun-lit sea. We hear much of organization; and this is
well, and even necessary, in its own place. But what we need,
far more than organization, is more life; we need, not merely the
building of the altar, but the descent of the heavenly fire. And
we need this, not only that we may advance, but that we may
withstand our spiritual adversaries, and hold our ground. If any
one, therefore, ask, Wherefore is it that the Lord goeth not
forth with our armies as heretofore?—the answer is, Why have
so many of us been too easily satisfied with our religious condition, and been content to know that we were far above the worst,
though we are far below the best? Why have we seen the great

gospel-commission floating over our heads, summoning us to work and pray that God's way may be known upon the earth, and yet have taken the great subject of the world's conversion and salvation so easily ? Why have we seen the cloud of blessing passing near us, and bending over us with heaven's choicest riches in it, while we have not made more of that spiritual wealth and strength our own, by more inwrought, united, persevering supplications that would take no denial ? Why have we been so slow to enter by the open doors of opportunity ? O, it is indeed time for us to awake out of sleep ! We have shown the weakness of our faith, or rather the sad prevalence of our unbelief, by the wonder we have expressed when the showers of blessing fell, whereas a strong faith would have wondered when the blessing was withheld. What is it that has been holding back the heavenly supplies, and delaying the advancing chariot of our Redeemer and Lord ? Come, Lord, and fit us for the blessing. Come, Lord, and command the blessing in its seven-fold plenitude. "Let thy work appear unto thy servants, and thy glory unto their children. And let the beauty of the Lord our God be upon us: and establish thou the work of our hands upon us; yea, the work of our hands, establish thou it." "God be merciful unto us, and bless us; and cause His face to shine upon us; that thy way may be known upon earth, thy saving health among all nations." Amen.

THE WELLS OF SALVATION:

A SERMON.

BY

Rev. THOMAS MACLAUCHLAN, LL.D.,

FREE ST. COLUMBA'S CHURCH, EDINBURGH.

" Therefore with joy shall ye draw water out of the wells of salvation."—
ISAIAH xii. 3.

THERE is no figure more generally used in Scripture to indicate
the Gospel than that of water. It pervades both the Old and New
Testaments. The stream from the smitten rock is shown by the
apostle to have been a type of Christ. "They drank of that rock
which followed them, and that rock was Christ." This prophet,
whose words we are considering, proclaims that great and gracious invitation, "Ho, ye that thirst, come ye to the waters."
What were the waters, or what was the value of the invitation,
unless they typified Christ? The Prophet Zechariah tells us of
a fountain to be "opened to the house of David and to the inhabitants of Jerusalem, for sin and for uncleanness." That fountain was Christ. In the New Testament the same significant
emblem is employed. As our Lord stood amidst the multitude
hurrying, in accordance with the words of our text and from a
full apprehension of their meaning, to the well of Siloam, on that
last and great day of the feast, He proclaimed with a loud voice,
"If any man thirst, let him come unto Me and drink." As He
stood by the brink of Jacob's well, He said to the woman of
Samaria, "If thou knewest the gift of God, and who it is that
saith unto thee, Give me to drink, thou wouldest have asked of
Him, and He would have given thee living water." Towards the
very close of the Divine record, these gracious words are written,
"Let him that is athirst come ; and whosoever will, let him take

of the water of life freely." And as if this were not enough,—as if it were needful that to the Word the sacrament should be added, we find, in the sacrament of Baptism, the same symbol employed to represent the excellency and efficacy of Christ. This figure then, water, is one of those most frequently employed in Scripture to represent the Gospel and its gracious provision for the redemption of the sinner. If this be so, are we not justified in viewing the wells here spoken of as representing those means and ordinances in which the Gospel is presented and offered to us? In this view of the passage let us consider—I. The wells. II. Drawing out of them. III. The joy of the Church in this exercise.

I. *The wells.*

God, in carrying on His government, has seen it wise to act usually through agencies and means. So soon as the world is called into being, He acts on this principle. He does not create man of nothing, as He does the mass of rude and unformed matter, but he takes of the dust of the earth, and out of that He moulds his body. From a rib out of man's side He makes her who was to be his help meet. He employs a Moses to deliver Israel, and lead them through the wilderness towards the land of promise. The rod of Moses is made apparently instrumental in working his many miracles. Christ employs the clay to anoint the blind man's eyes; and when the great Gospel of salvation is to be proclaimed, He employs a few men, many of them, seemingly, very ill fitted for the work, and makes them the means of working out His great design. Many may have asked, Would it not have been better if God had done all these things by direct interposition,—if He had thrown aside all subordinate agencies and become the great agent Himself,—if He had put aside imperfect and fallible men, and, as He did at first, done all things ever after by the word of His power? We do not mean to say which would be best, but we know what he has seen right to do, and we know, further, that an economy in which everything was done by the direct intervention of God would be an economy entirely different from ours, and, above all, in that which peculiarly distinguishes it,—from the whole system of human responsibility. It is because God employs agencies that agents are responsible, and that each of us has to see to it how we fill the place, and do the work which He has assigned to us.

God has provided means for carrying out His great and

gracious purposes in redemption, These are here presented to us as wells. Let us consider what they are.

1. *The preaching of the Gospel.* This was the first of the means instituted by our Lord, the first of the wells opened. Christ's first work upon earth was the preaching of His own truth. And, as it was the first, so it was the chief. The Apostle says, "Woe is unto me, if I preach not the Gospel. And, in contrast with other instrumentalities, he says, "Christ sent me, not to baptise, but to preach the Gospel." How unlike this to be the Apostle's boast, if baptism were the new birth! Would he not rather rejoice in the number he had baptised? And in thus instituting and giving such a place to the ordinance, is not Divine wisdom justified by the marvellous results? See these few first preachers of the Gospel going forth on their apparently hopeless mission. The whole world lay before them, and their work was to bring it to the foot of the Cross, to acknowledge Christ as the sent of God and the Saviour of the world. And remember that, while feeble and apparently contemptible themselves, the object they had to commend was not likely to attract, but rather to repel the minds and hearts of men. It was not a Christ appearing in all the glory of heaven, attended by hosts of angels shouting His praise. It was not a sceptred, crowned, and enthroned Christ they came to announce, but Jesus of Nazareth, the presumed son of a carpenter, the meek and the lowly one, the man of sorrows and acquainted with grief, the despised, the rejected, the crucified one,—one who, while he lived, was the mingled object of hatred and scorn. Nor were these things concealed, but announced: "It was Jesus Christ and Him crucified." Was it possible that such men could succeed with such a message? Yet they faltered not, but, like David with his sling and his small stone from the brook, they went forth in the Lord's strength. And when were there ever victories like theirs. When did the sword or the spear ever achieve such triumphs? These triumphs were over the intellects and hearts of men. It was not long until the Areopagus at Athens, and the very palace of Cæsar himself brought their ready tribute to the feet of Christ. A few centuries, and the known world acknowledged the mission and work of Jesus of Nazareth. And what was the instrumentality? The preaching of the Gospel. It is, indeed, called "the foolishness of preaching;" so well it may, in as far as it is man's instrument, but it is power in so far as it is God's. Let men say what they will, God's great instrument for spreading His own truth is the preaching of the Gospel. It

will never be supplanted by any other. Neither the sacraments
of the ritualist, nor the newer or more effective agencies which
modern theorists, who hold themselves wiser than God, would
supply, will ever supplant it. It is God's own; nor do we fear
that the future, any more than the past, will afford reason to
question the marvellous wisdom which presided at its institution.

2. *The sacraments are means of grace, or wells of salvation.*
This has often been realised in the experience of Christians. We
have an instance in the case of the Ethiopian eunuch. He was
travelling through the wilderness on his way to his native land.
As he travelled, he was led to peruse these prophecies of Isaiah.
Who knows but his eye may have rested on the words of our
text? As he read he became perplexed with passages which he
could not understand. One of the great prophecies concerning
the coming Messiah came before him. He knew not to whom it
referred. But God, who seeth all things, and who designed a work
of grace on the heart of that stranger, provided an interpreter.
Philip stood by him, and led him to see in these words Jesus of
Nazareth. He believes the truth. But he does no rest there. He
prizes Christ, and, because of that, he prizes His ordinances.
"What is to hinder that I should be baptized?" They descend
from the chariot, the ordinance is administered, and what is the
result? "He went on his way rejoicing." And may we not
believe, too, that the other sacrament, in which Christ is
represented under the symbols of the broken bread and the cup,
has been to tens of thousands of his people as a well of water in
the wilderness. How would the experience of His people, from
that first night when it was instituted among the twelve, in that
guest-chamber in Jerusalem, have accorded with the wisdom and
grace of its appointment?

3. *Another of those means of grace or wells of salvation is
prayer.* God is the hearer of prayer. In this character His
Word ever represents Him. "He will regard the prayer of the
destitute, and not despise their prayer." And he provides that
this manifestation of His grace shall not be in vain; that as He
is a prayer-hearing God, His people shall be a prayer-offering
people. His beneficence is not wasted. Fitting objects are provided for it. Nothing more distinguishes the character of God,
as revealed in the Gospel, than that He heareth prayer; nothing
more distinguishes His people than that they are a praying
people. The earliest testimony given to the conversion of Saul
of Tarsus was, "Behold, he prayeth." Here we have presented

to us the open fountain and the thirsting soul. Prayer is as natural to the believer as it is for the living child to cry for food. That cry is not the cry of sickness but the cry of health. The mother does not mourn over it, she rather rejoices in it. It does not arouse her anxiety, she is glad to hear it. It would be the absence of it that would fill her heart with alarm. It would be the stillness and silence of her child that would fill her soul with fears. So with prayer. The crying of the believer unto the Lord is not a sign of sickness and weakness, but of health and vigour. It is one of the necessary exercises of the spiritual life, and betokens that things are prospering with it. It is when the cry of prayer becomes faint and infrequent that there is reason to fear for the result. And thus nothing is more truly indicative of a man's state before God than his experience with respect to his need of prayer, and the life and earnestness that enter into the exercise. And how truly has the throne of grace been ever found by the Church of God as a well of water in the wilderness. Moses found it so. So did David. So did Paul. So did Cornelius, whose prayers came up with such effect before God.

These three, then, the Word, Sacraments, and Prayer, are God's ordinary means of salvation. We do not mean to say that He has confined Himself to these, and that he may not use other instrumentalities when he sees it good so to do. The conversion of Paul was irrespective of all ordinary means, and was the direct act of God himself. What he has done once he may do again; and we doubt not He has done so. The ungodly man has been arrested in the midst of his wickedness, no man being able to tell how. The arrow has pierced the heart of the impenitent, no man knowing from whose hand it came, or what eye directed it. God is sovereign in all He does. He made it a law of His universe that this globe of ours should revolve round the sun. And yet he could arrest its progress, and make it stand still, as the sun lighted Joshua's way to the destruction of the Canaanites, in the valley of Ajalon. And it is well it should be so. Were it nothing else, it is well for the blind that grace is not necessarily allied to the reading of the Word; it is well for the deaf that it is not necessarily allied to the hearing. And it is well for many now, that grace has various ways of access into the human heart, and that God may make use of such means as He may devise for bringing the sinner to Himself. Yet there is a law of His house; and it is not with these exceptional cases we have to do, as a rule for us, but with that law; and according to that law, the Word, Sacraments, and Prayer, are the means by which sinners are converted, and the Church edified.

And, in connection with these, let us dwell for a moment on two considerations. (1) They are God's ordinances. It is well to be able to realise this. It is well for ministers. There are times when they are ready to say, despondingly, "We have toiled and laboured, but where are the fruits?" Not that we have warrant to believe that any faithful minister of Christ is altogether without success in his ministry, but there are measures of success vouchsafed to some that are denied to others, and periods of success denied at other times. Yet, however little in the way of success we may be able to point to, we have this always to fall back upon—that these are God's ordinances—that, while we have nothing to do with the success, we have to do with duty, as indicated by Him; and that, whatsoever the results may be, we are, as obedient to Him, ever to Him as a sweet-smelling savour. And we are warned by this thought against having recourse to appliances of human devising, as if these could accomplish what God's ordinances could not, as if ordinances of human devising were more likely to be effectual than those which are Divine. And what is true of ministers is true of hearers. Let them remember, although they may not be able to see what they would like of fruits, that these are God's institutions, and that the only safe course is to hold by them. (2) Another important consideration is that the fruits of these ordinances, when administered, are of God. The institutions and their results are equally of Him. Paul may plant and Apollos water, but the increase is of God. The race is not necessarily to the swift, nor the battle to the strong. The ablest and most learned and eloquent of ministers have not always been the most successful. "God hath chosen the weak things of the world to confound the strong." With what emphasis does His dealing in this matter teach men to think humbly of themselves! Paul may plant— and where would you find husbandry like his—what skill, what zeal, what prayerfulness in carrying on his work! With what power he would have spoken of righteousness, temperance, and judgment to come! The trembling of Felix was a testimony to the power of his eloquence and faithfulness. And yet, of itself, this was insufficient. He had not converted himself;—"By the grace of God I am what I am." He could not convert others. "Through Christ strengthening me I can do all things." And the watering of Apollos was, like the planting of Paul, equally insufficient. And yet, with what skill he could have watered,—his watering a noble supplement to Paul's planting. His eloquence and knowledge of the Scriptures would have fitted him admirably for building up the Church. How he would have applied the truths of God's Word to the cases of believers, and, by the aptness and timeousness of his applications, helped them over their difficulties. Yet, after all, the plant would wither and die, but for a secret influence coming down direct from heaven, just like the dew, which, unseen and unheard itself, refreshes and fertilises the tender herb.

II. *The Drawing out of these wells.*

The Jews understood these words literally, and accordingly, on stated occasions, they all rushed to the Pool of Siloam to draw water. They substituted the form for the spirit, as we too often do, and gave to the sign the place of the thing signified. Our Saviour rebuked them, and called them to come unto Him and drink. He is the well; but it is needful to participate of its contents. A very trite remark; but can we be reminded of it too often?

1. *The existence of the means of grace is not enough.* When Eliezer of Damascus and his ten camels came to the well at the city of Nahor, that was not enough. They had had a long and tiresome journey under the heat of an eastern sun. They were parched and wearied, and it was cheering to find themselves on the brink of the well. But they might have perished even there, unless Rebekah had come forth with her vessel and given them to drink. The provision of the Gospel is precious—the feast of fat things full of marrow, and wine upon the lees, well refined; the fatted calf; the best robe; the abundance of a Father's house. But what is it all, unless it be appropriated and rightly employed? And, surely, while it is mournful to see a soul perishing eternally anywhere, nowhere is it so sad as amidst the light and the privileges of a Gospel land. Perishing, as it were, amidst the sound of a Saviour's voice,—almost within sight of the promised inheritance! If we would benefit by the Gospel, we must appropriate its blessings. We may live in the midst of them, we may tender them to others, and urge their acceptance, while strangers to them ourselves.

2. Nor is it less true, that *we never will appropriate those blessings until impelled by a sense of need.* It was their oppression by the Egyptians that made the Israelites look else-

where for rest. All that might be told them of the riches of
the Promised Land would have, of itself been insufficient. It
was their sense of need that made the blind men cry out, with
such earnestness and perseverance, " Jesus, thou Son of David,
have mercy on us." It was the same sense of need that brought
the woman with the issue of blood into the presence of our
Lord. There was much to deter her. She was poor; she was
weak; there was a great crowd. She had to resist the promptings of her timidity and her modesty; she had to press into
the crowd, and to force her way to where Jesus stood. But
she was in need; eight and twenty long years had she been a
sufferer, and she hoped for relief, and by her sense of misery
and danger is she urged on, in defiance of everything that would
deter her, until she is able to touch the hem of his garment,
and is made whole. And who are the despisers of Christ, of
whom we hear so much ? Who are the rejectors of the Gospel ?
Just the men who never felt their need of a Saviour. Let them
but once feel that; let them but feel that they have immortal
souls, and that these souls are in danger of perishing eternally,
and they will not any longer despise Christ. Men need to be
taught that they are sinners: this lies at the foundation of all
religion. We are but beating the wind in speaking of Christ and
the consolations of the Gospel to men at ease in sin. We need
to tell them of Him, to tell them that they are sinners ; we need
to pursue them into their refuges of lies, and drive them out.
We have to do with masses living in sin and at ease in Zion,
ready enough to commend the Gospel, because they have been
trained to do so, but never closing with it. Nothing can be more
plain than that until a great, humbling, alarming, and awakening sense of sin has lodged in the heart, all our offers of Christ
and commendation of Christ are but labour lost.

We must draw, then, as needy sinners, out of the fulness of
Christ. And what is this drawing ? How are we to appropriate
Christ in the Gospel ? To what is He tendered? Is it to our
reason ? Not primarily. Is it to our affections ? Not primarily.
Appropriating Christ is not an act of the human intellect, nor a
mere exciting towards a certain object of the emotions of the
heart. It is an act of faith,—that act which, above every other
exalts Christ and His efficacy, and shuts out human boasting,—
that act which serves so much to equalise men, presenting them
all as sinners in the sight of God,—that act which, above every
other, shows how little the human intellect can do, and how little

God designs to honour it in carrying out His great purposes. The
difference between one man and another waiting on the means of
grace, lies in his faith. Two men are engaged in perusing the
Scriptures. There is little apparent difference. There may be
equal intelligence, equal apparent solemnity. Yet the real difference may be tremendous, not less than that between life and death.
And where does it lie ? In this: the one is a believer, the other
is not. Two men may be engaged in prayer. There is nothing
to show that they differ. They may have the same forms, the
same words; and yet how wide may be the gulf that separates
them ! They may stand side by side in the same pew, and yet
the distance that divides them may be as great as that between
God and sin. And what is it that constitutes the difference ?
The one is a believer, the other is not. The line that separates
faith from unbelief is that which separates the Church from the
world. We may judge by other standards, and take other elements into account in estimating men. God values them in the
the measure of their faith. With what emphasis does our Lord
commend the woman of Canaan ! " Oh woman, great is thy faith."
Of the Centurion, Gentile though he was, Jesus says, " I have not
found so great faith, no, not in Israel." Nor need I stop to
show how consistent this doctrine is with that of the thirteenth
chapter of First Corinthians.

III. *The joy here spoken of.*

Surely there is joy—there must be—in finding salvation. As
cold water is to a thirsty soul, so is good news from a far
country. Would not the soul of Hagar have rejoiced when the
angel pointed to the well ? Would not the soul of the affrighted
jailor have rejoiced when a door of hope was opened to him ?
There are many things in Christ, as presented to us in the Gospel,
fitted to inspire joy.

1. *His adaptation to the wants of the sinner.* He is just
what he required. Christ is not only unspeakably excellent in
Himself, but His excellencies are in every way suited to the
wants of the soul. Gold is precious, but it will not satisfy the
man perishing of hunger or thirst. One morsel of food, or a
draught of cold water, would be more precious to him than thousands of gold and silver. The sinner had perhaps been led to
seek peace from other sources, but he had been grievously disappointed; and disappointment followed disappointment, until he
well-nigh thought that for him there was no peace, that there

was no balm in Gilead. He had found nothing but broken cisterns that can hold no water. But he was graciously led to the true Siloam, whose waters are so well denominated those of peace. Then, in the fulness of Christ, he found all he needed,—wisdom, righteousness, sanctification, and complete redemption. Is it any wonder although his soul should rejoice ?

2. *There is the fulness of Christ.* The supply is not only suitable, but it is abundant. And how could it be otherwise ? The Christ presented to the soul in the Gospel is an infinite Christ. His merits pass infinitely beyond the demerits of sin. Let the sinner but for a moment compare himself with the Saviour, the finite with the infinite ; and how inadequate must he find those views of the Saviour which would lead him to doubt the sufficiency of Christ for him ! Surely he must know but little of the height and depth, and length and breadth of the glorious provision made there, who sees room to fear that Christ is not able to save him.

3. *He is an eternal Christ.* Infinite, so that there is no sin for which there is not provision made in Him. Eternal, so that He fills all time. And, lest it should be possible that at any period, any hour or day of the sinner's existence, there might be room to doubt the all-sufficiency of Christ, we learn that He is an unchanging Christ, ever loving, ever pitying, ever ready to save all that cry unto Him. If such be the Christ presented in the ordinances of the Gospel, is it any wonder although the sinner should lay hold of Him with joy ?

4. *There is the cause of rejoicing in the terms on which He is tendered.* Many things are good which are not attainable. How often are the sick without the needful remedies because they have not the means to command them ! The physician orders his patient to take certain measures, perhaps to travel to some other land, and seek to breathe a kindlier air. But the remedy is beyond the patient's means. He may be assured of the certainty of his cure, but what of that, his circumstances are such that he must refrain, even if he should die : The Gospel is brought within our reach, the reach of the poorest, the most abject, the most hopeless. It addresses the sinner as an offer. Its language is not " Do." That would be vain. Nor is it, " Give." That, too, would be vain. Its language is " Take." Let him take the water of life freely. When Abigail came to David, she loaded her asses with the abundance of Nabal's household. She sought for peace, and she felt that she must purchase it. Nor was she un-

o

willing or unable to pay the needful price. But what have we
to bring to Christ? Let us load ourselves out of our stores, and
what have we? Nothing but an accumulation of sin and misery.
And yet, that is what he wants. We are warranted to say, that
never did a sinner appear before Him without aught save his
wounds, bruises, and putrifying sores, who was not infinitely
more welcome than if he carried the wealth of a world. And if
Christ be so free, is it any wonder if the sinner should not only
appropriate Him, but appropriate Him with joy?

Let us now apply what has been said. (1) How mournful it
is to want the wells. When there is no vision the people perish.
Who can tell the value of Christian ordinances—their value for
time, their value for eternity? What a wilderness this world
would be, what a wilderness this land in which we live, without
its Sabbaths, and its Bibles, and its sermons, and its Communions!
It is not for one class only to strive to maintain these ordinances among us. It is the duty and interest of all. (2) The
danger of polluted wells. To be wholesome the water must be
pure. We dare not mingle anything with Christ. Nothing we
can thus mingle can be so pure as Himself. Let us strive to exhibit
all Christ, and only Christ. (3) If we have Christ in the ordinances, let us strive to partake of His fulness. What is the use
of waiting upon the ordinances of Christ, if we despise Christ
Himself? There is no greater dishonour to Him than that of
approaching Him very nearly, and yet rejecting Him there—
coming into His very presence and there exclaiming, with them
of old, "Crucify Him! crucify Him." Let us embrace Him, that
we may have to say with the Church, "Thou hast put gladness in
my heart more than in the time that their corn and their wine
increased." Amen.

CHRISTIANS A ROYAL PRIESTHOOD:

A SERMON.

BY

Rev. WILLIAM NIXON,

MONTROSE.

" And hath made us kings and priests unto God and His Father."—Rev. i. 6.

THE ascription of praise to Christ, of which these words are a part, was called forth by the contemplation of His redeeming love. That love passeth knowledge. It is destined to fill for ever, with its praises, the boundless and eternal kingdom of God. It is the love of God incárnate, to mean, polluted, perishing creatures. This love of Christ led Him, from all eternity, to rejoice in their arranged redemption by His love. It led Him to reveal Himself, as the Redeemer, to our first parents when they fell, and to their posterity, age after age, until at length He came, God manifested in the flesh. During His personal abode and ministry in our nature on the earth, the love of Christ breathed in all His works of power and mercy, in all His words of grace and truth, in all His ready, patient submission to the sufferings which He endured from friends and foes, from the powers of darkness, and the wrath of God; in dying for His people's offences, that He might rise for their justification. His love is further displayed in His going up from this earth to prepare a place for them in the mansions of His Father's house; in making continual intercession with the Father for them; in sending down into their hearts the Spirit of truth, to sanctify and comfort them, and to lead them to His presence above; and in using His almighty power to bring them to eternal life, and for putting all His and their enemies under His feet.

The love of Christ is here magnified more specially for the

experience which believers daily have of it on earth, in their felt deliverance from the guilt and dominion of sin, in the spiritual power and dignity which they are enabled to wield and wear, and in the sacred services to which they are called, and in which they spend their being. He has loved them, and washed them from their sins in His own blood, and made them kings and priests unto God and His Father. The same view of the sacred dignity and power of true Christians is given by the Apostle Peter, when he speaks of them as a "holy" and a "royal priesthood."

I. *The functions or offices here assigned to believers. They are "made" by Christ "kings and priests unto God and His Father."*

The Lord Jesus is a King as well as a Priest. He is "a Priest for ever after the order of Melchizedeck." Melchizedeck was king and priest in one. He was "king in Salem, and priest of the most high God." And Jesus is the antitype of Melchizedeck That fact is especially set forth and dwelt upon in the Epistle to the Hebrews, in order to prove that His was a priesthood superior to that of the Jewish priests. They were nothing but priests. The kingly power in Israel belonged to a distinct class of men. In the person of Melchizedeck, however, the powers and functions of king and priest were united. In like manner, Jesus Christ is both King and Priest of His church. He is "a Priest upon His throne,"(Zech. vi.). He is to be seen on high as "the Lamb in the midst of the throne."

Now, so far as that is possible, all true Christians partake of both the royalty and the priesthood of Christ. They are made by Him "kings and priests unto God and His Father." They are "a royal priesthood."

1st. They are made *kings*.

Temporal power and dignity belong to earthly kings. To Christ, the great King, belong all divine power and glory. He has all power in heaven and on earth. To Him every knee shall bow. He is Head of all principalities and powers, and mights and dominions. He is thus Head over all things for the Church, which is His body, the fulness of Him that filleth all in all. And all His redeemed followers partake of His power and dignity. They are made by Him kings as well as priests to God. They inherit His kingdom, and sit with Him on His throne, wearing crowns of glory.

(1) Christians are kings in respect of their *power*.

In popular language, all men who wield a special influence in the world, are spoken of as kings among men. Poets, philosophers, statesmen, warriors, philanthropists, and benefactors, who, in their respective spheres of action, exercise a commanding power over others, are spoken of as kings. The justness of this idea is recognised in Scripture itself ; for, when the Corinthians acted as if they considered themselves signally gifted and authoritative persons, Paul said to them, " Now ye are rich, ye have reigned as kings without us : and I would to God ye did reign, that we also might reign with you " (1 Cor. iv. 8).

In the best and truest sense, Christians are kings in power. They have wonderful power over all their enemies, if they are but careful how to use it, and to put it forth. Thus they can resist the devil, until he flees from them ; and they can so keep themselves, that he is unable fatally to touch them. They can also resist their own evil tendencies, mortify the deeds of their bodies, crucify their flesh with its affections and lusts. And they can withstand the world, despising its allurements, and patiently enduring its frowns. They overcome, in short, all adversaries and all evil, by the blood of the Lamb, and by the word of His testimony. They are thus kings in power.

(2) Christians are also kings in *dignity*, as regards both their personal dignity and their borrowed glory.

They partake of the *personal dignity* of *kings*. They have in them a kingly nature. They partake of the Divine nature, of the holiness of God. There is a moral majesty in the character of all God's children. It may be said of them, as of the children of Gideon, and in a far higher sense, that each of them resembles the children of a king.

Christians also partake of a *borrowed dignity* that is *Divine*. They partake of the glory that belongs to the Divine Redeemer. They are arrayed in the robes of His righteousness. As He was made sin for them, so they are made the righteousness of God in Him. The eye of faith sees them as the Lamb's wife, already standing on His right hand, like the queen in gold of Ophir.

But some, when looking at the outward circumstances and appearances of many of them in the present world, will say the saints are often in temporal straits,—in want, in danger,—crushed by trials from the hand of God,—overwhelmed, to appearance, by reproach and violence at the hands of men. Are they even in such a condition, *kings?* They are. They are kings even in such circumstances ; for, even in such a state, they are still really overcoming all their enemies, and all evil, by the blood of the Lord, and by the word of His testimony.

Take, as an illustration, Dives and Lazarus,—the one within his house, clothed in purple and fine linen, and faring sumptuously every day; the other at the gate, living on the crumbs that reached him from the rich man's table, while the dogs came and licked his sores. Which was the real potentate—which the pauper? Dives was all the while a poor, perishing sinner, hastening to hell: Lazarus was all the while a holy, honoured, happy child of God, and an heir of everlasting glory. Dives was the slave of his own lusts, and demons hovered over him—yea, filled him, and held him fast in chains of adamant, until they dragged him down with them to the bottomless pit. Lazarus was, even on earth, the conqueror of sin and Satan, of death and hell; and angels of light guarded him, and ministered to him, though unseen, until they conveyed him to his everlasting rest.

Go to the dying-bed of a mighty, graceless monarch, and you find him, in the midst of weakness and of misery, hastening down to the sides of the pit. Go to the dying-bed of an humble child of God, and, though you find him on his pallet of straw, yielding to the power of dissolution; his face is radiant with the light of the Divine countenance lifted upon him, and with the hopes of glory that fill and cheer his heart; and already you see Satan, death, and hell dragged, as powerless, prostrate foes, at the chariot-wheels of his triumphing faith, and find him raising the song of victory over all his enemies, as one who already feels that in Christ he is more than conqueror.

2d. Christians are made *priests*.

Among the Jews, a priest was one who, under the Divine appointment and guidance, stood before the holy God in the room of the guilty, to offer that sacrifice for their sins by which reconciliation between God and them might be accomplished, and then on the footing of the sacrifice offered, made intercession on their behalf with God. This priestly work of offering sacrifice was performed by offering typical sacrifices of animals; and the priestly work of intercession was performed by burning incense on the golden altar, and by the priest offering his supplication for the people: "The Lord bless thee and keep thee; the Lord make his face to shine upon thee, and be gracious to thee; the Lord lift up his countenance upon thee, and give thee peace" (Numb. vi.)

Of course, there was no inherent saving virtue either in the sacrifices or the intercession offered by Jewish priests. They were but types and figures of Jesus Christ, the great High Priest, and of the sacrifice which He once offered, to take away sin; and of the intercession which He is continually making within the vail. Strictly speaking, there never has been on the earth, and there cannot ever be, any true priest, able to bring sinners nigh to God, as a reconciled God and Father, except his eternal Son and our Redeemer, the Lord Jesus Christ. He alone offered the only sacrifice which really takes sin away; and His blood cleanses from all sin. He alone appears in the presence of God for his people, presenting the merits of his sacrifice before the throne, and pleading so effectually for His people, as to prove himself able to save to the uttermost all that come unto God by Him. All those types of Him that were furnished in the persons of the many Jewish priests, from generation to generation, have died out, and passed away for ever. And there are no such priests now in the Church of God. Men, calling themselves priests, indeed, and pretending to make and to offer true sacrifices for sin, have arisen in what they call His church; but they are impostors and deceivers; and, as adversaries of Christ, and enemies of His cross, they ought to be abhorred and shunned accordingly. Ministers of the Gospel are not, in virtue of their office, possessed of any of the peculiar functions of a proper priesthood. They are teachers, pastors, watchmen, overseers, rulers within the Church. But they are not priests. They are charged with the keys of doctrine and discipline, whereby they open up the truth to the people for their instruction, and enforce the laws of Christ among the members of the Church. They are, in their performance of these duties, servants of Christ and of His people, for His sake. But they have no literal sacrifices to offer, and no visible altar on which to offer them; and they have no authority or warrant for presenting literal incense on golden altars, as typical intercessors with God. All such types, except those which antichristian imposture thrusts upon the Church of God, are for ever swallowed up in that one offering of Himself, by which Christ has for ever perfected them that are sanctified, and in that continual, all-prevailing intercession which secures to believers, one and all, the all-sufficient benefit and efficacy of His sole and unchangeable priesthood.

The only priesthood which is spoken of in the New Testament as still possessed under Christ, is that which he bestows on all His people, and on each of them. All whom He loves, and whom He washes from their sins in His blood, are made by Him priests as well as kings unto God and His Father. They are "a holy priesthood." They have boldness to enter into the holiest by the blood of Jesus, by a new and living way which he has consecrated for them through the vail, that is to say, his flesh." Having Christ, as the High Priest over the house of God, they draw near with true hearts, in the full assurance of faith, having their hearts sprinkled from an evil conscience, and their bodies washed with pure water.

The nature of the priesthood of all Christians may be understood by observing the following things :—

(1.) The *foundation* of it is their oneness with Christ. As bone of their bone, and flesh of their flesh, their surety and representative, their sin-bearer, their righteousness, and their life, all that He did and suffered for them, and is doing for them, they are dealt with as having done and suffered themselves, as now doing in and with Him. They thus share with Him in His priesthood, insomuch that, in His death and burial, they became dead and buried with Him (Rom. vi.); and in virtue of His living again, rising from the dead, and ascending up on high, they are "quickened together with Him" (Eph. ii.) "risen with Him" (Col. iii.) "raised up," "to sit with Him in the heavenly places" (Eph. iii.). Further, the spirit of Christ in them prompts them to render such spiritual and holy services as correspond, so far as that is possible, with those which He himself offered unto God. And the meannesses and defects of their services, and their personal unworthiness, are all so covered by the merits of His sacrifice, and the power of His intercession, that their persons and services habitually find gracious acceptance with God. Notice—

(2.) The introduction of Christians into their priesthood.

First—They are called to it by God. For no man taketh this honour to himself, but he that is called of God, as was Aaron. Believers are effectually called to their priesthood, by being born again, by being saved with the washing of regeneration, and the renewing of the Holy Ghost, shed on them abundantly through Jesus Christ, the Saviour. None can lawfully or truly enter on it in any other way. When any take to do with religion under the mere natural promptings of their own consciences and hearts, when they begin professedly to serve God without being taught of God, quickened by His spirit, or brought nigh to Him in

Christ, their persons and services do not find acceptance in His sight. It is when He is pleased to reveal His Son in any, and when, in consequence, they no longer confer with flesh and blood, but are called into the fellowship of His Son Jesus Christ our Lord, that they begin and continue acceptably to serve God.

Second—They are divinely qualified and prepared for their priestly work. They have been duly purified, being washed by Christ from their sins in His own blood. They are clothed in the necessary priestly vestments; for Christ has put upon them the garments of salvation; He has covered them with the robe of His righteousness (Isaiah lxi.); He has arrayed them in that fine linen, white and clean, which is the righteousness of saints (Rev. xix); and they have an unction from the Holy one, a divine anointing, an anointing of the Spirit, by which they are made to know and love their priestly work (1 John ii.). They are thus prepared to yield themselves unto God, as alive from the dead, through Jesus Christ. His blood, applied by the Spirit, purges their consciences from dead works to serve the living God. And so they hearken to the voice of Jesus, and set themselves at once to obey the commandments of His Word, and serve God with reverence and godly fear.

(3.) Thus called to their work, and qualified for it, they perform the duties of their priesthood, as the proper business of their life.

Prepared for their work as a holy priesthood, they henceforth live as in the presence of God, ministering before Him, and fulfilling their appointed services. They present their bodies a living sacrifice (Romans xii.). They present to God the sacrifice of a broken and contrite heart (Ps. li.). They offer the sacrifice of a living faith (Phil. ii.). They offer the sacrifice of praise and thanksgiving, or what are termed "the calves of their lips" (Hos. xii., Heb. xiii.). They lay on Christ, as their altar, the deeds of love done by them to others; remembering that with such sacrifices God is well pleased (Heb. xiii., Phil. iv.), and that they are the odour of a sweet smell, a sacrifice acceptable to God (Phil. iv.) Thus believers are "a holy priesthood."

II. *The inseparable connection between the royalty and the priesthood of Christians, between their work as kings and their work as priests.*

They have the *honour*, and exercise the *power*, of kings, because thus only can they be prepared to perform their duty as priests. For, as kings, they are laden with honours, make conquests, and in various ways put forth their power, and accumulate the fruits of its exercise, in order that, as priests, they may take their honours, resources, and conquests, and the varied fruits of their power, and consecrate them all to the service and glory of God.

In point of fact, they cannot be kings unto God at all, except as they put forth all their characteristic power, as from God, and as given to them to be used in His name, so as to fulfil His commandments and advance His praise. Their power as kings must be used by them in the sacred character of priests to God; for otherwise, with their power and honours, they serve themselves, and live to themselves, instead of living unto God and serving him; and, in doing so, they cease to be kings to God, and become in fact, at best, but the gilded slaves of the world, the devil, and the flesh.

On the other hand, they cannot be priests to God, except as they are also kings. For if they are not kings they can have nothing to offer as priests; they cannot command resources, accumulate fruits of wisdom, and accomplish holy, righteous, and loving services, which, as priests, they bring and offer up to God. Accordingly, that they must be a royal priesthood, if they are a priesthood at all. And thus becomes plain the necessary and indissoluble connection between their kingly and priestly office. This leads us to notice—

III. *The subordination of their kingly to their priestly office and work.*

The office of Christians, as priests, is higher than their office as kings. This is not the ordinary opinion of mankind, as to the two offices of king and priest. But it is the scriptural representation of the matter. And the reason is found in the very nature of the offices of believers, as kings and as priests to God. For, as *kings*, they but *rule* over *themselves*, and over *creation* around, *conquering* and *keeping under* the *enemies*, the spiritual enemies that fill and surround them, and causing the *creatures* around them to pay them tribute. But as *priests*, they turn their back upon creation, and their faces toward God, and stand in His immediate presence, and minister before His eternal throne. As kings, they but exhibit the honour with which they themselves are invested. But as priests, they are employed in giving all glory to God. They are thus not *priestly* KINGS, but *kingly* PRIESTS. They are a "*royal* PRIESTHOOD."

This view of the subordination of their kingly to their priestly office and work, becomes more evident and impressive when we consider how their office, as kings, shall at length be in a great measure absorbed in their office as priests. For when, as kings, they have conquered sin, and Satan, and death and hell, they shall come out of all their tribulation, and wash their robes, and make them white in the blood of the Lamb, and be before the throne of God, and, as priests, for ever serve him day and night in his temple. And though, as kings, they shall at last appear with crowns of glory, yet, as priests, they shall take their crowns, and cast them at the feet of Him who bought them with His blood ; and they shall then, and for ever, have it for their chief employment, to give, as priests, all glory to the Eternal.

It is appropriate to our present purpose to notice the way in which the kingly power of the Divine Mediator is rendered subservient to His work as priest. He is "a priest upon His throne." His throne is occupied by Him as a priest. His throne thus subserves the end of His priesthood, which bring sinners to God. And when, by his kingly power, He has redeemed all the sinners given to Him in the everlasting covenant, and prepared them for their blessed place among the works of God, in delivering up His mediatorial kingdom to the Father, the last act of Christ shall be to take His gathered saints, and, as a priest, offer them up to God, to serve Him henceforth and for ever and ever.

Then, throughout eternity the work performed by Christ in the midst of the ransomed and unfallen hosts of heaven, shall be work of a priestly nature, viz., that of leading the praises and services of God's holy and happy family. For we are told, manifestly with reference to Christ, " A voice came out of the throne, saying, Praise our God, all ye His servants, and ye that fear Him, both small and great." And, in response, there was heard, "the voice of a great multitude, and as the voice of many waters, and as the voice of mighty thunderings, saying, Alleluia, for the Lord God omnipotent reigneth" (Rev. xix.). While, to show that, under the leadership of the Divine Redeemer, this priestly work of praising and serving God is the principal, final, everlasting employment of the redeemed, as well as of the unfallen angels,— to show that the boundless and everlasting kingdom of God is a kingdom of priests employed for ever in ministering before Him, every creature is represented as heard joining in the chorus of the universe, "Blessing, and honour, and glory, and power be unto Him that sitteth upon the throne, and unto the Lamb, for ever and ever."

Thus, the work of Christ, as Mediatorial King, is subservient to His work as a priest. For, as His priestly work consists in opening up the way for the return of sinners to God, so His power as King is put forth to accomplish their return. By His power He subdues them to Himself, He rules and defends them, and restrains and conquers all His and their enemies. And when He has completed His work as Mediatorial King, in the final salvation of all the ransomed, He shall present them to His Father, as ready to enter on their course of perfect and unending obedience, and shall henceforth eternally lead in the praises and services which the redeemed and holy offer up before the throne of God and of the Lamb.

In like manner, the office of priests is the chief office which Christians execute in the house of God. No doubt they are said to have power with God; but the power thus spoken of, is power as priests, not as kings. It is power to entreat as suppliants, not to command. The power proper to believers, as kings, is power over the creatures around them, power over themselves, power over their sins, over their tempters, over satan and the world, over all evil. But the higher function proper to them, as priests, is to stand before God, to stand in His immediate presence, and to serve Him day and night in His temple.

To act as priests to God is the greatest honour, as well as the chief employment of believers. To serve God is the chief honour of the highest born of the sons of men. It is a satanic maxim, "better to reign in hell than serve in heaven." David appeared greatest, not when subduing his enemies, not when firmly seated on his throne, and receiving the homage of his people, and of his conquered foes; but when he sought out the ark, and brought it to its resting place on Zion; when he accumulated and dedicated to God the costly materials provided by him for the erection of the temple; and when, as the sweet singer of Israel, he penned those precious psalms which have been, in all ages, the vehicles of the praises of the Church of God. And Solomon, in all his glory, never occupied so exalted a place on earth, as when he stood in the midst of his princes, priests, and people, dedicating to God the temple which he built. Great as a conqueror looks, in vanquishing nation after nation, he appears far greater still in humbly, reverentially, and thankfully drawing near to God, saying, " Thine, O Lord, is the great-

ness, and the power, and the glory, and the victory, and the
majesty." The sovereign of this mighty empire of ours is not so
exalted in swaying the sceptre over such vast dominions, as
when, taking all her derived and dependent honours, authority,
and power, and as a sinful and redeemed servant of God, a
humble, happy worshipper of the Most High, offering up all that
she is, and has, at the footstool of the eternal throne. And the
mightiest of earthly rulers who forget this, who refuse to count
it their chief honour, as well as duty, to serve him by whom kings
reign and princes decree justice, shall speedily have all their
pride, and power, and honour brought low, and be found hiding
themselves in the dens and caves of the earth, and crying to the
mountains and hills to fall on them, and cover them from the
face of Him that sitteth upon the throne, and from the wrath of
the Lamb.

Thus, then, be your earthly position or prospects what they
may, your highest duty, honour, interest, and happiness, as believers, consist in taking all your talents, energies, substance,
influence, and time, and, as a royal priesthood, offering them up
continually in sacrifice to God.

Practical conclusion.

See to it, if you are believers, that you are by grace qualified
and rendered careful to spend your daily life in performing all
your duties as kings and priests to God.

As you would wish to be found, as *priests*, drawing near to
God, to minister before Him, take care that you are sincere and
holy. For their falsehood in pretending to give to the service of
God, that which they are really keeping back, Ananias and
Sapphira were struck dead in the presence of the first disciples.
For wickedly offering strange fire, which God commanded not,
Nadab and Abihu were consumed by fire from heaven. See,
then, that ye worship God ·in sincerity; that ye worship Him in
spirit and in truth, in the beauty of holiness.

You ought continually to put forth and employ all the power
which you have as kings, so as to enable you to fulfil your duty
as priests to God. Conquer sin, Satan, and the world. Rule
over yourselves. Live above the world. Quench the fiery darts
of the wicked one. Employ your faculties, your time, your substance, your influence over others, for spiritual and heavenly
ends. Bring all the successes which you thus achieve as
kings, and, as priests, lay them at the feet of Jesus. Thus,

whether ye eat or drink, or whatever ye do, do it to the glory of God.

Endeavour to have your character as kings and priests, attaching to all your thoughts, words, and actions. Live as those who have been set apart to the divine employment of living near to God, and serving Him. For this you have been cleansed by the blood of Christ from all your sins, and anointed with His Holy Spirit. Therefore, maintain your character at all times, and in all places. As anointed priests dedicate to God your souls and bodies, your time, and talents, and gains. Serve Him in all your relations, and in all conditions; serve Him in your closets; serve Him in your families; serve Him in your callings; serve Him in your recreations; serve Him in prosperity and adversity; serve Him with your one talent, or with your ten; serve Him in the church, and serve Him in the world; serve Him in the midst of His friends, and serve Him in the midst of His enemies; serve Him day and night; serve Him in health and in sickness; serve Him with your joys and with your sorrows; serve Him in life and in death. Cause your light continually to shine before men. Let the holy fire of love be ever kept alive and burning within your hearts. Let holiness to the Lord be engraven on all the thoughts, imaginations, and desires of your hearts, on your habitual conversation, and daily and hourly conduct. Let all the members of your body, and all the powers of your mind, as instruments of righteousness, be consecrated to His services. And thus, by a life spent in continual acts and exercises of piety, prepare for passing through the gates into the celestial city, there to serve God day and night in His temple for ever.

Such as are not thus living as kings and priests to God, are slaves of sin and servants of Satan. They worship and serve the creature more than the Creator. They employ their time and talents, their energies, resources, and influence, in ministering to the lust of the eye, the lust of the flesh, and the pride of life. And continuing so, they can have no share in the services of the heavenly temple, and no standing within its precincts.

JACOB'S DYING CHARGE:

A SERMON.

BY

WILLIAM BRUCE, D.D.,

INFIRMARY STREET CHURCH, EDINBURGH.

"And he charged them, and said unto them, I am to be gathered unto my people : bury me with my fathers in the cave that is in the field of Ephron the Hittite, in the cave that is in the field of Machpelah, which is before Mamre, in the land of Canaan, which Abraham bought with the field of Ephron the Hittite for a possession of a burying-place. There they buried Abraham and Sarah his wife ; there they buried Isaac and Rebekah his wife ; and there I buried Leah. The purchase of the field and of the cave that is therein was from the children of Heth. And when Jacob had made an end of commanding his sons, he gathered up his feet into the bed, and yielded up the ghost, and was gathered unto his people."—GEN. xlix. 29-33.

THERE ended the long and eventful life of the patriarch Jacob. He had schemed to obtain the birthright and blessing of his brother. He had borne the burden of toil and privation, through day-drought and night-frost, in the service of his uncle Laban in Padan-aram, meeting difficulties with resolution, and opposing craft to craft, that he might secure wealth and his union to his cousin Rachel. He had returned into Canaan, hoping to enjoy the comforts and luxuries of a prosperous condition, but only to find his latter days clouded by the jealousies and quarrels of his children. All these, however, were over now; and he was also leaving the honour and happiness experienced in Egypt, where the high rank and influence of his son Joseph had guarded and gladdened his declining years. How many vicissitudes he had survived ! How many obstacles he had surmounted ! How much of earthly good had been gained by him !—the father of a nume-rous family, the owner of large substance, a companion of nobles and princes, a man of repute and influence, not only among his own people, but among strangers ! What, think you, was his estimate of it all, when he charged his sons to bury him in the cave of Machpelah?

There ended also the religious privileges and exercises which had mingled with the current of his temporal labours and fortunes;—such visions as that which brightened his solitary unsheltered slumbers at the gate of Luz; such promises as that which pledged the God of Abraham and Isaac to be his guardian; such prayers as that which won for him, in the night-wrestling at Jabbok, his new and princely name of Israel; such thank-offerings as that which he laid on the altar of commemoration, in the place which he called Bethel.

But it was not the end of such things, as it was the end of all his worldly wealth and dignities. The latter terminated in the sense of ceasing for ever to have any special value in his eyes; they became to him as if they had never been,—as if schemes, and labours, and trials, and prosperings were the phantasms of a dream from which he was now awaking. But his religious experiences here ended, in the sense of being transformed and gloriously consummated, as the flower ends in the fruit, or the foreshadow in the antitype. No more visions of descending angels for him, who was about to join the multitude in the heavenly mansions; no more promises of Jehovah's blessing, because all that could be promised was on the point of being realised; no more prayers for defence in danger, because he was passing into the country where danger is never known; no more thank-offerings at earthly altars, because he was ready for the services of the upper Sanctuary. My friends, there is a vast difference between the earthly and the spiritual; and O, how impressively the death-bed teaches that the one is changeable, transient, and unsatisfying, — that only the spiritual is trustworthy and everlasting!

The dying words of the patriarch, recorded in the passage before us, are chiefly important as indicating his peace and faith in that hour. But we may first contemplate them shortly as *an expression of natural feeling*.

A natural feeling it is, a strong instinctive impulse of our humanity, this concern about the body, this concern about it to the last, this desire that, when the spirit has fled, it should not be neglected,—should not be thrown carelessly into the ground anywhere, but should receive a respectful interment where its mouldering remains may mingle with the dust of our nearest relatives. The soul, indeed, is the better part, the nobler element of our being, the seat of those rational and moral faculties which so unspeakably transcend in value the most curious and beautiful mechanisms. It can exist apart, can retain its consciousness, can exert its energy, can know, and love, and be happy, when its earthly house of this tabernacle is dissolved. But the body is its companion here, as one brought up with it, as one affectionately cherished by it; and we cling fondly to the hope that surviving friends will manifest some reverence and attachment to the stricken frame in which we once moved among them, and looked upon them, and talked with them.

We feel also, that, if there be one place in which our ashes may most fitly rest, it is the place which has already received into its silent chambers the remains of those who have been bound to us by the closest ties of kindred—whose fellowship we have loved, or whose memory we have venerated. " Bury me with my fathers," said the dying patriarch,—" Bury me with my fathers, in the cave which is in the field of Machpelah before Mamre ; there they buried Abraham and Sarah his wife ; there they buried Isaac and Rebekah his wife, and there I buried Leah." Who wonders that he uttered such a wish ? Even if it had not been prompted by the holier principle to which we shall afterwards advert, might it not have found a sufficient spring and motive of its exercise in the natural impulses of human feeling ? How instinctive the thought, that the dust in the family sepulchre has still some relationship to our material frame ! How instinctive the desire, that our bodies and those of our beloved friends should take the long, still sleep together !

Not less natural is the wish to be remembered—to be remembered in connection with those who have been so near to us in kindred and kindly fellowship. That our name shall be found among those of our household on the tombstone, that it shall be read along with theirs when the place is visited—that it shall link our memory to their memory, in the thoughts of the generation that follows us :—this may be a humble ambition, but it has a deep root and free growth in our human sensibility. There may have been no pillar erected, no scroll graven, above the quiet resting-place of the patriarchs at Machpelah. But that spot would be memorable and hallowed to their posterity ; and the thoughts of other generations, reverting to it, would dwell upon the characters and deeds of those whose bones had been laid in that unforgotten sepulchre. Did the dying man think of this ?

P

—did he think of the pious Hebrew, in after years, leading his children to the place, and saying, " This is the tomb of the good and great ones, whose blood is in our veins, and whose virtues we must imitate ; here they buried Abraham, and Sarah, his wife ; here they buried Isaac, and Rebekah, his wife ; here they buried also Jacob and Leah ? "   It was at least a natural wish, that there should be this additional link, binding his memory to the remembrance of his fathers.

Such feelings, my friends, are not unlawful ; but neither are they unprofitable.   If they be kept in their own place, if they be cherished in subordination to higher principles, if they be not permitted to overgrow and stifle the desires and expectations of that which is spiritual, they are neither unbecoming nor useless. We are the better of feeling that the body is a part of man, an integral part of our personal identity, and not lost, or unworthy of care, even in its dissolution.   We are the better of feeling that beyond death there is still some tie of kindred between our dust and the dust of our beloved relatives, as well as between our souls and their souls.   We are the better of feeling the wish to be remembered after we are no more seen in the world,—to be remembered in association with those whom we esteem and reverence. That is no civilised land—no land of social attractions and advantages—in which there is no concern felt about funerals and sepulchres.   That is no sound philosophy—no healthy training of the heart as well as the intellect — which would pity as sentimentalism, or stigmatise as superstition, the request of the patriarch to be laid beside his fathers.   Yet, if these words had breathed only what natural feeling dictates, if they had not embodied some higher and holier sentiments, we could hardly have expected to find them so specially recorded in the book which is designed to raise us, above the things that are seen and temporal, into the hope of the heavenly, and into fellowship with the divine.   The Word of God comes to make all things new in man ; and if a few flowers, remnants and memorials of a better day, still linger in the weed-cumbered garden, these must have a new tone of life infused into them, that they may again display the beauty and breathe the fragrance of holiness.

In their holier import, the words before us expressed the *peace and faith* of the dying patriarch.

He had reached a great age ; but he was still in full possession of his reason and consciousness.   His language shows clearly that there was neither weakness nor wandering of the intellect in that hour. He knew also the solemnity of the change now coming over him; he knew that he was then on the threshold of judgment and eternity—of a righteous judgment and an unchangeable eternity; he knew that he was about to pass for ever from this world, in which the offers of pardon are made, the opportunities of grace enjoyed, and the door of a divine salvation open. Yet, mark with what calmness he speaks, with what composure and tranquillity he anticipates his immediate departure. "I am to be gathered unto my people,"—"I am being gathered unto my people" seems to be the proper force of the expression, pointing rather to a present than to a future event. It was the language of one who felt that the last short journey was already commenced, that his feet were already dipping into the swellings of Jordan. But there was no appearance of alarm, no token of anxiety, no struggling search as if he wanted something to rest upon, or as if the anchor of the soul were not holding firmly. All is quiet, untroubled, and peaceful. Thus he passed down— down into the dark valley—down into the rushing river—as you might speak of going home from your day's work at evening. "I am now ready to be offered, and the time of my departure is at hand," said another, whose name is as familiar to you as that of the patriarch Jacob. The apostle was not destined to breathe out his spirit, in the bosom of an affectionate family, cheered by the presence and tended by the care of loving and loved ones. His course was to be checked by the cruel hand of persecution; and, from various allusions in his writings, it is evident that he expected his struggling bark to go down in some more violent gust of the storm which had been so long beating on it. Yet his reference to the catastrophe is in these calm words, "I am now ready to be offered, and the time of my departure is at hand." Were they not sufficient to prove that Paul had no dread of the issue—that he was filled with tranquillity and assurance in the prospect of putting off this tabernacle? It is equally obvious that Jacob had gotten the great victory, had surmounted that dark fear of death which subjects so many all their lifetime, and especially in the closing hours, to bondage. He died in peace; and most clearly was that attested when he uttered, in the face of the king of terrors, these few, simple, quiet words, "I am being gathered unto my people."

A similar inference may be drawn from the manner in which he conveyed to his sons the charge concerning his burial. Observe his careful, leisurely description of the place to which he referred, and its purchase by his grandfather : "Bury me in the cave which is in the field of Ephron the Hittite, in the cave which is in the field of Machpelah, which is before Mamre, which Abraham bought with the field of Ephron the Hittite, for a possession of a burying-place; the purchase of the field, and of the cave that is therein was from the children of Heth." That was no hurried glance at a secondary matter, amid the agony of an arduous and uncertain conflict,—no snatching of a moment out of engrossng anxieties and apprehensions about his spiritual interests, to indicate his desire regarding the body which was about to be resolved into the dust from which it had been taken. If he had not been at rest in reference to his undying soul, if he had not felt a quiet, holy confidence that it was safe, would he have been so deliberately careful in describing the situation and the pur- chase of the sepulchre ? Let us not marvel, my friends, that saints about to depart can dwell upon the thought of some earthly and temporal matter; neither should we grieve to hear them then speaking with interest about other things besides the spiritual and heavenly. It may be the very strength and quiet assurance of their hope of immortality that permit them to give some special attention still to the body, or the household, or the world which they are leaving.

Whence that peace, that terrorless tranquillity of Jacob in the death-hour ? Here he made no particular reference to the source of it. This was not necessary. He had indicated, by his religious profession, and by the consistent piety which adorned his life, especially the latter portion of it, that his trust was in the covenant mercy of Jehovah. In the prophetic blessing also, the sound of which had scarcely left the ears of his assembled children, he had spoken of the Shepherd, the Stone of Israel ; he had named the Shiloh, to whom the gathering of the nations would be ; and had concluded his prediction respecting one of the tribes with these words, " I have waited for Thy salvation, O Lord." Mark the connection in which this expression occurred. It followed the reference to Dan, whose emblem was "the serpent by the way, the adder in the path that biteth the horse heels, so that his rider shall fall backward." Injurious cunning, the cha- racteristic of the serpent, would be displayed by that tribe; and did not the patriarch then remember his own sin, the deceit which he had practised on his father, to the hurt of his brother Esau ? But he had waited, he said, for God's salvation—for salvation, for God's salvation he had waited; he had trusted the merciful God of his fathers to save him. There was no need of further explanation—there was no need for his declaring now that his peace was the fruit of faith, faith in the saving grace of that God who had given him the covenant with its blessings and promises, ratified by sacrifice and predictive of the Messiah.

The faith of Jacob was, like that of Abraham and Isaac, the substance of things hoped for, and the evidence of things not seen— a faith by which he embraced the promises afar off, and confessed himself a stranger and pilgrim on the earth, desiring a better country, that is, an heavenly. Yet his dying thoughts were on the earthly Canaan; and we can discern a special exercise of faith animating his wish to be buried in that land. The natural feelings of which we have spoken had their influence. But is it likely that he would have yielded to these, in the circumstances, if there had not been holier principles dictating the same desire, and more important ends to be secured by its fulfilment? The way was long from Goshen to the cave in which the ashes of his fathers lay; the funeral procession would have to travel a desert region, tediously, toilsomely, and not without danger. Yet the heart of the patriarch was set upon this interment in Canaan— so strongly set upon it, that he made it his dying charge to his children, the last utterance which they heard from him, too solemn to be forgotten, too sacred to be neglected. He had previously made special mention of it to Joseph, whose influence gave him peculiar facilities for carrying it out. Joseph also afterwards took a similar promise, upon oath, from his kinsmen; and the language of the inspired New Testament writer is, " By faith Joseph gave commandment concerning his bones." Canaan was the land of Jehovah's promise—his gift to the seed of Abraham—the heritage of the chosen people under the covenant of God's mercy. Jacob had removed from it, carrying his family and property into the territories of Pharaoh, where Joseph had married and become powerful. As years passed by, human judgment would be ready to say, the history of the Israelites is permanently merged in that of Egypt. But the Word of the Lord had spoken otherwise. In it Jacob had trusted; and his interment in Canaan would be to his seed, from generation to generation, the clear token of his belief that the covenant promise stood —that Canaan was the home country and the inheritance of Israel, in which the Most High would yet plant and prosper them.

There have been other deathbeds as peaceful as that of Jacob,
—others on which the failing breath could speak as calmly of
the approaching change, and of personal or family matters proper
to be attended to,—others which have conveyed to sorrowing
relatives the assurance that they were there to witness a believer's home-going. If it has been so in the case of beloved
relatives or friends of ours, should the remembrance of the
solemn scenes in which we saw their countenances changed be
only bitter, as if there had not been, amid the shadows, a fragrance of holiness, and a dawn-gleam of immortality? It may
have been a very pleasant voice that then ceased—a very sweet
and profitable fellowship that came to an end there; but if we
have seen the Saviour's promises fulfilled to the departing ones
—if we have beheld death without a sting, its bondage-fear
conquered, and its dark vail penetrated by rays from the eternal glory, should we not praise the grace of Him who has made
all things new to us, bringing life and immortality to light by
His Gospel? Again, let us not fear to anticipate our own departure. Let us be earnctly and trustfully preparing for it now,
in the faith of the Lord Jesus, for we know not what a day
or an hour may bring forth; and with reference to friends who
shall survive us, and sadly miss us from their side, let our
prayer be, that, whatever else we may leave to them, there shall
be, by God's grace, the legacy of those comforts and hopes which
flow from the Christian's deathbed. "Mark the perfect, behold
the upright; the end of that man is peace."

GOD CALLING THE WICKED TO REPENTANCE:

A SERMON.

BY

JOHN KENNEDY, D.D.,

DINGWALL.

" Say unto them, As I live, saith the Lord God, I have no pleasure in the death of the wicked, but that the wicked turn from his way and live : turn ye, turn ye from your evil ways ; for why will ye die, O house of Israel."— EZEK. xxxiii. 11.

THIS message from God contains, in the form of an oath, a declaration regarding Himself, and, with earnestness most intense, conveys a call to the house of Israel. The *declaration* and the *call* are therefore the two things to which the text demands our attention.

I. In considering the DECLARATION, we must first attend to the *import* and then to the *form* of it—to *what* God tells us, and to *how* He tells it.

1. The *import* of the declaration. It contains two statements. The first tells us, in what He hath not, and the second, in what He hath, pleasure. Let us consider each of these separately.

" *I have no pleasure in the death of the wicked.*" And yet the wicked dies. He who saith, " I have no pleasure in the death of the wicked," is He from whom came the message, " O wicked man, thou shalt surely die." The death of the finally impenitent is taken for granted. It is the mind of God regarding that certain event which the text calls us to consider. This passage gives no countenance to the idea that the death of the wicked is inconsistent with the mercy of God; for here we have divine mercy proclaimed right over it. In full view of this awful fact, Jehovah asserts His benevolence. Nor is it required, in order that we may reconcile it with the character of God as He is good, that we think of the death of the wicked as something less calamitous than eternal misery. Surely it is not mere temporary suffering, nor annihilation, over which Jehovah is exhibiting earnestness so intense. Only those who know not sin can be disposed to modify the retribution.

If a stranger, visiting this country, looked in on the homes made wretched by vice, some of which are not very far removed from the palace; or into the cells of our prisons, which are so prominent and so costly as government institutions, throughout our land; or on the sad scene of an execution, at which agents of the crown were present;—would he be justified in coming to the conclusion that our Sovereign was not benevolent—that such a state of things under her government was an evidence of our Queen's lack of clemency? If the crime, on account of which the wretchedness, the bondage, and the execution were elements in the condition of the kingdom, was ignored, it would be no wonder if a conclusion, adverse to the character of our Queen, were drawn from these facts. But let the crime be taken into account—trace to crime these instances of misery, and then not a shadow of suspicion appears to rest on the throne of our kingdom, nor on the name of our Sovereign. A ruler that would forbid the exact exercise of justice in dealing with crime, would, in effect, be quite as oppressive as the most cruel of all despots. The mercy that winked at crime would produce more calamitous results than the sternest tyranny. Even goodness demands a restraint on crime, and punishment for the convicted criminal.

And let it never be forgotten that the death we are now considering, in relation to the government and character of God, is "the death of the wicked." We must think of his crime when we think of his death—of his having resisted the will, disowned the authority, dishonoured the name, hated the being, and defied the power of God. Can we think of God as infinite in His being, glory, and goodness, without being constrained to conclude that eternal death is the wages due to all who thus sin against Him? Could we worship a God who, in the full knowledge of what He was, would award a punishment less than this? A God not necessarily to this extent just to Himself, could not be infinite, and could not be worshipped. Such awful justice as finds expression in the eternal death of the wicked, you must discover in the divine mode of government, ere you can either revere or love Him who is "over all." If you accept in faith the truth of God's infinity, you must accept as true the awful fact of the eternal death of all the wicked who remain unsaved.

The one pregnant difficulty is the existence of wickedness. While this fact must be assumed, it points to what must, to us, for ever remain an insoluble mystery in its relation to the will of God. But it is due to God, because of His infinite love of righteousness, that His relation to the origin of sin should be regarded without any suspicion; and it is also due to Him, as Supreme Governor, that to His mind alone the perfect rectitude of this relation should appear. It should be deemed enough by us, if to Him the existence of sin appears to be perfectly consistent with all the glory of His holiness and goodness. Into what awful darkness your mind must enter, if you presume to attempt to occupy, in relation to this, any position except that of adoring silence! Do not venture, with your imperfect conceptions of the Most High, to imagine that His way of dealing with sin cannot be right, because it appears not so to you. Ignorant of God and, therefore ignorant of sin, men often venture to pass judgment on the moral government of God, as if they had before them a finite being, dealing with some trivial offence. All error has its root in ignorance of God; all ignorance of what may and should be known of God, in hatred of the light; and all painful difficulty—all feelings that interfere with our adoration of God, and our admiration of His ways—in the pride which thrusts us beyond our place as creatures in considering the ways of God. At any rate, the existence of sin furnishes an occasion for the infinite display of the very attributes of God on which it seems to cast a shadow—His holiness and His goodness—and a proof that God alone is necessarily infallible; for it appears that no creature can become so, either in heaven or on earth, except when, by a sovereign exercise of His goodness or of His grace, He involves their life in His own unchangeableness. If the existence of sin forms a dark background before which the glory of Him who alone is immutable all the more brightly appears, let our thoughts regarding its relation to Jehovah's sovereign will, produce the calmness of adoring silence behind the awe which overwhelms us, as we think of its moral hideousness and of its everlasting results.

There is no malevolence in God which could be gratified in

the death of the creature of His hands. It is not because He
delights not in mercy that sin has been permitted to exist, and
death has been awarded as its wages. This is sufficiently proved
by His providence and by His Gospel. Does He not cause His
goodness to abound even to the evil and unthankful? Is not
the earth, at any rate, a scene on which He makes manifest, in
His providential dealings with sinful men, that He is "long-
suffering and slow to wrath?" Each moment between birth
and death is a fresh proof of this. And if, after a life made up
of moments, each of them brightened by the goodness of God,
the wicked dies at last, this calamity must be traced, not to lack
of benevolence in God, but to impartial justice. And how ample
the proof given in the cross that God hath no pleasure in the
death of the wicked! There, the death of wicked persons is seen
dissociated from them, and endured by a person who is the only
Begotten Son of God. There are the deaths of a countless multitude of wicked persons in one great retribution; and in the light
of that awful fire, in which the wrath of God is exhaustively
expressed, you may read the lesson of this text. They must die,
but they so die in Christ that they shall surely live. Their
deaths are swallowed up in the death of Him who is their Substitute; and because He alone is crucified, they all shall live.
Here we see God dealing with sin apart from the person of the
transgressor; and, instead of the guilty criminal, there stands
at His bar a person who is His own only Begotten Son. O,
how infinitely strong is the proof this affords, that it is from impartial justice, and not from malevolence towards the persons of
the guilty, that the sentence comes forth which awards death to
the wicked!

But there is more than this in the first statement, in God's
declaration regarding Himself, which we have in the text. It
tells us that *such is the character of God, as revealed in the
Gospel, that it is impossible for Him to find pleasure in the
death of the wicked.*

Now, it is not by ignoring the stern aspect of His character
presented by the law, that you can be enabled to have before
your mind the view of His character given in the text. Whatever was, is and must for ever be the character of God. He can
never cease to be all He was revealed as being in the days of old.
And by the law He reveals Himself now, just as He did then.
You, as a sinner, have to do with Him under the same aspect of
His character, and in the same relation, as Lawgiver and Judge,

as they who were under the former dispensation. And only in
a way which is quite consistent with all He was, and with all
He claimed, and with all He threatened, as the God of Sinai—
only when His name is so before you, that you can recognise
Him by the same glory which made awful the place of His
presence on " the mount that might be touched, and that burned
with fire"—can you possibly attain to hope in His mercy.

Nor is it by concluding that, because God is love, therefore
He loveth all, that you can have before you the view of His
character presented in the text.   Beware of being content with
a hope that springs from believing in a love of God, apart from
His Christ, and outside of the shelter of the Cross. It may
relieve you of a superficial fear. It may excite a feeling of joy
and gratitude in your heart. It may beget in you what you may
regard as love to God. This love, too, may be the mainspring of
very active movements in the bustle of external service ; but it
leaves you, after all, away from God, ignoring His majesty and
holiness, dispensing with His Christ, and enjoying a peace that
has been secured by a cheating, instead of a purging, of your
conscience. The time was, when men openly preached an un-
covenanted mercy as the resort of sinners, and laid the smoothness of that doctrine on the sores of the anxious.   " Universal love," in these days in which evangelism is in fashion, is
but another form in which the same " deceit " is presented to the
awakened.   This is something from which an unrenewed man
can take comfort. It is a pillow on which an alien can lay his
head and be at ease far off from God. It keeps out of view the
necessity of vital union to Christ, and of turning unto God ; and
the hope which it inspires can be attained without felt dependence on the sovereign grace, and without submitting to the renewing work of God the Holy Ghost.

" *God is love ;* " but when you hear this, you are not told
what must imply the declaration that He loves all, and that,
therefore, He loves you. *This tells us what He is, as revealed
to us in the Cross, and what all who come to Him through
Christ will find him to be.* It is on this that faith has to operate.
You have no right to regard that love, which is commended in
the death of the Son, as embracing you, if you have not yet
believed. It is only with the *character*, not at all with the *purpose* of God, that you have, in the first instance, to do. What
right have you to say that He loves all ? Have you seen into
the heart of God, that you should say, He loves you, until you

have reached, as a sinner, through faith, the bosom of His love in Christ? "But may I not think of God loving sinners without ascribing to Him any purpose to save?" God loving a sinner without a purpose to save him! The thing is inconceivable. I would reproach a fellow-sinner if I so conceived of his love. Love to one utterly ruined, and that love commanding resources that are sufficient for salvation, and yet no purpose to use them! Let not men so blaspheme the love of God. "But may I not conceive of God as loving men to the effect of providing salvation, and to the effect of purchasing redemption for them, without this being followed out to the result of His purpose taking actual effect in their salvation?" No, verily. For the love of God is one, as the love of the Three in One. The one love of the one God is the love of the Father, Son, and Holy Ghost. If that love generated in the person of the Father a purpose to provide, and in the person of the Son a purpose to redeem, it must have generated in the person of the Holy Ghost a purpose to apply. You cannot assign one set of objects to it, as the love of the Father, and a different set of objects to it, as "the love of the Spirit." And there can be no unaccomplished purpose of Jehovah. "My counsel shall stand," saith the Lord, "and I will do all my pleasure." "The world" which the Father loved and the Son redeemed, shall by the Spirit be convinced "of sin, righteousness, and judgment," and thus the Father's pleasure shall prosper, and the Son's "travail" be rewarded, through the efficient grace of God the Holy Ghost.

You have no right to attempt to look in on the relation of Divine love to individuals, till first you attain, through faith, to a place among His children. "Secret things belong unto the Lord;" do not, then, try to share them with Him. In considering the doctrine of the text, you have nothing to do with the question—"Does God love the wicked?" It is on the character of God that you are called to look, as He hath revealed this in the cross of His dear Son. You have no right to be influenced in judging of Divine procedure by preconceived ideas of Divine counsels, or of God Himself, but by the glory of His name, as He hath been pleased to reveal it. He does not tell me that He loves the wicked; but I am assured, when I look on Him as "He is love," that He hath no pleasure in his death. The fullest exhibition of His character, and the overwhelming proof of His having no pleasure in the death of the wicked, are given to us in the cross of Jesus Christ. "Yes," you say, "but it is in fulfilling a

sovereign purpose of grace that He has revealed Himself there."
True, but it is infinite love which He has revealed. It is by this
display of His love that you are to judge of the way in which it
shall fare with you, if you come to Him in response to His call.
Faith has infinite love on which to operate, in order to your encouragement. For, whatever be His purpose, it is abundantly
evident that "God is love." That is the character of Him to
whom you are called to return. That is the view presented to
you of Him to whom you are called to return, and it is with this
that you have to do. And when you think of the special purpose in fulfilling which He has so revealed Himself, you may be
all the more encouraged to return; for it is this which assures
you that a salvation both free and sure awaits you when you
come. The "purpose according to election," while casting no
shade on the infinity of the love, is a guarantee for the certainty
of the salvation which you are called to accept. For a people,
whom, in providing salvation for them, He accounted worthy of
death, He gave His only begotten Son, that, buying them by His
blood, He might save them by His power. You are called to
meet that love in the Son as Jesus the Christ, and to present
yourself on His blood as a suppliant for all the blessings of the
covenant of grace. What more can you desiderate? What
element of encouragement is wanting, in this form of doctrine,
which any of the systems of evangelical theology, or all of them
together, can supply?

But, 2. He tells us in what He hath pleasure—"that the
wicked turn from his way and live." The repentance of the
wicked is an occasion of delight to God; for it is the first
acknowledgment of His being "the true God;" the first tribute
to His godhead from the creature of His hand; the first movement of a lost one from "the wrath to come;" the first rupture
between him and that abominable thing which God hateth; the
first act of homage to His Anointed, who is also His Son; the
first fruit of the Spirit's work of grace—it is grace returning to
the fountain whence it came, and bringing a "wretched and
miserable, and poor, and blind, and naked" sinner back to be
"filled" with "all the fulness of God."

Repentance is the turning of the wicked "*from his way.*"
To this he was attached before, for in this he gratified the evil
desires of his heart. But from "his own way," as well as from
all besides that is sinful, the true penitent turns to God. But he
cannot do so without bringing the guilt and the source of his

wandering with him when he comes. And he turns to God. To Him he desires to come, to be a debtor for forgiveness to His mercy, and for salvation to His grace, and to consecrate himself without reserve to His service. And he comes through Christ to God, for He is "the way, and the truth, and the life," and "no man cometh to the Father but by" Him. He, as "the way," is all that God, in the interest of His glory, can desiderate, and that is required to make Him perfectly suited to the sinner's case. He who is "the way" is "the Word" "made flesh," made sin, and made a curse. Through His flesh, rent because of sin and by the execution of the curse, "a new and living way" was opened unto "the holiest." The entrance of this way is near to sinners in the Gospel—so near, that though the sinner can be brought nearer to it, it cannot be brought nearer to him. This way, no one but a sinner of our race may enter. It suits none else, and none besides is called. And his being a sinner is all regarding himself that is known to him who returns to God. It is not as a penitent, it is not as a loved one, it is as a "wicked" one, with all the guilt of his evil ways, and with all the corruption of the old heart, that he comes. And when, as such, he comes to God through Christ for salvation from all sin, "there is joy in heaven over" him.

And it is pleasant to God that the penitent should "*live;*" and He secures that live he shall, and live for ever. Finding the Son, he finds life, for he finds in Him a righteousness in which he is set free from condemnation, and has a right to all the bliss that flows from the favour of God. He has now a principle of spiritual life in him, and the Spirit of life Himself to preserve and perfect it; and even now, foretastes of life may be his through faith; while beyond, in the full view of God, and before the wistful gaze of his own dimmed eye, are the rest, and bliss, and glory of the perfect life in heaven.

There are three reasons, each infinitely strong, why this should be pleasing to God. As our greatest pains and pleasures reach our hearts through their love, the measure of love must indicate the capacity for joy. But who can conceive what must be the gladness, resulting from the gratification of infinite love! And there is a threefold love of God, through the gratification of which He receives pleasure from the penitence and life of the wicked.

(1.) *His infinite love to His people.* He embraces one whom He infinitely loves, when the repenting sinner reaches the bosom of His mercy. The loved one was lost, and the loved one was dead; and now the loved lost is found, and the loved dead is alive. It was only because this was ever present to His eternal mind, that Jehovah could have rested in His love to His chosen. But now the event is actual, and the divine joy is made known throughout all heaven. O, think of joy in heaven over one whose sins made the Son of God "a man of sorrows!"

(2.) *His infinite love to His Anointed One.* Each case of conversion is an instalment of reward to Him for doing the will, and glorifying the name, of Him who sent Him. The Father loveth Him because He laid down His life that He might take it again; and this love he expresses in fulfilling the promise, "He shall see of the travail of His soul and shall be satisfied." This He sees when He sees "His seed"—when the Father draws sinners unto Him, and follows this up by giving them, in Him, "all spiritual blessings" according to His intercession. The bestowal of such a reward, on such a One, must, to God, be the occasion of infinite delight.

(3.) *His infinite love to Himself, and to righteousness.* "God is love." He is so when contemplated *in the unity of the eternal Godhead.* But love requires an object; and He Himself who is love is the first object of the love He is. It is because His own infinite moral glory is ever present to His omniscience, that, through His love, it yields to Him who is "over all" such delight that He is "blessed for ever." And "God is love" as subsisting in a Trinity of Persons. "The Father loveth the Son," and that Son is, and ever was, "daily His delight." "I love the Father," saith the Son, and I was "rejoicing always before Him." And the Holy Spirit, who "proceedeth from the Father" and from the Son, lovingly fulfils the purpose of the Father through the Son. O, infinitely holy sphere! O, sphere of infinite loving —the unapproachable sphere of the interrelations and fellowship of the Father, Son, and Holy Ghost! And "God is love" to righteousness in His relation to His moral government. And when He makes manifest that He is love to His people, He does so in such a way as to secure that in their salvation there shall appear to His view, to His infinite delight, all to which He is love —as to afford an opportunity of expressing what He is as love to Himself, what the mutual love of the Trinity is, and how He loveth righteousness.

How the beauty of His holiness, to which He is love, appears in its having pleased Him to bruise His well Beloved, that there might be healing to diseased, and peace to guilty sinners!

How infinite must be His delight in this display of His glory, and how intent He must be on the salvation in securing which this joy was occasioned! Never did so much of His glorious character appear in any of His works as in the cross of Christ; but all this came forth in the prosecution of a scheme which bore on the salvation of sinners. True, all redemption work is before us in the cross. But the ulterior bearings of that work must be considered. Actual salvation is the terminating part of the divine scheme of grace, and each step of it must be brightened with the glory that shone forth in the course which led to it. If "truth met with mercy" in the cross, it was with a view to their coming forth together, from the presence of God on His throne, in the glad-tidings of the Gospel, to guide a sinner unto "the holiest," where alone He can obtain the blessing. If "righteousness and peace embraced each other," it was with a view to His being righteous to Christ, in giving peace, for His sake, to those who deserved to die. The infinite display, already given, finds its complement in a work of grace. To this new occasion of expressing Himself, He comes in all the glorious brightness of His name, as revealed in the cross. And in how many ways, in His work of grace, resulting in the penitence and life of the wicked, He manifests the glory of His power, wisdom, faithfulness, holiness, and love!

And how salvation furnishes an opportunity of exhibiting the mutual love of the Persons of the Godhead! The Father's love to the Son appears in His having delivered all things into His hand; and you are called to look, in the light of the Gospel, on this demonstration of that wondrous love. And the Son desired that the world should know how He loved the Father, by His obedience unto death, even the death of the cross. O, infinite wonder, that the blood which tells you there is peace for a sinner, is the demonstration which the Son has given to the universe of His love to the Father! And the Spirit, as the Comforter, takes the things of Christ, and of the Father, and, in fulfilment of the Father's purpose, and of the design of the Son's death, shows them to the sinners who are made heirs of salvation!

And how exhaustive, even as a revelation of divine glory, is the expression of His *love of righteousness* given in the death of His Son! The sins of a people eternally beloved, are imputed to Him who is His only-begotten Son; and for those sins, even He dies the death of the cross! O, how could any other exercise of justice, or all acts of justice that can occur in the course of His moral government together, express His love of righteousness as the atoning death of His dear Son hath done ? Only once did He, in the exercise of retributive justice, deal with one who was "His fellow," and only then could He, in one final transaction, give an exhaustive display of His righteousness. O sinner, all that God is, as He "is love," takes side with His mercy, when He receives and blesses him, who, at His call, comes to Him through Christ crucified!

2. *The declaration is in the form of an oath*—"As I live, saith the Lord." It is meet that such a declaration should have such a form, for thus only could earnestness, springing from infinite love, express itself fitly in words. What a proof this gives you of God's intense desire that you should believe what He declares! He swears by Himself in declaring to you that He hath no pleasure in your death, but that He hath pleasure in the repentance and life of all who turn to Him. Ought you not to fear remaining an unbeliever after all ? Is this divine earnestness to be met by indifference? Does this wave, coming from the divine sphere, in the eager movement of a solemn oath, strike on adamant when it reaches you ? Can you dare to dash it back by presenting to it a heart of stone ? Are you to be unmoved and callous before this display of divine earnestness infinitely intense ? Are you to sleep on, while this oath from heaven, uttered by the voice of God, strikes on your ear ? *For, does He not give Himself, in all the reality of His being and glory and blessedness, as security, for the truth of His declaration?* How real to God He Himself is ! But as He consciously lives in what He is, as infinite, glorious, and blessed, so is He true in the declaration of the text. What higher, firmer ground of assurance can even God give you than this ? O sinner, it is enough ! You might suspend on this ten thousand times ten thousand souls, each one as lost as the one soul you have, and you would run no risk. O, yield not to the unbelief that would dare to prefer a charge of perjury against Him for whom it is impossible to lie !

And does He not give Himself, in all the infinite resources that are His as God, in pledge of action according to the declaration of the text? Does not this suffice ? Can more be asked ? He shall cease to have, He shall cease to be, ere He can fail to be the God of salvation to you, if you return to Him at His call. O, what condescension is here ! O, how can you be at ease while the infinite Jehovah is thus in intensest earnestness bending over you ? O, lie in the dust before Him, as He approaches you in

Q

this marvellous act of condescension, and allow Him to lay the weight of His oath on your heart, to press out of it all its doubts regarding His truth and grace!

II. *The Call.*

From out of the midst of divine glory, from off the divine throne of grace, and intense with divine earnestness, comes the call to the house of Israel—"Turn ye, turn ye, from your evil ways." *Whence, whither, how* to turn, are the questions which these words require us to consider.

WHENCE? *"From your evil ways."* Every way in which you depart from the fellowship and service of God is "evil." Forsaking God is the great evil. It appears so to God as He looks on His own infinite glory, and on the provision of His everlasting love. How—because of His love to Himself, and of His zeal for His own glory—His holy indignation must rise into infinite flame, against that sin on the part of the creature of His hand! And how wonderful it is, that, in the full view of all that evil, and in His immovable resolution to deal out to all sin a full retribution according to justice, He should call the sinner from his evil ways, to be embraced on the bosom of His mercy! But the call is issued through the rent flesh of His own dear Son. The precious blood of His Lamb is before Him, as He calls the sinner from his evil ways; and to the praise of all His name, He can call the sinner to His mercy-seat. What the great High Priest presents meets all His holy indignation as it demanded expression in the infliction of the curse; and in gracious dealing, for His sake, with the wicked, it can be brought to bear, as consuming fire, on the sin whence sprang the guilt which atoning blood removed.

"From" *all* "your evil ways" you are called to turn; for there can be no turning unto God if there is any reserve of sin. Each evil way is oppossd, by an infinite contrariety, to the will of God. Sometimes the conscious reserve is reduced, under the pressure of conscience, to one evil way. What eager cries come from the flesh, for that one, and only that one reserve! And what attempts will be made to come to terms with God, while still cleaving to some darling sin! But it may not be. All sin must be forsaken by the will that inclineth Godwards. *How can Divine holiness admit of any reserve?* To cover any sin with your embrace, is to place yourself naked before the sword of God. He must strike at sin. O, beware lest He strike at sin through you! Come forth in your desire, away from, quite out of, all sin,

to God. " Cut off your right hand," " pluck out the right eye,"
rather than pass on to the fire that never shall be quenched.
And how can Divine grace admit of a reserve ? Salvation from
all sin is the boon which grace confers. Nought less than this
can express its bounty, and nought less than this can suffice for
you. Less than this you cannot have from the hand of God.
He cannot give you salvation to the dishonour of the law of
Christ, as the one authoritative rule of life. His holy grace under-
takes yet to give to the law, even in that form, its claims in full ;
and it begins to do so by bringing a sinner, with a heart broken
from all sin, under its holy yoke.

  " But must I rid myself of my guilt, and of my evil heart,
before I come back to God ? " Verily not. You are called to
come as you are, in the midst of your evil ways, with all the
guilt that lieth on you, and with all the fountain of evil in you.
Burdened and filled with sin, having no righteousness to cover
your persons, and no excuse to hide your guilt, and while there
is nothing in all your consciousness but sin, all over and all
through,—with no ability yours but the fell power to transgress,
—you are called to receive all the pardoning mercy and all the
saving grace you need.

  2. WHITHER ? To Himself God calls you. To Himself as
revealed in the declaration going before—to Himself as on His
throne of grace—to Himself through Jesus Christ. Beware of a
godless Christianity, as well as of a Christless religion. Souls, having only the uneasiness caused by the fear of death, are anxious
only for something that will take their blind dread away.
They have not known God in His awful glory as Lawgiver and
Judge, and they care not to realise Him in the person of the
Saviour. They feel not their need of a divine Saviour to remove
the guilt, and to subdue the power, of sin. And they ask not to
be admitted, under the Spirit's teaching, into the mystery of the
cross, to see a way for sinners unto God. The glory shining
from the face of Jesus draws them not through the Mediator unto
God. And they shrink from the pressure of Divine authority on
their conscience. But " he that believeth on me," saith Christ,
" believeth not on me, but on Him that sent me." By Christ you
must " believe in God who raised Him from the dead and gave
Him glory, that your faith and hope might be in God." " If
thou shalt confess with thy mouth the Lord Jesus, and shalt believe in thine heart that God hath raised Him from the dead,
thou shalt be saved." Believing thus, God shall be before you

244 THE MODERN SCOTTISH PULPIT.

in such an aspect of His character, and in such a relation to sinners through Christ,—in such marvellous love, and in such readiness to bless you when you come,—that you will be sweetly subdued into compliance with His call, and you cannot choose but to come. Divine glory, shining from the face of Jesus on a quickened soul, melts the heart, and causes it to flow down to the footstool of the throne of mercy. And the very view of God which wins his confidence, secures the homage of the penitent. He must appreciate His awful righteousness as displayed in the cross, as well as realise His majesty, ere he can have hope. And what he requires to encourage him, suffices to subdue him into an unreserved surrender of his whole being to God. The life that moves towards Him in hope, bows to His sovereign will, and lies in adoring worship at His footstool.

How ? In willingness to accept the terms proposed by God, as terms of salvation and of service. Even if you feel that you cannot come back to God—that, unless He, in His almighty grace, comes for you, you cannot come to Him—yea, even if you should shrink from asking Him to come,—if you only turn in the distant darkness to Him who is the way, and to God through Him, willing to owe Him the turning and drawing that you may come, as well as the blessing when you have come,—He " will pour out " His " Spirit unto you, and make known " His " words unto you." Turning thus, you will verily be debtors to His grace for all you need. And you may be hoping debtors, for He raiseth the poor from the dust, He bringeth the fallen from out of the horrible pit, and He gathereth, as He calleth, outcasts from the very ends of the earth.

Surely, then, God may ask the question, " WHY *will ye die?* " *You* have this question to answer. The reason for your dying is not on God's side. He has abundantly shown this. And on your side it is not found in your fall in Adam, nor in the ruin resulting from that fall. It is not in your helplessness, for you are called to lie under the gracious power of God to be saved by Him. It is not in the influence of the world, insidious and mighty though that be, for it cannot constrain you to be alien: from God. It is not in the might of the great enemy, nor in the multitude of his hosts, nor in the depth of his cunning, nor in the greatness of his cruelty ; for, " strong man " and " murderer " though he be, he cannot, for one moment, keep you away from Him who calleth you, if you are disposed to come.

Then " why WILL ye die ? " God meets you in the face, where

you are, and as you are, with this question. You are bound to give an answer, for only your own unwillingness to return can slay you. And are you to remain unwilling? If so, how can you justify yourself? 'My unwillingness,' you say, 'is just the lack of something which I can only have from God, and if He does not bestow it, then what can I do?' But, friend, do not think of your unwillingness as a mere negation—a blank for God to fill up. It is positive wickedness; it is sinful madness. It is an insult to God, implying contempt of His love, of His Son's precious blood, of His great salvation, and of His glorious name. To remain unwilling is to remain a rebel, disowning Divine authority, and bidding defiance to Divine power. And are you to choose this, rather than submit to be saved, ruled, and filled by God? 'Oh, but my unwillingness is the result of my being in a state of death as an alien from God, under the guilt and power of sin; how, then, can I help myself?' But, friend, the question is not, how you can help yourself, but, will you be indebted for all help to God? Will you die in your pride, even when confessedly helpless, rather than let Christ be "all in all" to you —rather than let the grace of God do all for you? To this point you are shut up, and this leaves your unwillingness exposed in all the nakedness of excuseless rebellion.

"*Why will* YE *die?*" Whatever may befall those who never heard the call to return to God, "why will *ye* die, O house of Israel?" "Line upon line, precept upon precept, here a little and there a little," have been given you, and is death to be *your* end? But the Gospel has been preached to the Gentiles, and to Gentiles also God hath granted repentance unto life. To each Gospel-hearer, therefore, this question is addressed by God. "The Son of man," who came "to seek and to save that which is lost," has come to you in your sinful helplessness, offering Himself to be to you all that you need, in order to your everlasting salvation; and, after all, will *ye* die?"

And "*why will ye* DIE? What is there in death, that you should choose it rather than life? And yet, every sinner who remains impenitent is charged with choosing death. God charges you with this when He addresses to you this question. And you are charged with *choosing* death because you *love* it, for He saith—"he that sinneth against me, wrongeth his own soul; all they that hate me love death." Rejecting the Gospel is sinning against Christ. You cannot do so without wronging your own soul. And this you do because you hate Christ. Not because you are merely indifferent. You would not sin against Him as you do, if you were merely indifferent. A consideration of your own interest would turn the scale, if there was an even balance. But it is not indifference, but hatred, that is your state of feeling towards Christ. And you cannot hate Him without loving death. 'O no,' you say, 'I cannot love death—I shrink from shame and agony, and both are implied in death.' True, what you regard as death you would fain escape from. But, in the view of Christ, it is death to be away from God. And you do love to be away from Him. And in loving this, you love death. And such is your love of this that you will not abandon it, though God tells you, and your conscience whispers to you, that if you abide an alien, you must perish for ever. You know that the death you love is linked to the death of woe from which your conscience makes you shrink, and that you cannot cleave to the former, without holding both in your grasp. And you never have at once any portion of time but the passing moment; and on that narrow foothold you always stand at the brink of hell. What you do there, is always finally done, for it is done by you on all you have of time. And there you keep fast your hold of that which must bring you down. Even now and there you do so. O "why will ye *die?*" Is there aught in "outer darkness" to commend it to you, so that you would choose to pass into the midst of it? Or is there aught in the "devouring fire," and the "everlasting burnings," to induce you to "dwell" with them for ever? Care ye to be in the bonds of despair, and under the fang of the "worm" that "dieth not." O, "why will ye" thus "*die?*" To God, who puts the question, give, if you can dare, the answer. And if you have no answer to give, fall silenced before the footstool of Him who calleth you. But break the silence of excuselessness by a prayer for mercy, and continue to cry, till an answer cometh from the mercy-seat, "Turn me, and I shall be turned."

THE EDIFYING OF THE BODY OF CHRIST:

A COMMUNION SERMON.

BY

REV. JOHN ALISON, M.A.,
NEWINGTON CHURCH, EDINBURGH.

" For the perfecting of the saints, for the work of the ministry, for the edifying of the body of Christ."—EPH. iv. 12.

THE first truth which may be pointed out as implied in the figure, 'the body of Christ," is the very close union between Jesus Christ, and those who are really His. It is a union similar to that of spirit and body. The Church of Christ is the body of Christ, and the Church consists of those, and of those only, who are thus one with Him.

We do not realize this sufficiently. Very many of those who swell the numbers of the visible Church are only on terms of ceremony with Jesus Christ. Is it otherwise with us? We are not necessarily of the body of Christ by having been baptised, or brought up in a Christian family, or having taken a ceremonial part in the communion. We may have eaten and drunk in His presence, yet not be recognised as His. "If any man have not the Spirit of Christ he is none of His." The Christ of the true Church is not a system of doctrine which may be learned by the intellect, nor a mystical or material person into which the bread and wine of a sacrament may be changed, and so received into our bodies. He is a pervading and animating Spirit; and that Spirit can pervade the whole Church only in one way—by animating the soul and body of each member of the Church.

How then may we attain this? By *yielding ourselves* to the Spirit of Christ. That is a very expressive phrase. It implies, first of all, not so much the zealous doing of something, as the letting ourselves be put right. It is more passive than active. It means the opening of our hearts to Christ. We cannot open our hearts by a resolution. We must yield them to the influence of such love as commends itself. We must let Him come in, because we have seen Him to be worthy. He stands at the door and knocks; at the common door, by which all loved ones come in, and He knocks just in their way. But when He comes in, it is not to have one of many seats at our table, but to be the new motive and spirit in us; to animate us as members of His own body. Jesus Christ must thus be in us, and to that end we must yield ourselves spiritually to Him. As a flower-bud yields itself to the rays of the sun, so will our hearts open to the felt love of Christ.

But we must yield ourselves to Him, in the other and harder sense of bringing our wills into subjection to His. What a stubborn and perverse thing our will is! It is like an old servant, who has long had his own way, but who has got a new master. He recognises his master's right to rule, but it is so hard to obey all at once. Self-will, long indulged, becomes stiff; it cannot bend easily to another's will.

In the unconverted soul, the will is in league with the appetite and desires and passions. The rightful ruler of them all, the spirit, has been so neglected, that if it speaks at all, it is in a weak way, without tone of authority. But when the Spirit of God quickens that spirit in us, straightway it rises in the consciousness of new strength and begins to take its rightful place, and to assert its true authority. Then the battle begins between the old servants who had been masters, and the new master over them. Then one can understand why the Spirit of God has laid so much stress on our overcoming; why so many promises have been given "to him that overcometh." We need daily grace for the conflict, else we should come under the dominion again of our own worse selves, and cease to be of the body of Christ.

You will see thus the true reason why, as believers in Christ, we should lead holy, loving lives; not merely because we have made a paction with Him, but because we are of Him; because His Spirit is in us, and we are again temples dedicated to the Lord. We ought to feel ourselves one with Him; identified with Him, in life as in interest. The union between the soul and the spirit of Christ is vital, a union of blended personality as soul pervades the body, and as spirit quickens the spirit in us.

The thought which is next suggested is the *unity* of the Church in itself. Probably there never has been an age when it was more difficult to recognise this unity of the body of Christ. One's first and natural idea of unity is that of external uniformity and external union; the opposites of these strike one more in these days. We have not only diversity, but separation, and in some cases not emulation merely, but enmity. Enmity between Christians is inexcusable—is almost a contradiction in terms; and it may well be doubted whether much of our separation into sects, while it has been overruled for much good, has not had in it the sin of schism. Whenever people fall out, and secede in anger, or jealousy, or uncharitableness, and are more ready to rejoice than sorrow over each other's failures or misfortunes, we may rest assured that the guilt of schism lies on them.

Still with much outward diversity, there may be real and conscious unity. There are diversities of tastes and diversities of operation, but the same spirit; and the great end may be best served by variety in the forms and by classification of the opinions in the Church, so that each may do his part in the way that suits him best, provided that the one thing needful is kept prominent.

This accordingly suggests the question—In what does this unity consist? In the unity of the faith.

"One faith," it may be necessary to say, does not mean, oneness of opinion in all things pertaining to our faith, or oneness in our ways of defining the faith; but unity in the faith itself. Regarded in this way, there is, when one thinks of it, far more real religious unity, even among those who seem to differ much, than they themselves quite realise. Taking faith as the reverent, filial, penitent trust of the soul in the living God and in Jesus Christ our Saviour, there is a large prevalent unity. But when people begin to define that which they cannot comprehend, and to magnify matters of opinion, they begin to differ, and quarrel, and separate, and hate one another. Given a number of men thoroughly in earnest, and with a fair knowledge of the facts and truths of the gospel, trying honestly to be true to their light, and bearing with one another in matters on which they do not see alike,—I am quite sure that, however men may judge, God sees their unity, and recognises them all as of the body of Christ.

Further; when we think of the figure by which St. Paul describes this unity, we discover some very important practical bearings of it. Two of the most obvious of these are the necessity of *mutual forbearance* and *mutual helpfulness*.

Every union implies a measure of restraint; each limits the freedom of the other. To be bound in a bundle when the separate members are free agents, is to feel restrained by the bond. Two horses or two oxen yoked together are not free to do as each pleases,; they must wait on each other, and learn to pull together. So, in all our associations, — and not least in the Church,—we have to learn the duty of considering and bearing with one another. You do not solve the problem by keeping apart from your neighbour as much as possible. You must draw near to him, speak to him, and act towards him as a brother, as a member with yourself of the living spiritual body of Christ; and when you and he cannot agree about some point of doctrine, or as to the best way of doing this or that, you must learn to forbear, by seeking some common ground, and cultivating the spirit of unity.

There is also the necessity of mutual helpfulness. The right purpose of a member of the body is not to seek its own good, but the good of the body of which it forms a part; and so the right attitude of a member of the Church, the body of Christ, is to seek not his own, but the things which are Jesus Christ's. Our true life thus is found in losing it. We find our truest good in crucifying self in faith and love.

We cannot be absolutely independent. It is a necessity of our nature that we should help one another, and the Spirit of Jesus Christ only makes the sense of this stronger. The very idea of the Church is that of an association, with a common faith and service, and bound by a spirit of mutual helpfulness. "The eye cannot say to the hands, I have no need of thee; neither the head to the feet, I have no need of you; nay much more, those members of the body which seem to be more feeble are necessary;" so in the Church, no one can say to his neighbour, I am entirely separate from, and independent of you; and as mutual dependence is a natural fact, so mutual helping is a Christian duty. If we are indeed one *with* Christ, we shall also be one *in* Him. Each will rejoice in another's success, and be ready to contribute to it. There should be no schism in the body. "Whether one member suffer, all the members suffer with it; or if one member be honoured, all the members rejoice with it."

There is certainly a great deal of this in the Church, and in the world through the influence of the Church. Not self-interest, but love, is the cement that binds the atoms of life into Christian unity. We readily forget whence some of our most noble and precious things have come. How few realise that all the charitable institutions of these times, all the sympathetic responses which famine and disaster, anywhere in the world, meet with from those more favoured, are due to the teaching and influence of Him who lived His simple life in Nazareth, and ministered in the towns and villages of Galilee and Judea! Christianity has told to a most blessed degree on the life and custom of the world; yet how much remains for it to do!

We are not true to Christ, else there would be far more mutual helpfulness. Not in trouble only, but in all circumstances, should we try to be as helpful as possible, that, "bearing one another's burdens, we may so fulfil the law of Christ."

The text suggests next, the *diversity* of *service*, as of gifts, in the Church. St Paul enlarges on this in the 12th chapter of 1st Corinthians, and also in the 12th chapter of the Epistle to the Romans, "As we have many members in one body, and all members have not the same office; so we, being many, are one body in Christ, and every one members one of another."

"The body," he says, "is not one member, but many," and then he shows the fitness of this, because of the many functions to be discharged. "If the whole body were an eye, where were the hearing? if the whole were hearing, where were the smelling?" The manifold usefulness of the body consists in its having many members, with diverse functions, able to work simultaneously. Such is the very condition of the Church's usefulness.

The apostolic rule is, "As every man hath received the gift, even so, minister the same one to another, as good stewards of the manifold grace of God." Let no man say, then, that he is not gifted. Every one is gifted. God has endowed all, though not all alike; but as He has not given to one the gifts of his neighbour, so He does not hold him responsible for them. If He has given you money, or a higher rank than some, put it to a Christian use. If your station be humble, you can there do service impossible to the rich. If you have a gift of teaching, use it; but if not, then do something else; for you may be sure that there is something which you are able, and expected to do.

Your presence at the Communion table was a practical acknowledgment of your privilege and responsibility as a member of the body of Christ, and a promise to do your best. Do not let your life belie your promise.

We are reminded, finally, of the end of this service, "the *edifying* of the body of Christ." To edify means to *build up*. Now, there are two kinds of edification implied here. There is the building up of the *individual*, and there is also the building up of *the Church*. Regarding personal edification, St Paul exhorts the Colossians, as they had received Christ, to be "rooted and built up in Him, and established in the faith." We should be very earnest in this. It is not enough to have been brought into vital union with Christ by faith. That life must continue to grow, striking its roots deeper and wider, and becoming both morally stronger and more productive. It must be built up, not so much as a house is built, but like anything with life and roots, increasing from within, through the influence of God's sunshine and by His storms also.

It is wonderful how God builds up His plants. Every spring repeats the wonder. The seed and the root are perfect of their kind, but God develops their perfection, drawing them out, and building layer on layer. From year to year it is the same plant, yet always changing. As soon as this process of building stops, the plant dies. So in the life of the soul; there must be a rooting, and stablishing, and growth in our faith; and one end of the offices which Christ appointed in His Church is, that this may be accomplished. "He gave some apostles, and some prophets, and some evangelists, and some pastors and teachers"—not merely that sinners might be arrested, turned, and brought to the mercy-seat, and into the company of Christ's redeemed, but that those, too, who have been so brought nigh by the blood of Christ might be edified, and the saints perfected. We must exhort one another, lest any of us be hardened. We must provoke one another unto love and good works. We must, "every one of us, please his neighbour for his good to edification." Only by this building up can we become able to bear the trials which may come to us. We cannot foresee them, we cannot tell the time or form in which they may come; but for any, or all, the one security is our edification in the faith.

There is also the other form of edification, the general building up of the Church. Too many give themselves no thought of this. They never try to realise the great world-wide purpose of God, and that every age, as well as each person, has a part to execute. The building up of the Church of Christ goes on like that of some of the great Cathedrals that have been built, or are still in course of completion, on the Continent. Two of the greatest and most notable in every way, at Cologne and Milan, are not yet finished. They were begun hundreds of years ago. No one generation could have done all the work, and so each in turn took up the architect's plan, and added a part; till now, in the one, only the pinnacles of the towers, and in the other, some carved work, high up, await the workmen. So "ye are God's building," and ye are set for the edification, according to your day and gifts, of the body of Christ.

It is our privilege and duty to care for the grand heritage which has come down to us, and to add to it. Stones for the walls of the great temple may be brought by us from waste places near and far. As in the Cathedral of St Mark's, in Venice, there are pillars brought from old heathen temples, and consecrated thus to holy Christian use; so, from the ruins of many idolatries, we may bring many precious living stones to build up and beautify the house of God. Every soul, indeed, that is won from the world to Christ, will contribute its precious things. "They that turn many to righteousness shall shine as the stars for ever;" and each of those so turned shall fill some place in the divinely-planned temple.

Each has his gift for the work. Some break up the fallow ground—tell, in their rude way, of sin, and hell, and Christ, and the blood, and salvation. Let us not despise them because they cannot do more,—because they have no system of thought that will bear criticism. They have their office. Others have the gift of sowing, or building up, leading out the new life to the food and work fit for it. Others, again, may have both gifts: and a still larger number can testify best, in the more common duties of ministration, of the love of Christ, and the life of faith. But whatsoever our hand findeth to do—just, because it has been put to our hand, and we can do it if we try—let us do it with our might.

This is the day of building, but there comes the night of taking down, that we may pass hence into the better country, that is, the heavenly, and from life in the visible body to the service of the Spirit, in the house not made with hands. Amen.

THE SOUL'S DESIRE FOR REST:

A SERMON.

BY

REV. JAMES JEFFREY, M.A.,
ERSKINE U.P. CHURCH, GLASGOW.

———

"And I said, O that I had wings like a dove! for then would I fly away and be at rest."—Ps. lv. 6.

ON the upland plains of Bethlehem, a shepherd lad might have been seen, in the olden times, playing on a rude musical instrument, as he watched his father's flocks. The boy was a born minstrel, and the long hours were beguiled by meditating on the glorious works of God around him, or by dreaming of the future.

There would be a strange feeling of restlessness in his breast, for the consciousness of growing power is very apt to make the young restless and discontented at home. Was his whole life to be spent in the humble occupation of a shepherd? Was he never to do more heroic acts than slay the lion and the bear in defence of his helpless flock? Were his brethren to serve the king, and live in the camp, and bear arms, and reap glory in war, while he was to be condemned to a life of peace, in which there seemed no prospect of winning renown? Such, I imagine, may have been the thoughts of the shepherd boy, as, sweeping his lyre, he expressed his restlessness in the beautiful words, "O that I had wings like a dove! for then would I fly away and be at rest."

The visit of Samuel to Bethlehem altered his whole life. We can fancy how his spirits rose, as the old prophet poured the anointing oil on his head, and disclosed his high destiny. We can fancy how he would live in the future, and would long for the time when he could throw aside his humble calling, and rise to the throne.

We follow him to the camp. We see him returning from the defeat and slaughter of the Philistine champion, the pride of the army, the hero of the day, the Court favourite, and we imagine that now surely the restless spirit must be satisfied; but we have only to remember the care and anxiety his advancement entailed, to understand how far off the desired rest seemed. From the day he returned to camp, bearing the head of his great adversary, the king looked upon him with a jealous eye, and he had soon to become an exile. For days and months he was hunted like a wild beast. His life was never safe. At one time he dreaded the fury of the king, at another, the faithlessness of his friends; and, as he fled from place to place, he may often have exclaimed, "O that I had wings like a dove! for then would I fly away and be at rest."

At last, that period of anxiety came to an end, and the outlaw found himself raised to the throne by the voice of the most powerful tribe. Now, surely his dreams were realised. Now, his ambition was gratified, and he might look forward to a few years of rest. It was not so, however. The beginning of his reign was clouded with civil war. Succeeding years found him engaged in war with some of the neighbouring tribes; and when his arms had been victorious everywhere, there came sore domestic trials. His favourite son rose against him, stole away the hearts of the people, and even threatened his life. Then it was that, full of trouble, not knowing what to do, or where to turn, David, the King of Israel, uttered the cry of the text, "O that I had wings like a dove! for then would I fly away and be at rest."

David is thus the type of man who "never is, but always to be blessed," who, from childhood, is looking for something more than he has to make him happy, and who, if he obtained every object of his desire, would still cry with David, "O, that I had wings like a dove! for then would I fly away and be at rest."

I propose to consider—

I. *The rest to be desired.*

II. *The means by which the Psalmist sought to attain the desired rest.*

In the first place, consider *the rest* the psalmist so eagerly desired.

We cannot say, with certainty, at what period of his life David wrote this psalm, and it really matters very little. The experience that gave rise to it was by no means an uncommon one with him. Many a time had he felt that if he could only rid himself of present entanglements, only get away from such men as Joab, only escape from the sea of cares in which he was plunged, he might be happy.

We all know the feeling. We all know what it is to have such a dissatisfied feeling with our present circumstances, that if we could just escape from them, in some way or other, we might be happy; and the only way of escape seems this, to be lifted out from the midst of them, and set down in perfect peace and solitude.

We may then, I think, find it interesting and profitable to inquire, what really is the rest which the soul craves; and what men mean when they utter this cry, "O that I had wings like a dove! for then would I fly away and be at rest."

1st. The rest without which, unquestionably, man can never be happy, is *reconciliation*. The soul can never entirely forget its relation to God. It may overlook this for a time; its claims may be unheeded for years, while men live for this world, and gratify every desire of their bodily nature. It may allow man to amass wealth, and court pleasure under any form in which it may present itself. It may allow him to pursue happiness wherever he thinks it is to be found. It may allow him to live as if there were no God, and no hereafter, and it may fancy it enjoys rest. But even as an eagle stirs up its nest, and compels its brood to take wing, so will it unsettle man's rest, by reminding him that his end is drawing near, and that God is about to require his account, and will force from him the cry, "O that I had wings like a dove! for then would I fly away and be at rest." It is astonishing what a trifling matter may disturb the soul's rest. A man may retire to his luxurious mansion, to the happiness of his domestic circle, to the companionship of his books, to the society of his friends, and yet fail to find rest, because he has spoken a hasty word that has severed him from one of his dearest friends. So, at the back of all the uneasiness of men, is the feeling that their hearts are not right with God, a feeling of which it is impossible to rid themselves, till they obtain peace with him through Jesus Christ.

You perhaps wonder why the gratification of your desires does not make you happy; the reason is, that the soul cannot be happy until it has made friends with God, and realised the blessed peace which they alone know whose sins have been forgiven through the blood of Christ. Flee, then from the wrath to come, to the love that is now eager for your salvation, and you will find rest in your present circumstances, but not otherwise. The rest of which you are in quest is not to be found in business, or pleasure, or intellectual pursuits, or the gratification of ambition,—it is to be found only in returning to God, and obtaining acceptance with Him through Jesus Christ. Do not, then, seek your happiness in these things; for, if you do, you will only engage in a butterfly chase, and you will never, never in this world get your weary longing satisfied. But if you will begin with Jesus, if you will accede to his invitation, "Come unto me all ye that labour and are heavy laden," then I can promise you rest, on the assurance of God Himself.

2nd. The rest so eagerly desired is *deliverance from trouble.* The cry, "Oh that I had wings like a dove! for then would I fly away and be at rest," came from an afflicted, persecuted, and sorely tried man. He felt himself surrounded with enemies; he knew not whom to trust. His spirit was wounded and crushed. He was haunted by the suspicion of personal danger. If he could escape into some solitary wilderness, he might feel safe, and might there find the rest that was denied him at home. Now, that feeling is one with which the most of us can have full sympathy. We may have had such severe bodily pain that our sleep has been disturbed, and our nervous system worn out. We would give all we have in the world to be able to fly away and be at rest, or to be delivered from our trouble. Or it may be, that some sudden bereavement or crushing calamity has overwhelmed us, and nothing we can do or think of can ease the pain we feel at heart, or lift the weary burden that oppresses us. Life is completely changed. It has lost its sunshine for us; and in the extremity and hopelessness of our condition, we have perhaps cried, "O that I had wings like a dove! for then would I fly away and be at rest." Or the Christian may be tried in a more painful way. He may be exposed to strong temptations, that try his faith and integrity very sorely; and as he finds himself exposed, day after day, to the same ordeal, as he finds temptation renewed with even greater persistency and force, he may eagerly desire rest; and, deserting his post of duty, he may hope, like Elijah, to find the long-sought rest. Others, again, may be tormented with doubt, and, with a serious anxiety to find the way

R

of peace, may be surrounding and hedging it with difficulties which they cannot themselves remove.

Such a state of mental and spiritual unrest is very distressing. It keeps the mind uncertain about the highest verities of life,—a condition in which no right-minded person can remain. The spirit cries, "O that I had wings like a dove! for then would I fly away and be at rest"—rest in the certainty either of faith or in utter scepticism, only it must have some resting-place. Like Noah's dove, it cannot flutter above the waters, it must have rest; and that rest is to be found only in returning to God, and in the simple dependence of faith on Him.

Again, this cry for rest is the cry of the dying saint. It is the cry of the soul for rest, which, after all, it cannot find on earth. There are few who can carry about with them such a confident assurance of their interest in Christ that they are never troubled with doubts or disturbed with fears. But the hour draws near when the journey is almost ended, and the city of God comes into view. From his dying bed, the believer catches a glimpse of it, and the glimpse is enough. He knows that there, and there alone, is to be found the perfect peace of an unwavering faith; that there, and there alone, is to be found the rest of a painless and sorrowless state of being; and he would gladly escape from his bed of suffering, to enter that blessed rest. The cry of the text is like the swan-song of many a saint, "O that I had wings like a dove! for then would I fly away and be at rest." Let us thank God for the rest of heaven. Our life of feverish anxiety, and ceaseless toil, and great sorrow, is coming to an end. The sun setting in storm may rise in calm and brightness; and the soul that leaves this world amid suffering and sorrow shall enter the other world in everlasting joy and peace. The desire of the soul shall be fulfilled then, as, with swift flight, it passes from the unrest of this earth to "the rest that remains for the people of God." No anxious thought, no fretting care, no depressing sorrow, no subtle temptation, shall even for a moment disturb that rest. It is secure against every interruption with which we are only too familiar here; and never again shall there escape from the redeemed and glorified saint that cry which has been so often heard here, "O that I had wings like a dove! for then would I fly away and be at rest."

In the second place, I go on to consider the *means* by which the psalmist sought to attain the desired rest, "O that I had

wings like a dove!" What did he mean by using this beautiful figure, and what are the wings that speed the soul on its
return to its rest? The first idea suggested by the figure is
an instinctive desire for home as the resting-place. There
is evident reference here to the wonderful instinct of the
carrier-pigeon. Instances have been recorded, in which the
bird has been carried hundreds of miles from its home, and
then set free; in a moment it has winged itself far over-
head, and then, fluttering for a little as it rested on the wing,
it has, with unerring instinct, directed its flight homewards.
The bird was drawn to its home by an invisible cord. So the
soul longs to return to what is its true home and resting-
place in the favour and friendship of God. This is the unerring
instinct of human nature, which has found expression in all the
religions of the world, and manifests itself, even in the most careless, in the moment of sudden calamity.

The first movement of the awakened soul is toward God,
though it by no means follows that it continues to seek Him.
But, deep down in our poor human nature, God has implanted
this instinct, which if obeyed, would lead the soul back to Himself. There lives and rules, even in the most degraded of our
race, what we call conscience, and the movement of the conscience, whatever men may say to the contrary, is Godward. In
those better moments that sometimes come to men's hearts, you
feel the desire to be reconciled to God, and thus obtain deliverance from the fear you entertain at the thought of meeting Him.
You have felt like a child away from home, who fancies all
would be well with him if he were again at home. The bio-
grapher of Michael Bruce tells us that, when he felt he was
dying, " the young heart yearned for home—for a mother's hand,
a mother's face, a mother's kiss, a mother's love"—so have you
felt the desire for home, wondering, it may be, how to get back
to God, and how to make your peace with Him, but conscious
that your heart will not be at rest until you have the light of His
countenance lifted up upon you; and your cry is, with the
psalmist, " O that I had wings like a dove! for then would I
fly away and be at rest." Now, this instinct is true. It has
been implanted by God. It is the dim memory, in the race, of a
time when God and man were friends, when the home of man
was made glad with the Divine presence, and man was not
afraid to meet God. And it is the true prophecy of a time when
that shall again be the case. But it is more; it may, by the

Divine blessing, become the means of again giving you this happiness on earth. The prodigal on the hillside, in utter want, was thoroughly miserable. He could get nothing to satisfy his hunger, or relieve his wretchedness, when, dove-like, the instinct of his heart sent his thoughts homeward,—"I will arise and go to my father;" and with the wings of a dove he sped homewards to his rest. And if I speak to any who are restless and dissatisfied with the life of sin, and whose consciences are speaking to them of God their Father, I would say to them, Listen to the voice of conscience—Return to God, and you will find your sins forgiven, your fears removed, the past forgotten, and the future radiant with hope. Come home, poor prodigal, come home, is the call of your father. The door is open. He is awaiting you with boundless compassion. You have cried, "O that I had wings like a dove," and He gives them to you, He attracts you home. Yield now to His gracious drawing; come home, poor prodigal, come home; and, in the enjoyment of your Father's love and favour, you will experience a happiness such as nothing in this world could ever give you.

The second idea suggested by this figure, is the directness of the dove's flight home. When instinct has taught the bird where home lies, it makes straight for it—you cannot hinder its flight, or turn it aside. Instinct will not allow it to rest until it has returned to the dove-cot. So, when the weary spirit desires the wings of the dove, it indicates that only at home can it find rest, and it seeks to get home speedily and directly. It is only by a direct return to God that the soul can come into the enjoyment of peace.

Now, there is something very suggestive in the idea of the soul going direct to God for its rest; for it is just between the awakening of the desire and the attempt to satisfy it, that many have failed to obtain rest. They know that God alone can give rest to the soul, but they mistake the way back to God. They have not been able to find as direct a course Godward, as the dove takes homeward. Who can ever forget Luther, with true instinct, toiling wearily in his efforts to get back to God? No dove-like flight was his, but a long round of useless ceremonies, that brought him no nearer home. And when, in utter disgust, he turned aside, still longing for rest, there rose before him the steep hill of difficulty, up which he was told the path to God lay; for he then sought peace in the faultless performance of every duty. But it was all unavailing. The direct road to God is through Jesus Christ. The only way of acceptance is by faith in His dear Son. To get back to our Father's home, we must come by the door, and Christ is the door; and the restless soul that comes to Christ and by Christ, finds itself home at once, and in full possession of that rest which He offers to the weary and the heavy laden. You may have rest at once if you will take God's way, but not so long as you prefer an easier method of your own. When walking in a part of the country that is new to us, we often feel a strange inclination to take some by-path which has the appearance of being shorter, but which too often turns out utterly misleading. It is the same in the matter of salvation. We have a natural inclination to try some other method more pleasing to ourselves than that provided in the gospel. But that is so easy and so well defined that no poor sinner need miss the road. It lies by the cross of Christ. It is by the death of the cross, and the life of the cross, that you get home to God; and you will display true wisdom if, with the wings of a dove, you fly away to your rest in God.

The third idea suggested by this figure, is the swiftness of the dove's flight home. Give the carrier-pigeon the wing, and not only does it make direct for home, but with an easy speed that distances the fastest train. Its eagerness to return gives speed to its flight, as, with unwearied wing, it pursues its homeward journey. So will it be with the soul that has not only been awakened, but has discovered the direct way to return. It will hasten to be at rest. The flight of the dove, is, after all, slow compared with the act which takes the soul to God in Christ. Swift, indeed, is the flight of the dove. Rising into the upper air, it cleaves it with beating pinion, and pushes on, hindered by no obstacles. Rivers, mountains, seas, forests,—all are alike to it. Raised above them all, it makes for home with a swiftness and sureness in comparison with which "the tempest is slow and the arrow uncertain." But swifter far is the act by which a poor sinner believes on Christ, and thus enters into peace. In a moment the soul is borne, over seas of doubt and mountains of difficulty, to its home in God, to find there the rest which God desires to be its portion. It may have taken a long time to reach the distance at which it finds itself from God, but the return may be accompanied with the speed of lightning. Some have called in question the genuineness of sudden conversions, and have scouted the idea of a man changing his whole course of life in a moment. But experience has shown that he can. Why,—not to speak of the great spiritual change,—many a man has, by great spiritual effort, broken loose from some evil habit and become entirely changed. And, with the Word of God in my hands, I dare not deny the possibility of sudden conversions. The first step in any great act of reformation must be taken in a moment; and in the return of the soul to God, the first step is one of the most important. Could anything have been swifter than the act of mind that brought the dying thief home to God, and gave him a peace that passed all understanding? Could anything have been more sudden than the act of mind that transformed Saul the persecutor into Paul the preacher? And it may be so with some whom I address. You may not merely cry, with so many, "O that I had wings like a dove," but you may even now return to God who is your rest. One look to Jesus will do it, and the unrest of a life-time will give place to joy and peace in believing.

And what are the wings that bear the soul to its rest? We can understand how the dove wings its way homeward. We can understand how the wanderer returns home—but how does the soul get back to God? or, in other words, how does the soul become reconciled to God, and how does it realise deliverance from trial? To this I answer, the soul returns to God on the wings of faith. A great modern critic has given a beautiful description of the dove's wing; but no language can sufficiently describe the nature and simplicity of faith. It is on the wings of faith that the soul makes much of its progress in knowledge; and for the most important of all knowledge, the knowledge of the way of salvation, it must make use of the same means, for that is the revelation from God Himself. In order to reach some distant land, we must have perfect confidence in the directions of those who have already visited it, and have furnished us with all the necessary information. And in order to return to God, we must attend to and believe the directions given us in His word, which are so plain that "he who runs may read." And what are these? The way to heaven lies through the valley of repentance, past the cross of Christ, into the highway of holiness. The truth revealed for the salvation of the sinner is the good news of the Gospel,— that the love of God has provided, in the death of His Son, an atonement for the sin of the world; and pardon is offered to every individual who trusts the work of Jesus for his salvation.

Thus it is that the penitent soul may mount, in a moment, from the pit of ruin to the rest of home, and the prodigal may return home on the wings of faith with swifter motion than the dove to its rest. Then come and be at rest. Do not delay. Come, rise up from your sin and worldliness, from your vanities and follies, and, with the wings of a dove, fly away and be at rest.

Again, the soul is borne to rest on the wings of hope. I have heard that the blind do often in sleep receive their eyesight, that is, in sleep-life, the pictures presented to the mind are those impressed on it when they enjoyed their sight; and they take pleasure in dwelling on these old mind-pictures. A man acts in a somewhat similar manner. When his life is compassed with care and sorrow, when he is brought through severe trials, he rises on the wings of hope, and, viewing the land of rest and peace to which he is fast travelling, he anticipates the joy of perfect rest. Like Moses, he climbs his Pisgah, and views the good land into which he will soon enter. How easy it is thus to escape from the sorrows of the present. The body may be imprisoned, but the soul flies away on the wings of a dove to its rest. A prisoner in Patmos, John soared on the wings of hope, and experienced the peace and joy of heaven. Bunyan's soul had many a happy flight into heaven when he sat in his cell in Bedford Gaol, and from many a sickbed has the wearied spirit been borne, on the wings of hope, to the mansions of the Father's house.

And lastly, the soul separated from the body will rise on angel's wings to God. The hour dreaded by so many is the hour expected by the Christian. It is the time when his desire is about to be fulfilled. Often has he cried, in weariness and distress, " O that I had wings like a dove ! for then would I fly away and be at rest," and now he gets them. Death removes all hindrances. Death opens the doors of the cage, and the soul mounts to God. Blessed be God for the assurance, that the glorious life of His people will begin at death ; that, when the heart ceases to beat, the spirit wings its flight to God. The one moment, the sufferer has cried, " O that I had wings like a dove ! for then would I fly away and be at rest;" the next, the free spirit has entered into rest ; for, says the Book of God, " Blessed are the dead that die in the Lord, for they rest from their labours." That, indeed, is to come ; but to all of you, I do once more offer a present rest, the earnest and the foretaste of the eternal. To all of you, I do once more address the Master's invitation, " Come unto Me all ye that labour and are heavy laden, and I will give you rest."

CHRIST OUR ADVOCATE WITH THE FATHER:

A SERMON.

BY

Rev. JAMES FENTON, M.A.

DUNDEE.

"My little children, these things write I unto you, that ye sin not. And if any man sin, we have an Advocate with the Father, Jesus Christ the righteous : and He is the propitiation for our sins ; and not for ours only, but also for the whole world."—1 John ii. 1, 2.

THE Christian life is variously regarded by the New Testament writers as a walk, a race, a warfare, a passing through the fire, and a fellowship. These expressions suggest to us appropriate analogies between our natural life and the workings of our spiritual nature. What a man experiences in his struggle for life in the world, the soul experiences in its struggle for life in God. This experience, in its relation to God, is aptly described as a walk or fellowship with Him ; and, in its relation to our spiritual aims and difficulties, as a race, a warfare, a passing through the fire.

Now, although our spiritual life is all these and more, and although all these views of it may have been occasionally present to the minds of the New Testament writers, yet each of them has his own favourite view of it, to which he often returns. To Paul, for example, whose life was an intensely active one, and whose mind was of an argumentative cast, it is especially a race and a warfare. "So *run*, that ye may obtain," he says. "Forgetting the things that are behind, and *reaching forth* unto those things which are before, I press toward the mark." "Fight the *good fight* of faith ; lay hold on eternal life." And when, as the close of his earthly career drew nigh, he looked back upon the years he had spent in the service of his Lord and Saviour, he still regarded them as a time of warfare and pressing forward under difficulties, —"I have fought a good *fight*, I have finished my *course*, I have kept the faith." To Peter, again, who was of a fiery and impulsive nature, the spiritual life was a passing through the fire. It is he who writes, " that the trial of your faith, being much more precious than of gold that perisheth, though it be tried *with fire,* might be found unto praise, and honour, and glory, at the appearing of Jesus Christ." " Beloved, think it not strange concerning the *fiery trial* which is to try you, as though some strange thing happened unto you." And, as if all outward nature were but a symbol of the believer's inner life, he reveals to us that the new heavens and the new earth will appear only after the old have passed through the fire. "Seeing, then, that these things shall be dissolved," he says, "what manner of persons ought ye to be, in all holy conversation and godliness, looking for, and hasting unto the coming of the day of God, wherein the heavens, *being on fire,* shall be dissolved, and the elements shall *melt with fervent heat.*" And now to John, the writer of this epistle, the spiritual life was, above all things, as it was to Enoch, a *walk* or *fellowship* with God. He it was, you remember, that leaned upon the bosom of our Lord as they reclined at the Last Supper; and the idea of nearness to Christ, which this act suggests, was that which rose above all others in the mind of John, as he thought of the countless blessings of a Christian life. This is clearly shewn in the preceding chapter of this epistle: "That which we have seen and heard declare we unto you, that ye also may have fellowship with us; and truly *our fellowship* is with the Father and with His Son Jesus Christ." To John, all believers were but one society or brotherhood, having fellowship one with another, through their common fellowship with a Heavenly Father and His Divine Son. They were one family, under one Father, admitted to everlasting communion with the Father through the one Mediator Jesus Christ. This fellowship, you will observe, is possessed by the believer here and now. "Truly our fellowship *is* with the Father;" not *shall be.* Doubtless, it shall be enjoyed also in the new heavens and the new earth, but it begins now. No sooner do we rest upon Christ for our salvation than the Father begins to commune with us, and we with Him. This same truth is again taught us by John in his gospel: "He that believeth on the Son *hath* everlasting life," hath it now, though not in that fulness which shall be enjoyed in a state of perfection hereafter. And this is everlasting life, to know,—to have an intimate acquaintance, a close and near fellowship with,—"the only true God, and Jesus Christ whom Thou hast sent." This, in

John's view, is the chiefest glory in a believer's life. Nothing can for a moment be compared with the joy of knowing that, even upon earth, the Father and Son are with us, revealing to us by degrees the blessedness of a sinless character and the mysteries of the heavenly kingdom, talking with us by the way as we journey on towards our everlasting home. This is what our spiritual life ought to be—a walk with God in light, where there is no suspicion, no misunderstanding, no distrust. And this it shall be in perfection hereafter. But alas! it is not altogether this upon earth. There are occasional misunderstandings on our part; for we sometimes think that the Father has forgotten to be gracious, and that His dealings with us in providence and grace are not actuated by love. And there are occasions when the Father does leave off communing with us, and retires within the veil into His holy habitation. As He says in Jer. xl. 47, "I have forsaken mine house, I have left mine heritage, I have given the dearly-beloved of my soul into the hand of her enemies."

I. *The fact and presence of sin.*

Now, whence come these misconceptions and hard thoughts on our part, and these withdrawals on the part of God? Whence come these breaks in our fellowship? From the *presence of sin* in the believer's soul. Sin is darkness, while God is light. And "what communion hath light with darkness?" "God is light," says John, "and in Him is no darkness at all. If we say that we have fellowship with Him, and walk in darkness, we lie, and do not the truth." While the sun is shining upon this side of the globe, we have light; but away on the other side it is night; because the whole earth lies between it and the sun. And so, between the unregenerate man and God there lies the whole world of evil, with its depths of corruption and mountains of guilt; accordingly he walks in darkness, and, except he be brought back to the light, darkness must be his everlasting portion. But even over him who has been brought back and may, in general terms, be said to walk in the light, there hangs an occasional gloom. Why is this? Not that God the Light has lost His power, but because sin has risen like smoke, or the vapour which forms the clouds, and dimmed to his eye the lustre of the Divine glory. It is sin in the believer's heart which produces mistrust and disagreement, and, since "two cannot walk together except they be agreed," his walk or fellowship with God is, for the time, clouded or broken off. The apostle, knowing this, yet earnestly desiring that men should enjoy this fellowship —not occasionally, but at all times—exhorts us, with all the earnestness and tenderness of his affectionate nature, to be free from this cause of alienation from God. " My little children, these things "—viz., that God is light, and sin is darkness, and that they who live in sin cannot have fellowship with God,— these things " I write unto you so that ye may not sin."

Consider for a little the true nature of the apostolic exhortation, "*that ye sin not.*" The command is, not that we be as little as possible defiled with sin, but that we be absolutely and entirely undefiled. You must not imagine, Christian believer, that, because you are one with Christ by faith and God regards you in love for the Son's sake, He will not be offended by your transgression. With all the greatness of His love for you, He retains His infinite hatred towards your sin ; for He cannot look upon sin,—any sin, whether it defile His friend or enemy. His love for you cannot make Him blind to your faults, or regardless of their pollution. Our fellowship with God does not influence His holy nature as the fellowship of men often influences us. The latter makes us blind to their faults. It wears away the pain we may have felt at first when we heard their profanity, their unchaste conversation, or their words of pride, envy, or bitterness. But our fellowship with God has no such tendency or influence upon Him. It cannot lessen in any degree ·the grief for sin, or anger against it, which He felt at first when the rebel angels were driven from His presence. Even if we should think of the closeness of the relationship subsisting between God and us,—a family relationship, in which God is the Father and we His children,—we must be careful to remember, that, on this point, there is a wide difference between the household of faith, and an earthly household. In the latter, a son or daughter may commit a fault without causing grief or anger in the parents' minds, either because they are ignorant of the fault, or because, being sinful and weak of themselves, they lightly regard the fault committed. But it is not so in the household of faith. Every transgression and disobedience is known to the Father ; and because He knows, not only the act, but also the eternally ruinous effect of it, He will not,—nay, He cannot,—lightly regard it, or pass it by with easy indifference. He folds around Him His garment of light ; and as, when the sun rises, darkness flies away, so when God appears, the soul that is defiled with sin seeks to flee from His presence. One sin is sufficient to effect this. It required but one sin to break Adam's fellowship with God. After one sin, he could not look upon God, —he hid himself from His presence among the trees of the garden; and, on the other hand, God could not look with favour upon the sinner; "He drove out the man." Every thick cloud that comes between us and the sun has a twofold effect; it both hides the sun's face from us, and darkens and cools the ground. So every act of sin both deprives us of the light of God's countenance and casts a gloom and chill over our whole spiritual nature. Hence, the apostle commands us to be clean, spotlessly pure, to have nothing and do nothing that will break the continuity of His fellowship with us. "These things I write unto you, *that ye sin not.*"

Now, the sins which believers commit against God may be divided into these two great classes:—(1.) Sins of ignorance and weakness. Paul was thinking of these when he wrote to the Roman converts,—"The good that I would, I do not; but the evil which I would not, that I do." For those who may feel oppressed with this sense of shortcoming, we shall find a word of comfort and guidance as we proceed. At present, I invite your attention, for a moment, to the second class of sins. (2.) Sins of presumption, offences committed with a high hand, in face of the teaching of God's Word and the promptings of His Holy Spirit. The teaching of Scripture with regard to this subject is fitted to strike us with fear and trembling. For, the law laid down in Numb. xv. 30, 31, runs thus: "The soul that doeth ought *presumptuously*, whether he be born in the land or a stranger, the same reproacheth the Lord; and that soul shall be cut off from among His people. Because he hath despised the word of the Lord, and hath broken His commandment, that soul shall utterly be cut off; his iniquity shall be upon him." The law of Old Testament sacrifice provided no atonement for wilful or presumptuous sin, but commanded the sinner to be cut off. And in the New Testament we have very much the same law; for, in Hebrews x. 26, the apostle writes, "If we sin *wilfully* after that we have received the knowledge of the truth, there remaineth no more sacrifice for sins, but a certain fearful looking for of judgment and fiery indignation, which shall devour the adversaries." Now, it is quite true that this passage in Hebrews refers more to the *habit* of sinning wilfully, than to one or several *acts* of wilful transgression. And it is quite true that even Abraham was guilty of wilful sin, when he represented to Pharaoh that Sarah was his sister; that David was guilty of wilful sin when he planned the death of Uriah; that Jonah was guilty of wilful sin, when he fled from the presence of the Lord instead of obeying His command, " Arise, go to Nineveh;" that Peter was guilty of wilful sin, when he denied his Lord, saying, " I know not the man." All this is undoubtedly true ; and because their sins were pardoned, and they were restored to God's favour, the believer who feels that he has wilfully sinned against light, is saved from utter despair. But we ask, Is there not great reason for the avoidance of even one wilful sin, when we think of the trials and tears, and heart-broken cries that followed their wilful transgression ; and how, even after their restoration, they seem not to have enjoyed that untroubled peace which comes through unclouded faith in God ? And further, Is there not much cause for serious alarm, seeing that *acts* of wilful sin soon develope the *habit* of wilful sinning, which is nothing short of apostacy from the faith as it is in Christ ? Examine yourselves, therefore, believers. See that there be no secret cherishing of sin in the life, no wilful breaking of the Divine law in business, no obstinate, implacable hatred against friend or enemy. Forgive as you hope to be forgiven. Let profits go, if they can come only by falsehood and dishonesty. Cut off the right hand, pluck out the right eye, part with all that is dearest, if these stand between you and the crown of righteousness. For the Holy Spirit, speaking through the apostle, says, " These things I write unto you, that ye sin not." He who in presumption rushes into sin, merely because he knows there is an Advocate with the Father, is like a man who throws himself into the sea because he knows there is one on the bank able to save him. He is like one who carries a naked light into a powder-magazine, or a carelessly covered light into a pit full of fire-damp. There is but a step between him and death ! and he knows not how soon the step may be taken which shall eternally separate between his soul and its life. Let our prayer, then, in all honesty and seriousness, be, " Keep back thy servant from presumptuous sins : let them not have dominion over me."

II. *The provision for sin : an Advocate.*

Now we shall look at the provision made for the removal of sin—a provision we all require ; for, even if we should be innocent of wilful transgressions, we are at least guilty of sins of ignorance and weakness. " If I justify myself," says Job, " mine own mouth shall condemn me. If I say, I am perfect," as some now-a-days do, " it shall also prove me perverse." My very claim to perfection would establish the perverseness of my heart and life. And John, in the preceding chapter, writes, " If we say that we have no sin, we deceive ourselves, and the truth is not in us." What hope, then, remains for us that our fellowship with the Father and Son shall be continuous, or, if broken, be renewed ? Since every act of sin breaks that fellowship, as every fault in an electric wire stops the current, and since conscience brings home to us, not one, but a multitude of transgressions, how can we ex- pect the current between us and God continually to flow, bring- ing into our empty souls the fulness of His grace, and carrying back to His throne the praise and thanksgiving of hearts en- riched by Himself ? The apostle answers, " We have an Advocate with the Father."

I invite your attention to the expression here used ; for it is one we do not meet with in the ordinary language of the world. We hear of men being advocates with a judge, or intercessors with a father ; but nowhere except in this passage do we find the expression, " an advocate with the Father." The explanation of this strange phrase we take to be this : John is manifestly addressing *believers*, for it is only to them that God would say, " My little children." This is also shown by the words, " If any man sin ; " for in the more full and exact form, this should read, " If any man *have committed an act* of sin." The apostle is addressing, not those who live in sin and walk in darkness, but those who walk in light and have fellowship with God, whose walk and fellowship, however, may have been broken through some act of sin. It is to believers, therefore, that John is writing. And since all believers, at conversion, enter into a family relationship with God, and since that is the highest and closest in which we can stand towards Him, the apostle wishes believers to remember that, notwithstanding their sin, God still remains their Father. He is their Creator, and Judge, and King, as well as Father ; but *Father* implies the nearest and dearest relationship, a relationship which unbelievers cannot claim, and one which believers do not lose, even when they commit some act of sin. And therefore, for the comfort of believers who may be mourning over their infirmity and short- coming, and doubting whether there can be a restoration to peace with Him who had cleansed their garments which they have sullied again, the apostle reminds them that the filial relationship is not lost by their coming short of God's glory through the weakness of the flesh. And so he writes, not " an advocate with the Judge," which would be quite correct, but "an advocate with *the Father.*"

But, next, why *an advocate*, and not an intercessor? Because the apostle is dealing, not merely with the sonship of believers, but with that sonship as affected by sin. And sin is a violation of God's holy law; a violation of the law of that kingdom in which the Father is Lawgiver and Judge. The *Father* is *Judge.* When the believer, therefore, yields to temptation and breaks the law of the heavenly kingdom, God, notwithstanding that He still remains his Father, appears also as his Judge, and calls him, for his sin, to the bar. And when a criminal is brought to the bar in a court of justice, what he wants is, not an intercessor, but an advocate. If a believer were in all things obedient to the Divine will, as the angels in heaven are, it might suffice him to have an intercessor with the Father, who should daily procure for him the blessings of the everlasting covenant; but this will not suffice a believer who has proved disobedient to the Divine law. He requires an advocate. And hence, John writes, "If any man sin, we have *an advocate* with the Father." We draw your attention to this; for if it was the fault of the theology of a former age, to represent God only as a Judge, and to maintain Divine justice at the expense of Divine love, it is becoming no less the fault of the theology of this age to represent Him only as a Father, and maintain the Divine love at the expense of Divine justice. Not only Deists or Unitarians, but even some of God's children, seem to imagine that, since God is the Father, and His name is Love, He will pass by their sin as an indulgent parent disregards the waywardness of a favourite child. Now, it is quite true that God is ready to forgive—let His name be ever honoured and adored for the blessed truth—still, He is ready to forgive, not as an indulgent father, nor as a lax judge, but only through the irresistible might and right of Christ's advocacy. There is no force in the argument that, because God is love and man is morally weak, He will mercifully overlook our sins. "If the righteous scarcely be saved, where shall the ungodly sinner appear?" If even believers, who, through Christ and the spirit of adoption can say, '*Abba, Father,*' require for their salvation the power of Christ's advocacy, how shall it be with them to whom God is not Father, but only Judge and King, and who reject the effectual advocacy of His dear Son? Every sin calls for judgment. It is an offence against the righteous law of

God, which must be vindicated. He who commits the sin is made, sooner or later, to discover that he requires one holding the position of an advocate to plead for him at the judgment-bar. God is *the Judge of all*, as He is also *the Father of believers*. And therefore, if any believer have committed an act of sin, it becomes him to find his refuge in this grand truth, " We have an advocate with the Father."

III. *The believers' advocate Jesus Christ the righteous.*

This advocate, observe, is not the sinner himself. It is a common remark about law-courts, that "he who appears as his own advocate has a fool for his client." If this be true in an earthly court of justice, it is no less true in the court of heaven. For he who is arraigned at God's bar is altogether unfit to plead his own case. Let us here consider, first, the fitness or unfitness of the unbeliever for this work. (1) He is ignorant of God's law. The wicked say unto God, " Depart from us, for we desire not the knowledge of Thy ways." (2) He is ignorant of his own sin. "Lord, when saw we Thee an hungered, or athirst, or sick, or in prison, and did not minister unto Thee?" (3) He is ignorant of the ruin which sin works. " He hath said in his heart, I shall not be moved, for I shall never be in adversity." And (4) he is ignorant of the holiness and justice of God. " Thou thoughtest that I was altogether such an one as thyself." It is manifest that the unbeliever is altogether unfit to be his own advocate, and yet this is the office which those who reject Christ try to fill for themselves. It need not surprise us, therefore, if, when sentence is executed against them and they share the doom of the fallen angels, from the abyss of hell they should impugn the wisdom, goodness, and grace of God. " Nay father Abraham, but if one went unto them from the dead, they will repent."

But the question may now perhaps be asked, 'Does the *believer* really require an advocate ? He is not entirely ignorant of God's law and his own sin ; he feels, in some degree, the misery which sin entails ; and he acknowledges that "God is Light," as much as "He is Love," Does he, then, require an advocate, seeing he knows all this ?' Yes, and just because he knows all this. For he feels that his knowledge of God's nature, and God's law, and his own sin, is very imperfect, and that his statement of them must partake of its imperfection. But, what is more to the point, his knowledge of these, however imperfect it may be, is yet sufficient to show him the utter hopelessness of his case. " He putteth his mouth in the dust, if so be there may be hope." He prays for a daysman who may put his hand upon Judge and sinner, and the Father Himself has provided One. " We have an Advocate with the Father, *Jesus Christ* the righteous."

Now, when I consider the character and work of this Advocate, I feel it will be wise for me, not to act as the Unitarian and try to plead my own case, but to leave my case entirely in His hands. And, in approaching Jesus Christ, I do not feel, with the Romanist, any need for the intercession of the Virgin, the prayers of glorified saints, or the intervention of a human priesthood. They who, in the least degree, rely on these, cast a sinful reflection, a dark shadow, over the advocacy of Christ. Why should I require the intercession of the Virgin? Is her love for the sinner greater than Christ's love? Is she more long-suffering, or more easy-to-be-entreated? Are there any misconceptions in the mind of Christ which she can remove? Perish the thought. Christ knows us, as God the Father knows us; Christ loves us with a love that is infinite and everlasting. And who can be more easy-to-be-entreated than He who gives this gracious invitation, " Come unto me, all ye that labour and are heavy laden, and I will give you rest ?" We say, further, that when Christ appears before the Father on behalf of a believer who has sinned, it is not as an intercessor,—at least, such an intercessor as Mary and the saints are represented by the Romish Church. Christ must not be thought of as loving us more than the Father loves us, as more longsuffering, more easy-to-be-entreated, showing us more sympathy, or knowing better the weakness of our nature. In these, as in their power and glory, the Father and Son are equal. The Father loves us as dearly as the Son. " God so loved the world that He gave His only Begotten Son." This was the love which the *Father* bore to us, one that is only equalled by the Son's, who gave Himself. And, on the other hand, Christ hates sin, even as the Father hates it. It is He who shall say, " Depart from *me*, ye cursed, into everlasting fire." Hence, we repeat, when Christ appears before the Judge and Father for a believer who has sinned, it is not with any weak form of intercession, but as our Advocate at God's bar of judgment.

To that bar throng the witnesses against us. The accuser of the brethren is there, with his train of malignant spirits. Conscience is also there. The accusation is supported, possibly by the evidence of our fellow-men, certainly by the law of God and books of remembrance written in heaven. And when hell, earth,

S

and heaven have all testified against us, the Advocate begins to plead.

Does He deny the evidence, or try to tone down its effect? Does He represent the sin as a small one, unworthy to be brought before God? Does He allege that the law is too strict, or the penalty greater than the offence warrants? Does He plead the previous good character of the accused, shewing how often or how long he has observed the law? Does He attribute the sin to the force of circumstances, the strength of the temptation, or the weakness of our moral nature? No. These are the pleas-in-law which sinners urge who appear as their own advocates before God. But our advocate is Jesus Christ *the righteous*. And because He is righteous,—a righteous Advocate in heaven as He was a righteous Man on earth,—He will neither extenuate our sin, nor seek excuses for it in our circumstances or weak moral nature; nor will He charge the law or character of the Father with undue severity. He admits the sin; He approves of the law; he acknowledges the justice of the penalty; and yet, strange to say, He obtains for the accused a discharge from the bar. And why? Because He is *the propitiation for our sin.*

It is this which crowns the fitness of Christ for being the be-liever's Advocate. It is not His righteousness alone that fits Him. The unfallen angels are righteous, yet their advocacy would be of no avail. It is not because he came to earth, and gave us a revelation of, or from the Father. The angels, Moses, and the prophets have favoured us with a revelation, given under the Holy Spirit's influence. It is not because He gave us an ex-ample, that we should follow in His steps; nor because He was self-denying, even to death upon a cross. In these points, Jesus Christ would only stand higher than, but not outside the ranks of, mere men. No, it is because He is the propitiation for our sin —the sin-offering provided by God and approved of God—the Lamb of God slain from the foundation of the world. Unless Christ be the sin-offering, bearing away, in His body upon the tree, my sin,—suffering there, in my room and stead, the punish-ment incurred by my sin;—then, I say,—and this with the most profound reverence,—that all the suffering He endured in life, and all the agony of His cross in death, will not fit him for being an Advocate whose work shall bring rest and peace to my guilty soul. For—and here we sum up the course of our argu-ment—I have sinned. Sin brings me to God's judgment-bar. There I require an advocate; one who can plead that the penalty has been paid. Otherwise, the law must take its course, and I become an eternal outcast from the presence of God. But blessed be God who redeemeth our life from destruction; He has provided for us an Advocate whom He always hears, because that Advocate is righteous and also the propitiation—priest, altar, and sacrifice—for our sin. If then, burdened with sin and guilt, we are at any time ready to halt, and almost ready to despair, let us think of Jesus Christ as our Advocate with the Judge and Father,—the same who, on Calvary, laid down his life for us. Thus shall we be able, with another apostle, to raise the note of triumph: "Who shall lay anything to the charge of God's elect? It is God that justifieth. Who is he that condemneth? It is Christ that died, yea, rather that is risen again, who is even at the right hand of God, who also maketh intercession for us."

Now we must close. We have dealt with the passage as referring exclusively to believers. Thus, we believe, the apostle intended we should deal with it. Is there, then, no word here for unbelievers, for those who may be out of Christ, but are anxious to be found in Him, not having their own righteousness, but that which is of God, through faith? Yes, in the words that follow—"Not for ours only, but also for the whole world." We do not understand this clause as touching upon the debated question, 'Whether Christ pleads for all, or only for some,' at least, we do not mean at present to deal with that point. We call upon the unregenerate not to perplex themselves with that question; it is one with which they have nothing to do, so long as they are outside the kingdom. What they should now consider is, that, if they are willing to be God's children, and desirous to be free from sin's curse and power, their way is open to them. The Advocate who pleads for an offending believer is also ready to plead for an anxious sinner. And for the latter, as for the former, there is no other Advocate. There is but "one Mediator between God and men, the man Christ Jesus." "There is none other name under heaven given among men whereby we must be saved." Let the anxious inquirer after salvation, then, meditate on this last clause: Christ is the propitiation for *their* sins, as well as for the sins of believers who have erred. The Advocate who pleads for believers so effectually that they are kept within the kingdom, is also ready to plead for the anxious sinner, that he may be admitted into the kingdom. That you may believe this, and trust to it, and act as those who in truth so believe and trust, is the prayer of the Church on your behalf. Amen.

GOD IS LOVE:

A SERMON.

Rev. JAMES ORR, B.D.,
HAWICK.

" God is love."—1 John iv. 16.

God's world might teach us to hope,—God's Word alone can give us the immoveable certainty, that He in whom we live and move and have our being, the Author of this universal frame, whose presence is manifested in every part of it,—is Love. It seems to us so simple, so self-evident a proposition, that we may wonder how the faintest shadow of doubt could ever rest upon it. Yet it is unquestionable that, as proclaimed by Christianity, now eighteen hundred years ago, this truth, God is Love, burst on the world with all the power of a grand discovery. Unaided by the disclosures of God's character made in the person and work of Jesus Christ,—as in a less perfect form in the teaching of the law and prophets,—it would seem to have been beyond man's strength, we do not say to rise to a firm persuasion of this truth, but even to frame an elementary conception of it. No single religion of antiquity, no one sage unenlightened by Revelation, ever attained to it. Those who did approach it thought that this good God could not be the Creator of the existing world. The nature-worships of the East found a multitude of powers in Creation, some beneficent, some noxious, some awful and avenging. Deifying all, they loved, feared, or propitiated each, according to its character. The bright sky, the fertilising rain, the sweet influences of dawn, were figured as genial deities, and hymns sung in praise of them were like far-off echoes of the saying of this text. But what could be said of the terrific earthquake, the dread simoon, the devastating flood, the glaring sun, withering the produce of the fields? If these powers were to be adored, man could only prostrate himself before them in shuddering fear. Asiatic religions, had they been interrogated, might have murmured, "God is Mystery." Greece with her Olympus, the bright reflection of her own free, æsthetic temperament, would have said, "God is Beauty." Rome's majesty would have answered, "God is Law." From the hardier northern races would have come the reply, "God is Prowess —God is Strength." Christianity alone, fresh from the vision of her Lord, and penetrated by the sorrows of His cross, has ventured on the sublime announcement, "God is Love." Truly a glorious statement! We are to ask to-day what it means, and how the Gospel has succeeded in raising it to the rank of a great spiritual certainty. But, as a preliminary to this, we may inquire —Whence the acknowledged inability of the world to reach this great truth for itself? How came mankind so universally to miss it?

I. "*God is Love*"—*a truth unknown to the wisdom of the world.*

We take for granted that man, at the commencement of his history, knew God as Love—knew Him as a wise, kind, and beneficent Friend, and loved Him as such in return. But this did not endure. Sin entered, perverting the will, darkening the mind, and degrading the affections. So to the simplicity of early faith succeeded heathenism with its impure worship of nature, savagery with its grovelling idolatries, and pagan culture with its refined but licentious gods of marble and gold. "When they knew God, they glorified Him not as God, neither were thankful, but became vain in their imaginations, and their foolish heart was darkened. Professing themselves to be wise, they became fools, and changed the glory of the uncorruptible God into an image made like to corruptible man, and to birds, and four-footed beasts, and creeping things" (Rom. i. 21-24). The knowledge of the true God was thus lost; and when earnest spirits, groping upward, tried to win it back, they found the ascents to the truth all too steep for them. Not one of them rose, or could rise, to this summit of sun-clear certainty—"God is Love." Now, why was this?

One cause of the failure must be sought for *in the spirituality and elevation of the idea itself.* As displayed in Christ, the love which is declared to be the essence of God's character rises above everything ever thought of in the world before. It is a love of purity so dazzling, of sweetness so tender, of sub-

limity so majestic, of self-sacrifice so unique, as to form a study
entirely by itself. Just as it is the glory of a painter to give
to the world a new ideal of beauty on canvas,—an ideal, the
grace and the perfection of which all can recognise when presented to them, but which they could never have conceived or
reduced to embodied expression for themselves—so with this
new ideal of transcendent, pure, self-sacrificing love given in Christ.
It was loftier, immeasurably loftier, than anything which past
experience enabled men to image to their thoughts.   It was a
new thing on the earth, an original creation, an ideal of love
which could not by any means have risen in the minds of men
breathing a pagan atmosphere, and nourished by pagan ideas.
Jesus therefore has done a yet greater work than teach us the
simple fact that "God is Love;" He has taught us what love in
God is; He has, out of His own life, filled up this word with an
unspeakable significance.   He has flashed on the world the vision
of a superhuman loveliness, creating the idea as well as certifying
the truth.   And this is not the least important part of the debt
which the world owes to the Gospel.

But a second consideration on this subject is, that *in the
scale of reason, the question of God's love must often seem a
balanced one.*   There is much in nature which supports, but it
must be admitted that there is much also which seems to discredit, belief in the entire goodness of God.   Our first impressions
of nature are joyous and optimistic.   From every opening leaf,
as in every passing breeze, we seem to hear it whispered, "God is
love."   The gay sunshine, the skies bending over us in the deep
purity of their heavenly blue, the brooks purling with soft music
through shady glades, the warble of birds, the general happiness
of the various creature-tribes, between which and their surround-
ings there exists so wise and beautiful a harmony ; the summer's
flowers, the fields yellow with the rich ripe grain in autumn, the
golden colours of the sunsets,—were these the only hues woven
into this living garment of God which we call creation, it would
be difficult indeed to resist the conclusion that God was nought
but good.   But they are not the only hues.   They are not always
the predominating ones.   Lift the veil a little, and beneath these
tender and caressing aspects of nature, how much lies hid that is
stern and inexorable,—one is almost compelled at times to say,
mercilessly cruel!   If we have summer's breezes, have we not
also terrific and destructive hurricanes ?   If we have fair meadows,
have we not also pestilential swamps, reeking with malaria ?   If

we have fertilising rains, have we not also furious and inundat-
ing floods? If we have fostering sunshine, have we not also
scorching heat, burning up the herbage over vast tracts of the
globe, and sucking the life from myriads of wretched beings, who
perish from drought and famine? If we have animal enjoyment,
have we not also the red tooth and claw of the beast of prey,
shrieking against our creed? If we have abodes of peace, have we
not also the brutalities and crimes of war? If we have smiling
landscapes, have we not also Vesuvian eruptions, Lisbon earth-
quakes, Alpine avalanches, the tornado, and the thunderbolt? If
we have life in its heyday of healthful mirth, have we not also
foul disease, decrepit old age, the sickening sights of the hospital,
and finally, for all—death? Now, put away your Bibles, and
looking these facts in the face, ask nature boldly, Is God love?
Does it give you an answer on which you think you can
depend? Very obvious is it that if love, as expressive of God's
essence, be that mere indulgent amiability which some who speak
of it seem to suppose, then God, as revealed by his works, is not
love. Whatever love in God is, it is not a love which cannot
both do and look upon things which are very terrible. It is not
a love which is regardless of law. It is not a love which cannot
punish. It is not a love which is incompatible with a holy intolerance of wrong, and a certain awful sternness of rule. There
are difficulties here which natural religion cannot successfully
cope with, which even revealed religion is compelled to recognise.
So that not from this source, if from any, can the mind of man
rise to the serene and joyous confidence, "God is love," In proportion to his thoughtfulness will he be baffled and perplexed,
and be tempted, if not to a denial of God's goodness, at least to a
limitation of God's omnipotence, or to a cheerless Manichæan
dualism. With only nature's book to read from. "The Father of
all," as Plato said, "is hard to find."

Yet a third cause of the failure of the world to apprehend
this great truth, and perhaps the deepest of all, is—*the workings of an evil conscience.* The voice of conscience in man,
accusing him of sin, can never be entirely stifled. The heathen,
as well as others, "show the work of the law written in their
hearts, their conscience also bearing witness, and their thoughts
the meanwhile accusing or else excusing one another" (Rom.
ii. 15). Now, conscience in a sinful heart invariably makes a
man distrustful of the love of God. It robs him of his peace,
disquiets him in presence of Deity, makes him quick to discern,

in any untoward event of life, or in any startling appearance of nature, a token of the displeasure of his gods. Fear and despair are felt to be tugging at the heart-strings of every pagan faith. The anger of the gods is a prominent feature in them all. Here, indeed, the question touches ourselves. Nature may suggest that God, in His natural relations to mankind, is love; but what is He in His moral relations to transgressors? Shall we say here "God is love?" or, "God revengeth? It is not enough for me to know that God is good to birds, and beasts, and insects? The question is—Is He good to sinners also? Can He undo their evil? Can He forgive and restore them? Can He turn back, from its avenging course, that terrible law of retribution which seems to hold them in its grasp? Revelation speaks of the angels who sinned, whom God cast down to hell. What if the same judgment awaits a world which also has broken loose from the restraints of law? Who shall say it does not? Who shall certify that God forgives? Pagan faiths have never been able to solve these questions satisfactorily. They have had their altars and their ritual, they have brought sacrifices, they have offered deprecatory prayers, they have sued for forgiveness from the gods as for a hard-won favour; yet, when they have done all, they have not made the consciences of their worshippers perfect. The peace of forgiveness is not in the pagan soul—trust in the favour of God is not re-established in the pagan heart. There is still a terror, a suspicion, a dread. God, in these faiths, is *not* love.

How, then, it may well be asked, are we to attain to certainty on this subject of the love of God? Science cannot help us. The voices of the age are perplexed and conflicting. "God?" says one, "There is no such Being." "God?" says another, "All is God; God has no reality save as His essence is expressed in the world around you, and in your own thoughts and feelings." "God?" says a third, "It is but a name for the dread, mysterious, inscrutable Power on which all depends. The highest worship is at the altar of the Unknowable." "God?" says another, "It is possible that He exists, but He is far too exalted a Being to disturb Himself with you and your petty cares."

Only on one point do these voices seem to agree, and that is, that God is not a Being whom we can love and trust—not a Father. "What, then," we perhaps ask ourselves, in some disquieted mood, "what if this sad, sad view of the universe should turn out to be the true one? How am I to be sure it is not?" So the strong craving rises for some distinct manifestation of God which will set the question for ever at rest. "Show us the Father." If God really exist, if He be really love, let Him break His awful silence. For, given one absolutely certain and convincing demonstration of God's love, we can bear to wait for an explanation of all else that is dark. It is here, I need hardly say, that the Christian Gospel meets us, and gives to the baffled soul precisely what it wants. No mere assertion, no vague assurance, no proof from doubtsome, visionary appearances; but in the face and person of His own Son, manifest in the flesh, has God given us that for which our souls crave. We are thus led to consider

II. *God is love—a truth revealed and certified in Christ.*

Even taking Jesus as man, and regarding him simply,—as most are willing now to view Him,—as the highest expression of the Divine who has yet appeared on earth, we would still be entitled to say, judging from his life and history—" God is love." His revelation means nothing, or it means that. What soul in distress need ever have hesitated to apply to Jesus? What penitent need have feared to trust Him? What friend could doubt His faithfulness or His love, even unto death!

But how much grander an aspect does the argument assume when we remember that this Jesus, whom we adore, was not mere man, but God's own eternal Son, and the world's Divine Redeemer! The facts of Christ's revelation can be squared with no theory which stops short of the recognition of His full divinity. "The life was manifested," says John, "that eternal life which was with the Father;" "and," he adds, "we have seen it" (i. 4). "We beheld His glory, the glory as of the only Begotten of the Father, full of grace and truth" (John i. 14). In Jesus, therefore, God was present, tabernacled in flesh, and was manifested bodily to men. In seeing Him, we see the Father. He is the Father's very mould and impress. It is God's love with the fulness of which He is filled. Now, was not the very appearance of this great and holy One on earth, engaged in labours for the recovery of the lost, itself a convincing proof of God's love? Had God not loved us, is it conceivable that Jesus should have been here at all, doing what He did, humbling Himself to what He suffered?

A higher certainty, however, is wrought in us when we view Him in the exquisite unfoldings of His character. If this be God who is seen mingling with the lowliest, receiving sinners and eating with them, weeping at the sight of Jerusalem, enduring so

meekly the contradiction of sinners against Himself, engaged
continually in ministries of mercy to sick bodies and sick souls,
yearning with exhaustless compassion over the fickle multitudes
who flocked to His teaching—if this be God, then who will doubt
that "God is love?" "Looking unto Jesus," every doubt is
silenced, every fear is swept away.

But there is given us, through this Son of God, a still grander
demonstration of the same truth. Love in Jesus is peculiarly
the love of self sacrifice. His life, from its first step to its last,
was a life of self-sacrifice; and in the cross, sacrifice reaches the
point in which God's love and man's sin meet as they never met
before, the one to receive its complete defeat and condemnation
through the other. For, what see we there? The Holy One
taking upon Himself the sin of the world, and offering Himself
up to the holy endurance of all sorrow for man's redemption. It
was not enough that He came to live *with* sinners; he must
insert Himself into their lot, take their place, bear their curse,
and die their death. He gave Himself for us, His life for our
life, His soul for our soul, and so He has made propitiation for
our sins. Who shall estimate the transcendency of this expression of God's love in the surrender of His Son to an opprobrious
death for sinners! The cross is, in a sense, the Father's sacrifice
of Himself for men as well as Christ's; for the Father, too, was
in the act, yielding up, for a world that did not love Him, the
dearest treasure of His life. Well may John say, "Herein is
love"—herein, as if all other manifestations were eclipsed in
this, "not that we loved God, but that He loved us, and sent His
Son to be the propitiation for our sins" (v. 10). And well may
another apostle reason—"He that spared not His own Son, but
delivered Him up for us all, how shall He not with Him also
freely give us all things" (Rom. viii. 32)? If, gazing on the
character of Christ, we cannot doubt that "God is love," it is still
more impossible to question it when we ponder the meaning of
the cross. Even Divine love could mount no higher, stoop no
lower, make no costlier sacrifice, enshrine itself in no greater
glories than it did there. The heart that comes to know and
believe the love that God has to it in Christ, will doubt no more
the depths of His affection.

Now, as to the love thus revealed, various points strike us as
of great moment. One is, *It is a love not out of harmony with
the sterner aspects of God's government, as seen in the world
around us.* We have seen that, whatever view we take of God's

love, it must have space in it for the undeniable facts of life, and
some of these are very awful. But, how does God's love appear
to us in the Gospel? Is it as a weak, indulgent feeling, regardless of law, looking lightly on transgression, shrinking at the
touch or spectacle of pain? We must all feel that it is something
very different. The love of Jesus was no soft amiability. Think
of Him forgiving the fallen, yet, for their redemption, submitting
in His own person to the law's just and inflexible demands.
Think of His dealings with different classes of His contempo-
raries — sensitive and sympathetic, with more than a woman's
tenderness, yet denouncing the severest woes against the obdurate; infinitely pitiful to sinners, yet waging war to the death
with sin. There was a certain granitic sternness in the character of Christ, as well as soft and gentle words and smiles.
And as for pain, think of the bitter cross, and of God not sparing
His own Son there. "God is love;" but love though He be, the
Gospel teaches us that God's love is a very high, very holy, very
awful love, and assuredly not to be trifled with by presumptuous
transgressors.

But notice next, *the place to which the Gospel raises love in
the character of God.* It does not say simply God loves, but "God
is Love." It identifies love with God's essence, with the very
root of His character and life. God is unshadowed, unstained
love,—pure and unmingled goodness. A pagan said, "When God
was about to make the world, He transformed Himself into love."
But the Christian Gospel goes beyond this, and declares that God
eternally *is* love. This is a conception so deep and far-reaching
as to pass in its length and breadth beyond our grasp. If God is
love, and love constitutes His essence, then must love dominate,
wield, work through all His other perfections, using all for its
own purposes, transmuting all into its own nature. There can be
no discord or division in the breast of the Eternal. What God
is, He must ever have been, must be at all times, in all His works,
and under all forms of His manifestation. He must eternally
be love, and naught else but love.

But we would be faithless to our text if we failed finally
to direct attention to this point—*the Gospel is pre-eminently
a revelation of God's love to sinners.* And this, as we have seen,
is the one thing that most concerns us. Only assure me that
God is love to *me*, though I have sinned against Him—that, like
the father in the incomparable story of the prodigal, He will
not reject me if I return to Him, but will take me back, with

overflowing affection and without upbraiding, to his heart—that
His mercy towards me, in all my sins, and faults, and weak-
nesses, is something I may fall back upon, and trust implicitly,
—and what more do I need to perfect my peace and joy ?
Tell me that God is One on whom, in all my feebleness, I may
safely rely ; to whom, in all my troubles, I can confidently pray ;
who will be to me as a strong tower in the day that I need a refuge,
and whose fatherly care, encircling me every moment, and keeping me in all my ways, will never leave me without support and
guidance,—and surely I may well be content to carry the heaviest
cross His wisdom shall appoint.   But need I say that promises
of just this character are the pith and marrow of the Gospel ?
If it tells me ,"God is love," it bids me look for love's highest
and sublimest manifestation in the propitiatory cross, and in the
endless treasures of forgiving and cleansing grace, open to us all
in the Well-Beloved. "In this was manifested the love of God
toward us, because that God sent His only begotten Son into the
world, that we might live through Him "(ver. 9).   It is this love,
above all other manifestations of love, which is to attract and
enchain ours, casting out fear, purging us from our dross, lifting
us up into bosom-fellowship with the Father and the Son. "We
love Him because He first loved us" (ver. 19).   Here, therefore, we
may fitly pause.   We have seen how the Gospel has made that a
great spiritual certainty to us, which we could never of ourselves
have dared to believe.   But, once the disclosure has been made,
do we not feel how worthy it is of God, how harmonious with
the ideas which our quickened minds are compelled to cherish of
the All-Perfect One ?   Has not the conviction become part of our
spiritual nature, that either God is love, or there is no God at all ?
A God who was not love, would be at least no God to us—no being
whom we could love, and trust, and worship, in recognition of his
perfections.   And it would be impossible to believe in a God whose
breast was presumed to harbour one trace of *un*lovingness, or who
was held capable of pursuing any of his creatures with vindictive
hatred, or even of looking with stony indifference upon their
woes.   The God whom Christ reveals, delights in the death of
none; He is not willing that any should perish, but that all
should come to Him and live.   All this has now, through the
Gospel, become a great lamp of certainty, shedding light and consolation into the darkest corners of our troubled existence.   Shall
we not receive the salvation which this love brings ?   Shall
we not yield ourselves up to its constraining power in faith

and self-surrender ?   O the guilt of despising this love!   O the blessedness of granting it an entrance to our hearts !   It is now a drawing, pleading, tender, and beseeching love !   May we all receive it, ere its holy purity flames out against its adversaries as consuming fire !

www.ingramcontent.com/pod-product-compliance
Lightning Source LLC
Chambersburg PA
CBHW020508270326
41926CB00008B/794